World's Best

Jokes &
Humor

World's Best

Jokes & Humor

Oliver Roydhouse

Sonya Plowman

SUMMIT
PRESS

950 Stud Road, Rowville
Victoria 3178 Australia
Phone: +61 3 8756 5500
Email: publishing@fivemile.com.au

This edition first published 2002
Reprinted 2004

Editors: Oliver Roydhouse and Sonya Plowman
Cartoons: Geoff Hocking
Formatting: Peter Bourne

Printed in Australia by Griffin Press

National Library of Australia Cataloguing-in-Publication data

ISBN 1 86503 760 5

1. Wit and humor. 2. Joking. I. Plowman, Sonya, 1972-.
II. Roydhouse, Oliver, 1977- World's best humour. III.
Plowman, Sonya, 1972- Great Aussie jokes. IV. Title.

808.87

Contents

World's Best
Jokes

Compiled by Sonya Plowman
Illustrated by Geoff Hocking

Contents

Have You Heard the One About...

An elephant, a penguin, and an
Irishman walk into a pub.
'What's going on?' asks the bartender
suspiciously. 'Is this supposed to be a joke?'

★

Some people love reading jokes, some love
telling them. Still others (we'll call them the
slightly thick ones) just like knowing the
punchline in advance so they're not left with a
vacant look as everyone around them guffaws
at a joke. Whether you are on the telling or receiving end of a joke, this collection will give
you enough material to ensure you'll never again

have to face those embarrassing end-of-joke silences that cause your name to be permanently banished from party invitation lists.

The jokes here run the gauntlet from those you could tell your Gran through to those you wouldn't dare tell your partner. But one thing's for sure: they've all been scientifically tested and there are gut aches to prove it!

The Sick, Dirty and Downright Disgusting chapter should, by its heading alone, warn you not to enter if you're at all easily offended. But if you don't like jokes that are lewd, crude and smutty, you're missing out on the best of them.

So read on...there are blonde jokes aplenty, and male chauvinist pigs have their very own chapter. You'd be wise not to tell any of *those* jokes to your girlfriend – it could mean a black eye or two! Of course, if she's *blonde* she probably wouldn't get them anyway...

Sonya Plowman

Sex, Love and Marriage

Nicki accompanied her husband to the doctor's office. After the check-up the doctor took Nicki aside and said, 'Your husband is suffering from severe long-term stress and it's affecting his health. If you don't do the following four things, your husband will surely die. First, each morning, fix him a tasty breakfast and send him off to work happy. Second, at lunch time, make him a warm, nutritious meal and give him a whole lot of kisses before he goes back to work. Third, after dinner, give him a massage and make sure you don't nag him about anything. Fourth, and most important for relieving stress, have sex with him every day in whatever position he fancies.' On the way home in the car, the husband turned to Nicki and said, 'So, I saw the doctor talking to you and he sure seemed serious. What did he tell you?'

'You're going to die,' she replied.

★

One day a simple lad visits a brothel and knocks on the door and says to the Madam opening it, 'I want a woman!' The Madam looks at him and says, 'You want a woman, huh? Have you done this before?' the Madam asks, doubtful. 'No.' The Madam laughs and says, 'I'll tell you what, you go and practise with the knotholes in those trees and when you know what you're doing, you come back and see me.' So the lad goes out and finds a knothole. Two weeks later he goes back to the brothel and says to the Madam, 'I want a woman. I know how to do it now!' So the Madam sends him off with one of her girls. When they get to the room the lad tells her to take off her clothes and bend over. When she does he takes out a length of wood and smacks her on the butt. 'What the hell did you do that for?' she exclaims. The lad replies, 'Checking for bees.'

★

Policemen had been working for months on a murder case and had just been given a valuable lead. The suspect was known in the criminal world as Alan Shagbreak. Sheriff Wagner drove around to the suspect's place of employment and said to the woman at reception, 'Have you got a Shagbreak here?' She scoffed, 'You have got to be kidding. The boss is so cheap we don't even get a coffee break.'

★

A woman is in hospital, about to give birth to her first child. She gives a big gasp, and suddenly the baby's head appears. The baby turns to the first man he sees and says, 'Are you my father?' The man replies that he is the doctor, and that the father had not made it to the hospital yet. So the baby says, 'Well, I'm not coming out until my father shows up. Tap three times on my mother's stomach when he arrives and then I'll come out.' With that he returns to his mother's womb. The father arrives an hour later. The doctor duly taps on the mother's stomach three times and down comes the baby. He looks around, sees his father and calls him over. With his little finger he pokes the father's nose, eye, and ear. While the father is wincing he says, 'So now you know how it feels. Not very nice, is it?'

★

A weary traveler stopped at a motel in the middle of the night, only to be told that there were no rooms available. 'You've got to have something,' pleaded the traveler. 'Even a spare bed somewhere will do.'

The motel manager thought for a moment, then said, 'Well, we do have one spare bed, but it's in a room with a really loud snorer. This guy snores so loudly that everyone has been complaining about him. You probably won't get any sleep if you share a room with him.'

'I don't care – I'll take it!' said the traveler with relief. The next morning he went down to breakfast bright-eyed and refreshed. 'So the snorer wasn't a problem for you then?' asked the motel manager, surprised.

'Nup. As we were going to bed, I bent over him, kissed him and said, "Good night, gorgeous" and he stayed awake all night watching me!'

★

Sometimes I wake up grumpy; other times I let her sleep.

★

Thomas and Melanie found it hard to get a babysitter and they decided that the only way to make love at home was to send their eight-year-old-son out on the balcony. The boy, pretending to be a super spy, began to report all the neighborhood activities. 'Mrs Smith is hanging out her washing,' he said. 'A taxi just drove by.' A few moments passed. 'Andrew's riding his new bicycle and the Coopers are having sex.' Thomas and Melanie shot up in bed. 'How do you know that?' demanded Thomas. 'Their kid is standing out on the balcony too,' his son replied.

★

Adam came first. But then, men always do.

★

Cheng Fut ran a Chinese take-out store in the red light district. Girls were always coming into the store in their skimpy clothes, telling each other about their last customer and swapping penis size stories. Cheng Fut became so horny one evening he bolted home as soon as he had served his last meal of the day.
'How about a 69?' he asked his wife.
'Are you joking?' she said grumpily. 'Why in hell would I want chop suey and noodles at this time of night?'

★

An old man with chest pains visits his doctor.
'You are very ill,' says the doctor. 'There must be no smoking, no drinking, and no sex.'
'I can't live like that!' protests the old man.
'Okay,' says the doctor, 'have one cigarette a day, and one glass of wine.'
'What about sex?' asks the old man.
'Only with your wife,' replies the doctor. 'You need to avoid all excitement.'

★

10 REASONS WHY CHOCOLATE IS
BETTER THAN SEX

1. You can *get* chocolate.

2. You can share chocolate with a group of friends without being considered obscene.

3. Chocolate satisfies even when it has gone soft.

4. You can have chocolate in front of your parents.

5. If you bite the nuts too hard the chocolate won't mind.

6. Two people of the same sex can have chocolate without being called nasty names.

7. The word 'commitment' doesn't scare off chocolate.

8. You can have chocolate in your office without upsetting your colleagues.

9. Chocolate is just as attractive when you are sober.

10. A big piece of chocolate is of course better, but even a small piece satisfies.

★

PLAYING THE SAX

Do I have to be married to play sax safely?
No, although married people play sax, many single people play sax with complete strangers every day.

My parents say they didn't play sax until they were 21. How old do you think someone should be, before they can play sax?
Sax playing is better left until adulthood — the necessary organs are at that stage better developed.

There is an area in the neighborhood where you can go and pay for sax lessons. Is this legal?
Yes. Many people have no other way of learning to play sax and must pay a professional to teach them.

Should a cover always be used for the sax?
Unless you are really sure of the person who last used your sax, a cover should always be used to ensure safe sax.

What happens if I get nervous and play sax prematurely?
DON'T PANIC! Many people prematurely play sax when they are young. Just wait until you're older before you try again.

★

A well-to-do Englishman found himself walking in a neighborhood a class or two below his own. It happened to be a windy day and as he passed a young woman the wind caught her skirt and lifted it above her head. 'Oh, it's airy, isn't it?' said the man. The young woman replied, 'Yeah, what did you expect? Feathers?'

★

Two old ladies are sitting in a park, when a flasher walks up, yanks open his raincoat and exposes himself totally to them. This is an enormous shock to the ladies and one of them has a stroke right away! The other one can't quite reach.

As the old farmer lay dying, his wife held his hand and murmured sweet nothings in his ear. The farmer, using the last ounce of energy he had, said, 'Mary, you've been with me through all my bad times. When all my cows died, you were there. When Oakey, the best dog ever to have chased sheep, was run over by a plough and killed, you were there. And when I fell into the water drum and almost drowned, you were there too. And now that I am about to leave this earth, you are still here. You know what Mary? I'm beginning to think you're bad luck!'

★

A little old woman walks into a sex shop. She goes up to the counter and says, 'Ex-ex-ex-excuse m-me, y-y-young m-man, b-b-b-but d-d-d-do y-you s-sell v-v-v-vibrators?'
'Why, yes we do.'
She holds her hands about 18 inches apart and says, 'D-d-d-d-do y-y-you h-h-h-have a-a-ny o-o-ones ab-b-bout th-th-this l-l-long?'
'Why yes we do.'
'W-w-w-well t-t-ell m-m-m-me, h-h-h-how d-d-do y-y-y-ou t-t-t-turn it-t-t o-o-o-off?'

★

Bud is a handsome guy, and recently he started going out with the most attractive girl in the neighborhood. The only problem he has is his lips — they seemed to always be chapped and dry, and now that he was going out with such a stunner, he made sure he carried a jar of vaseline with him so he could keep his lips moistened. Anyway, one day his girlfriend suggests he meet her parents over dinner, so he goes over to her place in his best clothes. When he gets there, he finds her waiting for him on the pavement out front.

'No matter what happens tonight, don't say a word,' she warns. 'Our family hates cleaning up. Whoever speaks first at dinner tonight will have to clean the house, and that would not be fun!' She then leads him into the house, where he is hit by the most incredible smell. Piles upon piles of trash lie on the floor. Empty milk cartons, candy wrappers, broken eggshells, banana skins... the place looks like a dump truck has dropped its entire load in the middle of the den. His girlfriend takes him into the dining room, where he nods at the parents, who nod back. They start the meal, and nobody says anything at all. So Bud decides to have a little fun. He grabs his girlfriend, throws her down on the table and has wild sex with her in front of her parents. His girlfriend is embarrassed, her dad wildly angry, and her mom horrified when they sit back down, but no one says a word. A few minutes later he grabs her mom, throws her on the table and does a repeat performance. Now his girlfriend is furious, her dad is boiling, and the mother incredibly shocked. But still there is complete silence at the table. All of a sudden Bud starts feeling a little nervous about what he has done, and his mouth becomes dry. He takes the vaseline out of his pocket, smears it on his fingers and is just about to apply it to his lips when the girlfriend's father frantically jumps up and screams, 'OKAY, OKAY, I'LL DO THE GODDAMN DISHES!'

★

DICTIONARY ENTRIES

Bitch (bich) n.
female: The woman who stole your boyfriend.
male: The hot, sexy chick at reception.

Butt (but) n.
female: The body part that every item of clothing makes 'look bigger.'
male: The organ of mooning, farting, and number two-ing.

Commitment (ko-mit-ment) n.
female: The desire to marry and raise a family.
male: A female-specific term; not relevant to the male species.

Communication (ko-myoo-ni-kay-shun) n.
female: The sharing of emotions and deep-seated feeling with one's partner.
male: The sharing of jokes with one's pals.

Entertainment (en-ter-tayn-ment) n.
female: A good movie, concert, play or book.
male: Anything involving alcohol, table tops, and women dressed in material only half an inch in width.

Flatulence (flach-u-lents) n.
female: A by-product of digestion.
male: An endless source of entertainment, self-expression and male bonding.

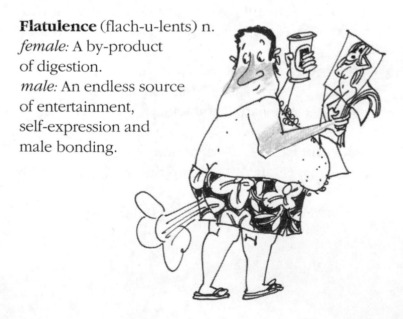

Making love (may-king luv) n.
female: The greatest expression of intimacy a couple can achieve.
male: What men must remember to call 'making love' to entice women to do so.

Needs (need-z) n.
female: The delicate balance of emotional, physical and psychological longing one seeks to have fulfilled in a relationship.
male: Food, sex and beer.

Taste (tayst) v.
female: Something you do frequently to whatever you're cooking, to make sure it's good.
male: Something you must do to anything you think has gone bad, prior to tossing it out.

Thingy (thing-ee) n.
female: Any part of a car's mechanics.
male: Any part of the female anatomy.

Vulnerable (vul-ne-ra-bull) adj.
female: Fully opening up one's self emotionally to another.
male: Playing gridiron without a ball protector.

★

An elementary school teacher thought it would be interesting for her students to learn to identify different names for the various kinds of meats. One day, she cooked up several different meats and labelled them. As each student took a bite they were asked to identify the animal. Little Rani took a bite of the meat labelled beef and correctly said that it came from a cow. Jared took a bite of pork and also correctly identified the meat as coming from a pig. The last meat was labelled venison. The children chewed and chewed and after numerous incorrect guesses the teacher attempted to give them a hint. 'What does your mommy call your daddy when he comes home from work at night?' she asked. All of a sudden little Joey jumped up from the back of the classroom and yelled, 'Jesus Christ! Spit it out! It's Asshole!'

★

Familiarity breeds children.

★

Cinderella had been invited to a ball but her wicked stepmother was being a bitch and reminded her that she did not have the right clothes, and she sure as hell wasn't going to buy her any. Cinderella sat about looking glum, until suddenly her Fairy Godmother appeared with some good news: she would give Cinderella a beautiful dress and matching shoes as long as Cinderella met her two conditions. The first condition was that she had to wear a diaphragm. Cinderella's mouth dropped open and she said, 'You must be crazy! I'm on the Pill, I don't need to wear a diaphragm.' When the Fairy Godmother reminded Cinderella that the alternative was to sit at home watching *Frasier*, Cinderella agreed to wear one. 'Well, what's the second condition?' Cinderella asked. The Fairy Godmother replied, 'You must be back home at midnight.' Cinderella couldn't believe this — a midnight curfew most definitely precluded getting drunk and partying all night. The Fairy Godmother told Cinderella that if she wasn't home by midnight, her diaphragm would turn into a pumpkin, so Cinderella again reluctantly agreed to meet this condition. At midnight though, Cinderella wasn't to be seen... at 1 a.m., no Cinderella... 3 a.m., no Cinderella... finally, at 5 a.m., Cinderella showed up at the door with a huge smirk on her face. The Fairy

Godmother looked angrily at Cinderella and said, 'Where the hell have you been? Your diaphragm was supposed to turn into a pumpkin five hours ago!' Cinderella told the Fairy Godmother all about the wonderful Prince she had met and how he had taken care of it for her. The Fairy Godmother had never heard of a Prince having such powers and asked Cinderella for his name. She replied, 'I can't remember exactly, but it was Peter Peter something or other...'

★

An old man walked slowly into the clinic. 'You gotta help me, Doc,' he said. 'You've got to help me lower my sex drive.'

'C'mon, who are you kidding?' said the doctor. 'We both know that your sex drive is all in your head.'

'That's what I mean. You've got to do something to lower it!'

★

A city slicker was tearing through the country one day in his new sportscar when out of nowhere appeared a bull on the road. Unable to avoid it, the guy drove right into the bull, killing it instantly. Feeling very guilty, he walked over to the farmhouse and knocked on the door. 'I'm so sorry, madam, I've killed your bull. I'd very much like to replace him.'
'Oh, okay,' replied the farmer's wife. 'Go around to the side and you'll find the cows in the barn.'

★

A man from the city was driving in the country when he came across a farmer sowing the fields without any trousers. 'How come you're not wearing any trousers?' he asked in astonishment. 'Well, buddy, the other day I went out into the field and I forgot to wear my shirt. That night my neck was stiffer than a door. So this is my wife's idea.'

★

What do men have in common with a toilet bowl, anniversaries and a clitoris? *They always miss them.*

★

It was Sam the Milkman's last day on the job after 40 years of delivering milk to the same neighborhood. When he arrived at the first house on his route he was greeted by the whole family, who congratulated him for his many years of good work and sent him on his way with an envelope filled with money. At the second house he was presented with a box of fine cigars. The folks at the third house handed him some fine Swiss chocolates and some vintage red wine. At the fourth house he was met at the door by a strikingly beautiful woman in a revealing negligee. She took him by the hand, led him through the door and took him upstairs to the bedroom where they

had the most passionate sex he had ever experienced. Afterwards they went downstairs, where she fixed him a giant breakfast: eggs, bacon, pancakes, and freshly squeezed orange juice. When he was truly full she poured him a cup of steaming coffee. As she was pouring, he noticed a dollar bill sitting on the table, with his name written on a piece of paper right next to it. 'All this is just too wonderful for words,' he said, 'but what's the dollar for?'
'Well,' she replied, 'I told my husband that today would be your last day, and that we should do something special for you. I asked him what to give you. He said, "F*** him, give him a dollar." The breakfast was my idea.'

★

The census taker told the sheriff of a small town that there was something wrong with the population figures. 'For the last ten years the population had been the same: 2058.'

'Yeah, that's right,' said the sheriff. 'It's always been 2058.'

'But surely someone has a baby every so often?'

'Sure,' replied the sheriff. 'And every time it happens some guy has to leave town.'

★

A man had decided to see a prostitute for the first time, but when he went to the address his pal had told him about, it looked like the place had shut down. 'Hey,' he yelled. 'I want to come in.'

'Okay, then put $100 through the mail slot.' He did. But nothing happened and no one came out. 'Hey, I came here to be screwed!'

'What?' called out a woman's voice. 'Again?'

★

What is the difference between
a golf ball and a g-spot?
*A man will spend 20 minutes
looking for a golf ball.*

★

'What do you think, Roger,' began Andy.
'Is it okay to talk to your wife when you
make love?'
'Oh I guess it would be all right,' replied Roger
thoughtfully. 'If there's a phone by the bed.'

★

39

One night a husband came home to his wife with a black eye.
'What happened to you?' she asked.
'I got into a fight with the Super. He said he had slept with every woman in this apartment building except for one.'
'Hmm,' his wife replied. 'I bet it's that ugly woman on the second floor.'

★

Frustrated by her husband's insistence that they make love in the dark, a wife switched on her bedlight one night in the middle of a romp — only to find a cucumber in his hand.
'Is THIS,' she asked, pointing to the vegetable, 'what you've been using on me for the last five years?'
'Honey, let me explain ...'
'Why, you cheating son of a —.' she screamed.
'Cheating huh?!' interrupted her husband indignantly. 'Perhaps you'd care to explain our three kids?'

★

'How many wives have you had?' Mr Brown
asked Mr Schwartz. 'Five,' replied Mr Schwartz.
'But only one of them was my own.'

★

A woman was in hospital, going through the
final stages of labor. As she was experiencing
quite a bit of pain, their doctor asked the
husband if he'd like to participate in the
birthing process and take some of the pain
away from his wife. The husband agreed, so
the doctor got out a strange machine with a red

lever. He set the lever to 10 percent, telling the husband that even 10 percent was probably more pain than he'd ever experienced. But the man didn't feel a thing. Being the egotistical guy that he was, he was sure that he could handle as much pain as his wife so he insisted that the doctor crank the lever up to 100 percent. After it was over, the man stood up, stretched a little. Both he and his wife felt great. Later, when they took the baby home, they found the milkman dead on their doorstep.

★

What are the three words you don't want to hear while making love?
'Honey, I'm home.'

★

A man rang home in the early afternoon one day to speak to his wife. The maid answered the phone and told him that his wife was upstairs in the bedroom with her lover. After ranting and raving for a minute, the man asked the maid if she'd like to make a quick $10,000. 'Sure,' she said enthusiastically. 'What do I have to do?'

'Take the gun from my desk and shoot both of them.' The maid went upstairs and did as she had been instructed. She came back down the stairs, picked up the phone, and said, 'Now what do I do with the bodies?' The man said, 'Take them out the back and throw them in the pool.'

'What pool?' asked the maid. After a moment of silence, the man said, 'Is this 555-555?'

★

Two business men, working away from home a lot, decided to share a mistress. They set her up in her own apartment, sharing the expenses equally between them. One day the mistress told the two men she was pregnant. Wanting to do the right thing, the men agreed to split the costs of bringing up the child.

When the mistress went into hospital, only one of the businessmen was in town to be there for the birth of the baby. When the other one returned, he went to the hospital to visit the newborn. His friend was sitting on the hospital steps looking depressed. 'What's wrong? Were there problems with the birth?'

'Oh, she's fine, but I have some bad news. She had twins, and mine died.'

★

A man, somewhat sceptical, went to see a gypsy fortune teller. 'I see you are the father of two children,' began the gypsy.
'Great, I knew this was all nonsense. I'm actually the father of three children.'
'That's what you think,' smiled the gypsy.

★

One evening, a boy sat down to say his prayers before going to bed. His father walked past at this moment and paused to listen. 'God bless Mommy and Daddy and Grandpa. And bye bye Grandma.' The father thought this was a little strange, but thought nothing more of it until the next day when Grandma had a heart attack and died. A week later, he happened to overhear his son again saying his prayers, and listened more intently this time. 'God bless Mommy and Daddy. Goodbye Grandpa.' Sure enough, the next day Grandpa suffered a stroke and died instantly. A month later, once again the father heard his son praying. 'God bless Mommy. Bye bye Daddy.' The father was mortified. He went to work, but was too scared to do anything in case he had an accident. When he got home from work, he told his wife what an awfully worrying day he'd had. His wife simply scoffed. 'You think you've had it bad? I've had a terrible day. I got up this morning and opened the door to discover the postman dead in our garden.'

★

One day this guy called Ari died. When he arrived to be judged, he was told that he had cheated on his income taxes, and therefore would not be allowed to go to Heaven unless he spent the next five years with a 400-pound, stupid, ugly woman. Ari decided that this was a small price to pay for an eternity in Heaven. So off he went with this enormous, vile woman. As they were walking along, he saw his friend Matty ahead. Matty was with a big, incredibly ugly woman too. When he approached Matty he asked him what was going on, and Matty replied, 'I cheated on my income taxes.' They both shook their heads in understanding and figured that as long as they have to be with these women, they might as well hang out together to make it easier to bear. So the four of them were walking along, minding their own business when Ari and Matty could have sworn that they saw their friend Nick up ahead, only this man was with an absolutely gorgeous centrefold. Stunned, Ari and Matty approached the man, and in fact it was their friend Nick. They asked him how he had managed to land this unbelievable goddess, while they were stuck with these god-awful women. Nick replied, 'I have no idea, and I'm definitely not complaining. This has been absolutely the best time of my life, and I have had five years of the best sex any man could hope to look forward to. There is only one thing that I can't seem to understand. After every time we have sex, she rolls over and murmurs to herself, "Damn income taxes!!"'

★

If a man is alone in the woods talking to himself, with no women around for miles, is he STILL wrong?

★

Adam had been going out with Sally for several months, but still had not managed to sleep with her. One night he tried to cajole her into it. 'But I'm afraid to,' she said. 'Won't you lose respect for me in the morning?'
'Of course not,' he reassured her. 'Provided you're good at it.'

★

What's the difference between a woman and a battery?
A battery has a positive side.

★

One day upon arriving home from work, Anton's wife informed him she was interested in having breast enlargement surgery. When he asked why, she said, 'Because it will make me more attractive to you.'
He asked her how much the operation was, and she replied, '$4,000 per breast.' He exclaimed, '$4,000 per breast?! That's ridiculous. We can't afford that! Have you tried the toilet paper method?' She looked puzzled. 'Sure – each night before you go to bed, rub toilet paper between your breasts, and over a period of time, they should grow.' She said, 'That won't work!'
Anton replied, 'It worked on your butt!'

★

CLASSES FOR MEN

1. How to Find the Vacuum

2. Yes, We Call that an Iron

3. If You Want Her to Wear Sexy Underwear, You've Got to Pay for It

4. Understanding the Female Response to Your Coming Home Late

5. You — the Weaker Sex

6. Drooling at Other Women — Yes there is a Cure

7. PMT — Feel It, Cry About It, Offer Sympathy

8. How to Stay Awake After Sex

9. The Trash Can — Taking it Out

10. How to Wrap Your Own Sandwiches

11. Watching the Game All Weekend is Not Fun

12. Bragging About No. Twos — How Not to

13. Remote Control 101 — Overcoming Your Dependency

14. Remote Control 102 — It Lives Not on the TV

15. Romanticism — Ideas Other Than Sex

16. She Does Not Want to Hear Your Farts

17. Mother-in-Laws — They are People Too

18. The Art of Changing Diapers

19. Separation Anxiety — You Don't Need that Beer

20. You Too Can Host a Dinner Party

21. How to Lose that Beer Gut

★

CLASSES FOR WOMEN

1. Are You Ready? — Definition of the Word 'Yes'

2. Elementary Map Reading

3. Basic Car Mechanics

4. Shopping 101 — Going Without Your Man

5. Shopping 102 — Using Your Own Credit Card

6. Gaining Five Pounds Vs the End of the World: A Study in Contrast

7. Gift-giving Fundamentals (was: Ties Bad — Pin-up Girl Calendar Good)

8. Driving 101: Introducing the Manual Transmission

9. Driving 102: Checking the Oil

10. Jealousy — Doing Without

11. How to Earn Your Own Money

12. How to Leave the Toilet Seat Up

13. Why It's Unacceptable to Talk About the Menstrual Cycle During Lunch

14. Nagging — An Evil Word

15. Sex is Not a Forum for Playing Dead

★

Two deaf men were discussing their night out the previous evening. The first man said, 'My wife was asleep when I got home, so I was able to sneak into bed, and not get into trouble.'
The second deaf man said, 'Boy you're lucky. My wife was wide awake, waiting for me in bed, and she started swearing at me and giving me hell for being out so late.'
The first deaf man asked, 'So what did you do?'
I turned out the light,' the second man replied.

Seems God was ahead of schedule in creating the universe and had a bit of spare time and a few leftover things to play with, so he dropped in to visit Adam and Eve. He told the couple that one of the things he had to give away was the ability to stand up and pee. 'It's a very handy thing,' God told the couple.

Adam popped a cork. Jumped up and begged, 'Oh, give that to me! I'd love to be able to do that! Oh please, oh please, oh please, let me have that ability. It'd be great! I'm working in the garden, and instead of running to the bathroom, I could just pull it out, it'd be so cool. Oh please, God, let it be me who you give that gift to, let me stand and pee, oh please...' On and on he went like an excited little boy (who had to pee). Eve just smiled and shook her head at the display. She told God that if Adam really wanted it so badly, and it sure seemed to be the sort of thing that would make him happy, she really wouldn't mind if God gave it to him. 'Fine,' God said, and the deed was done. He looked again into his bag of leftover gifts. 'Now, what else is here? Oh yes, multiple orgasms...'

★

AAH!

DOING IT

Help desk people tell you how to do it, hang up the phone, and laugh at you with their co-workers.

Firemen do it with a big hose.

Crooks do it with a gun in their pocket.

Telemarketers do it with their mouths.

Physicists do it with a big bang.

Pet shop owners do it with hamsters.

Consultants tell you how to do it, charge you a fortune, but never actually do it themselves.

Spies do it under cover.

Statisticians are 95% confident that they do it.

Hackers do it with bugs.

Mortgage bankers do it with interest.

Radio operators do it with frequency.

Blondes do it with anyone.

Golfers do it in 18 holes.

Deep-sea divers do it under extreme pressure.

Radio DJs do it on request.

★

DISADVANTAGES OF BOY SUPERHEROES

They'd much rather stay in and play Nintendo than go out on patrol.

They blush and stutter when confronted by a female supervillain.

They pick their noses when you're with the FBI.

They go into a sulk if you won't play Dungeons and Dragons with them.

When they've caught a villain, they sound silly when they say, 'Stick them up, dude!'

When they pull out their gun, it sometimes has old bubblegum stuck to it.

They think it's funny to suddenly fart in public.

They can easily be taunted by supervillains.

They get carsick in the Crimemobile.

It doesn't sound too convincing yelling, 'Stop or die!' when their voice breaks mid-sentence.

★

DISADVANTAGES OF GIRL SUPERHEROES

They're always holding slumber parties in the Crimecave.

One tiny zit and they won't leave the house.

They insist on criminals not seeing them in the same clothes twice.

They won't fight crime if Oprah is on.

They won't fight crime if they're waiting for a phone call from that cute guy they met a few days ago.

Batman or Spiderman may try to steal her away from you.

They kill people when they're premenstrual.

They won't use their fists to fight supervillains in case they break a nail.

They get crushes on villians because 'He's like so totally dark an' mysterious an' moody.'

If they're having a bad hair day, forget it.

★

Corey and Ben were sharing a few beers. 'So how come you and your girl broke up?' asked Ben. Corey was rather quiet. 'Sickness,' was all he said. 'I don't remember either of you being sick.' Corey shrugged. 'It was sickness. I just got sick of her, that's all.'

★

Two buddies were talking about Freudian slips. 'I made the worst Freudian slip last night,' said the first guy. 'What was it?' asked the other. 'Well, my wife and I were having dinner and I meant to say, "Please pass the salt," but instead, by mistake... it just slipped out of my mouth: "YOU'RE RUINING MY LIFE YOU GOD-AWFUL BITCH!"'

★

James told his girlfriend, 'There's one word you could say that would make me the happiest dude around when I ask you the question, "will you marry me?"'
'No,' said the girl.
'Thanks,' said James. 'That was the word.'

★

How many men does it take to change a roll of toilet paper?
I don't know. It's never happened.

★

A couple go to a bull auction in the country one weekend. The auctioneer begins his spiel for the first bull. He says, 'A fine specimen, this bull reproduced 60 times last year.'

The wife nudges her husband and says, 'Wow – more than five times a month!'

The auctioneer then calls out, 'Another fine specimen, this bull reproduced 120 times last year.'

Again the wife nudges her husband. 'Hey, that's some 10 times a month. What do you say about that?!'

Her husband is getting really annoyed with this comparison. The third bull is up for sale: 'And this extraordinary specimen reproduced 365 times last year!'

The wife slaps her husband on the arm and yells, 'That's once a day! How about YOU?!'

The husband was pretty irritated by now, and yells back, 'Big deal, once a day! I bet he didn't have to do it with the same cow!'

There are several men in the locker room of a private club after exercising. Suddenly, a cellphone that was on one of the benches rings. A man picks it up and the following conversation ensues:

'Hello?'

'Honey, it's me! Are you at the club?'

'Yes.'

'Great! I'm at the mall. I saw a beautiful mink coat... it is absolutely gorgeous! Can I buy it?'

'How much is it, honey?'

'Only $6000.'

'Okay, go ahead and get it if you like it that much.'

'Thanks! Well, I also stopped by at the Mercedes-Benz dealership and saw the latest models. The salesman gave me a really good price on a trade-in for our current car. You'd just love it, sweetheart.'

'Well, what price did he give?'

'Only $60,000!'

'Okay, but for that price I want it with all the options, petal.'

'Great! Before I go, there's something else...'

'What, sweetheart?'

'Well, I stopped by the real estate window and saw the house we looked at last year, with the pool, acre of English gardens and views over the beach. It's now on sale!'

'Wow! How much are they asking?'

'Just $800,000.'
'What do you know, I think we should buy it!
It sounds like a fantastic deal. Go in and make
an offer, pumpkin.'
'Thanks, sweetheart! I love you so much!'
'You too, baby...'
And then the man hangs up, closes the
cellphone's flap and asks all those present...
'So, does anyone know who this phone
belongs to?'

★

A WOMAN'S FOUR FAVORITE ANIMALS

A mink in the closet
A jaguar in the garage
A tiger in the bedroom
And an ass to pay for it all!

★

TOP 10 DATING TIPS FOR WOMEN

1. Enjoy talking about football. It's a very intellectual game.

2. Learn the precise art of pouring a beer. And then pour many.

3. Bring your own jacket.

4. Don't make him hold your purse.

5. Shopping is not fascinating.

6. Men don't want to talk about marriage on the first date. Or after the first year. Or at all.

7. Don't act clucky when you see little kids.

8. When he asks for a threesome with you and your best friend, he is only joking.

9. Unless the answer is yes. In which case, can he videotape it?

10. And show his buddies the next day?

★

DATING DEFINITIONS

Dating: The process of spending lots of money and time in order to sleep with someone.

Eye contact: Used to signal interest. Many women have difficulty looking a man directly in the eyes, not due to shyness, but because a woman's eyes are not located in her chest.

Indifference: A woman's feeling towards a man, which is interpreted by the man as 'playing hard to get.'

One night stand: What you call a date where you really like somebody and want to start a relationship, but they don't like you enough to bother ringing again.

Nymphomaniac: A man's term for a woman who wants to do it more often than he does.

Love at first sight: What you experience on the basis of looks alone before you actually realize what a loser the other person is.

Law of relativity: How attractive a given person appears to be is directly proportionate to how drunk you are.

★

15 REASONS WHY IT IS BETTER BEING A WOMAN

1. Free drinks.

2. Free dinners.

3. You can hug your friend without wondering if she thinks you're gay.

4. You know The Truth about whether size matters.

5. Speeding ticket? Why officer, what's that?

6. You've never experienced walking around school with a sweater strategically placed in front of your crotch.

7. Condoms do not affect your enjoyment of sex.

8. You can sleep your way to the top.

9. Nothing crucial can be cut off with one clean sweep.

10. It's possible to live your whole life without taking a group shower.

11. If you cheat on your boyfriend, people assume it's because you've been emotionally neglected.

12. You'll never have to punch a hole through anything with your fist.

13. You can quickly end any fight by crying.

14. You're allowed to be afraid of spiders and other creepy crawlies.

15. You can talk to people of the opposite sex without picturing them naked.

★

One day Gerry asks Fiona out to a movie. She accepts and they have a pretty good time. A few nights later, he asks her out to dinner and again they enjoy themselves. They continue to see each other regularly and after a while neither of them is seeing anyone else.

And then one evening when they're driving home, a thought occurs to Fiona and without really thinking she says it out aloud: 'Do you realize that as of tonight, we've been seeing each other for exactly six months?'

And then there is silence in the car.

To Fiona it seems like a very loud silence.

She thinks to herself:

Sheesh, I wonder if it bothers him that I said that. Maybe he's been feeling confined by our relationship; maybe he thinks I'm trying to push him into some kind of obligation that he doesn't want, or isn't sure of.

And Gerry is thinking:

Gosh. Six months.

And Fiona is thinking:

But hey, I'm not sure I want this kind of relationship either. Sometimes I wish I had a little more space, so I'd have time to think about whether I really want us to keep going the way we are, moving steadily toward... I mean, where are we going? Are we just going to keep seeing each other at this level of intimacy? Are we heading toward marriage? Toward children? Toward a lifetime together? Am I ready for that level of commitment? Do I really even know this person?

And Gerry is thinking:

So... that means it was... let's see... it was February when we started going out, which was right after I had the car at the dealer's which means... let me check the odometer...

Whoah! I am way overdue for an oil change here.

And Fiona is thinking:

He's upset. I can see it on his face. Maybe I'm reading this completely wrong. Maybe he wants more from our relationship, more intimacy, more commitment. Maybe he has sensed — even before I sensed it — that I was feeling some reservations. Yes, I bet that's it. That's why he's so reluctant to say anything about his own feelings. He's afraid of being rejected.

And Gerry is thinking:

And I'm gonna have them take a look at the transmission again. I don't care what those morons say, it's still not working right. And they better not try to blame it on the cold weather this time. What cold weather? It's 86 degrees out and this thing is shifting like a damn dump truck — and I paid those incompetent thieves $800.

And Fiona is thinking:

He's angry. And I don't blame him — I'd be angry too. I feel so guilty putting him through this, but I can't help the way I feel. I'm just not sure.

And Gerry is thinking:

They'll probably say it's only a 90-day warranty. That's exactly what they're gonna say, those slimebags.

And Fiona is thinking:

Maybe I'm just too idealistic, waiting for a knight to come riding up on his white horse, when I'm sitting next to a perfectly good person. A person I enjoy being with, a person I truly do care about, a person who seems to truly care about me. A person who is in pain because of my romantic fantasy.

And Gerry is thinking:

Warranty? I'll give them a damn warranty. I'll take their warranty and stick it up their...

'Gerry?' Fiona says.
'What?' says Gerry, startled.
'Please don't torture yourself like this,' says Fiona, her eyes beginning to brim with tears.
'Maybe I should never have... I feel so...'
She breaks down sobbing.
'What?' says Gerry.
'I'm such a fool,' Fiona sobs. 'I mean, I know there's no knight. I really know that. There's no knight, and there's no horse.'
'There's no night? No horse?' says Gerry, baffled.

'You think I'm a fool, don't you?' Fiona says.

'No!' says Gerry, playing it safe.

'It's just that... it's just that I... I need more time,' says Fiona. There is a fifteen second pause while Gerry, thinking as fast as he can, tries to think of a safe response. Finally he comes with one that he thinks might work.

'Yes,' he says.

Fiona, deeply moved, touches his hand. 'Oh Gerry, do you really feel that way?' she says.

'What way?' says Gerry.

'That way about time,' says Fiona.

'Oh,' says Gerry, glancing at his watch. 'No. I mean, yes.'

Fiona turns to face him and gazes deeply into his eyes, causing him to become very nervous about what she might say next, especially if it involves a horse. At last she speaks. 'Thank you, Gerry,' she says.

'Er, yeah,' says Gerry uncertainly.

Then he takes her home and Fiona lies on her bed, a conflicted, tortured soul, and weeps until dawn. Whereas when Gerry gets back to his place, he opens a bag of pretzels, turns on the TV and immediately becomes deeply involved in a re-run of a tennis match between two Czechoslovakians he has never heard of. A tiny voice in the far recesses of his mind tells him that something major was going on back there in the car, but he is pretty sure there is no way he would ever understand what, and so he figures it's better if he doesn't think about it. This is also Gerry's policy regarding world hunger.

The next day Fiona will call her closest friend, or perhaps two of them and they will talk about this situation for six straight hours. In painstaking detail, they will analyze everything she said and everything he said, going over it time and time again, exploring every word, expression and gesture for nuances of meaning, considering every possible ramification. They will continue to discuss this subject on and off, for weeks, maybe months, never reaching any definite conclusions, but never getting bored with it either.

Meanwhile, Gerry, while playing tennis one day with a mutual friend of his and Fiona's, will pause just before serving, frown and say, 'Scott? Did Fiona ever ride a horse at night?'

★

25 THINGS NOT TO SAY DURING SEX

1. But everybody looks funny naked!

2. You woke me up for that?

3. Try breathing through your nose.

4. Is that a Medic-Alert Pendant?

5. But whipped cream makes me break out.

6. On second thought, let's turn off the lights.

7. I thought you had the keys to the handcuffs!

8. I want a baby!

9. What *is* that?

10. Maybe we should call Dr. Ruth.

11. Did you know the ceiling needs painting?

12. I think you have it on backwards.

13. Oops! Did I remember to take my pill?

14. I told you it wouldn't work without batteries!

15. Did I tell you my Aunt Martha died in this bed?

16. No, really... I do this part better myself!

17. Perhaps you're just out of practice.

18. You remind me of my cousin.

19. I have a confession...

20. I really hate people who actually think sex means something!

21. Did you come yet, dear?

22. I'll tell you who I'm fantasizing about if you tell me who you're fantasizing about...

23. When would you like to meet my parents?

24. Long kisses clog my sinuses...

25. Was *what* good for me?

★

An elderly woman is on a plane, politely making small-talk with the young man that is seated beside her. Abour half an hour after take-off, the young man sneezed. But instead of emitting the usual 'aatchoo!', the young man writhed about in his seat screaming 'YES, YES, YES!' before rolling over and taking a nap. The lady found this behavior a little strange, but decided not to say anything. After all, he was a nice young man.

About fifteen minutes later, the young man awoke and sneezed for a second time, and, once again, writhed about in ecstasy. This time he jumped up and down, slapped his thighs, and screamed 'Whoah, baby! YES! YES! YES'.

before rolling over and taking a nap.

The elderly woman was shocked and rather miffed at his strange behavior, and thought to herself, 'If he does that again, I'm definitely going to tell him to settle down.'

Another 15 minutes went by and the young man sneezed again. This time he proceeded even bigger and better than before. He leaped, bellowed, writhed and wiggled into the aisle of the plane, knocking over the drinks trolley, whilst doing cartwheels up and down the cabin. Fed up, the elderly woman turned to the young man and chided, 'Excuse me, young man! Must you really create such an embarrassing ruckus everytime you sneeze?'

The young man apologized, and explained that he was suffering from a medical condition, 'You see, everytime I sneeze, I have an orgasm,' he explained.

'My goodness!' exclaimed the old woman, 'So what do you take for it?'

'Pepper' the young man replied.

★

An old man of 90 years marries a lovely woman in her early twenties, and they are on their honeymoon. Because the woman is worried about her new husband exerting himself, she tells him they should have separate suites. That night a knock comes on her door and her groom is ready for action. They unite in conjugal union and all goes well whereupon he takes his leave of her and she prepares to go to sleep for the night.

After a few minutes there's a knock on the door and there the old guy is again, ready for more action. Somewhat surprised she consents to further coupling which is again successful after which he bids her a fond goodnight and leaves.

She is certainly ready for slumber at this point and is close to sleep for the second time. There is another knock at the door, and there he is again, as fresh as someone her own age and ready for more. Once again they do the horizontal tango. As they're lying in afterglow the young bride says to him, 'I am really impressed that a guy your age has enough juice to go for it three times. I've been with guys more than half your age who could only manage to do it once.'

The old guy looks puzzled and turns to her and says, 'Was I already here?'

★

Dumb, Blonde and Stupid

Laugh alone and the world thinks you're an idiot.

★

What do you call someone who hangs out with musicians?
A drummer.

★

What does it mean when a drummer is drooling out of both sides of his mouth?
The stage is level.

★

The light at the end of the tunnel is an oncoming freight train.

★

What's long and hard on a drummer?
The third grade.

★

Judge: Do you know how many months pregnant you are right now?

Woman: I will be three months on the first of December.

Judge: So the date of conception was the first of September?

Woman: Yes.

Judge: What were you and your husband doing at that time?

★

A popular rock band began a tour of the world, hoping to gain some new fans and sell a lot of records. The band's first destination was Scotland. As they had some time to kill before their first gig, the two drummers of the band went on a day trip to Edinburgh. They soon began arguing about how to pronounce it. 'It's "Ed-in-burra",' said the first one. 'No way, you pronounce it "Ed-in-berg",' said the second. To settle it once and for all they decided to ask a local. Stopping at a burger joint, they asked the blonde behind the counter, 'How do you pronounce the name of this place?' She looked at them strangely for a minute, then said slowly and carefully, 'Mac-don-alds.'

★

A blonde needed to send a message to her mother who was overseas. She went into the communications centre, but was told it would cost $50. She said, 'I'm desperate to talk to Mom, but I don't have any money. Please, I'll do anything for you if you would help me!' The man arched an eyebrow. 'Anything?' 'Yes, anything,' promised the blonde. So the man took her into a room down the hall and

shut the door. Then he said, 'Get down on your knees.' She did. Then he said, 'Undo my zipper.' She did. The man closed his eyes, and whispered, 'Okay, go for it!'
The blonde edged closer to his groin, slightly puzzled, but keen to speak to her mother, and yelled into his Y-Fronts 'Hello, Mom?'

★

Why do blondes take the pill?
So they know which day of the week it is.

★

Why are blondes so attractive to men?
God had to give them something good to compensate for their lack of intelligence.

★

How does a blonde turn on the light after sex?
She opens the car door.

★

Why did the blonde stare at the orange juice bottle for two hours?
Because it said 'Concentrate'.

★

What do you call a blonde with half a brain?
Gifted.

★

Why can't you ever trust a blonde to dial 911?
She'll spend ages trying to find the 'eleven'.

★

What's the first thing a blonde does when she wakes up?
She goes home.

What happened to the blonde who took an IQ test?
The results were negative.

A blonde started her first day at her new high school with a pair of headphones on. Her teacher, realizing how difficult it was starting a new school, did not want to embarrass the girl so said nothing. The next day, and the next day again, the blonde continued to wear the headphones. Finally, the teacher asked her to take the headphones off. She refused. He let the issue rest for a while, but as another week went on and she still wore them he called her aside after class and demanded that she remove them. She looked at him sullenly and said nothing. Exasperated, he ripped them off, whereupon she immediately fell to the floor, dead. After the ambulance had taken her body away, he picked up the headphones to see what she had been listening to. He put them on and heard, 'Breathe in ... breathe out ... breathe in ... breathe out.'

★

Driving down a road, a guy flashes his lights at a cute blonde he sees in the next lane and signals for her to pull over. He gets out of the car, goes over to her window and unzips his trousers. The blonde rolls her eyes and says, 'Wow, this is my fourth Breathalyzer test in a week!'

★

Two blondes are walking through the woods. One looks down and says, 'Hey, look at the deer tracks.' The other blonde takes a closer look and scoffs, 'Those aren't deer tracks, silly! They're too big! Those are definitely moose tracks.' The two blondes argue back and forth about which animal's tracks they are. Eventually, they are hit by a train.

★

A blonde bought a book at the local bookstore called *Flight to France*. She got back home and was told it was volume four of the encyclopedia.

★

Why does a blonde keep a coathanger in the back seat of her car?
In case she locks her keys in the car.

★

Why do blondes like lightning?
They think someone is taking their picture.

★

Why do blondes hate M&Ms?
They take too long to peel.

★

A scantily-clad woman is sitting in a bar.
Having never shaved in her life, she has a
thick black bush of hair in each armpit. She
chugs down drinks like a man; every 10
minutes she raises her arm and flags the
bartender for another bourbon. Each time she
does the other drinkers at the bar are given an
eyeful of her hairy pits. After a few hours, a
drunk at the other end of the bar says to the
bartender, 'Hey, I'd like to buy Miss Ballerina
here a drink.' The bartender replies, 'She's not
a ballerina. What makes you think she's a
ballerina?' The drunk says, 'Any girl that can lift
her leg that high *has* to be a ballerina!'

★

Papa Bear and Baby Bear went into the kitchen for breakfast one morning. 'Someone's eaten my porridge!' wailed Baby Bear. 'And someone has eaten my porridge,' grumbled Papa Bear. 'You morons!' yelled Mama Bear. 'I haven't even made the damn stuff yet.'

★

Why do blondes wear underwear?
So their ankles don't get cold.

★

What do blondes put behind their ears to attract men?
Their knees.

★

HELP!!

Did you hear the one about the blonde who was trapped in a mall during a blackout?
She was stuck on the escalator for four hours!

★

What's the definition of mass confusion?
A room full of blondes.

★

Why do blonde girls have bruises around their belly buttons?
Because blonde guys are stupid too.

★

A pretty blonde goes out on a date to a carnival. After walking around for an hour the boy asks, 'What do you want to do now?' 'I want a weigh,' she says. So they go over to the fortune scales and weigh her. They walk around a little more and the boy asks again, 'So what do you want to do now?' 'I want a weigh,' she says. *Again?* The boy is puzzled, but takes her over to the fortune scales again. They both weigh themselves then go and grab some food. 'Now what?' asks the boy. 'I want a weigh,' says the girl. *What a weirdo*, thinks the boy. *Definitely too strange for me.* He takes her over to the fortune scales again and she weighs herself for the third time, before he drives her home. As she walks into her house her sister asks, 'How was your date?' 'Wousy.'

★

Why did the chef cross the road?
He was frying the chicken.

★

Why does it take one million sperm to fertilize one egg?
They won't stop to ask for directions.

★

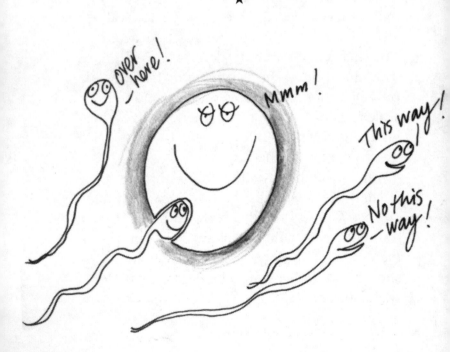

Two vampire bats are hanging in a tree just before dawn, when one says to the other, 'Did you hear that? My belly just rumbled. I've gotta get some more food.' His pal tells him that it is far too dangerous as the sun will be up soon, but he promises to be quick, and takes off. Within a minute, he's back on the branch, blood dripping from his mouth.

'That was quick, where did you go?' asks his pal in astonishment.

'Well see that tree over there?'

'Yeah.'

'Well I didn't.'

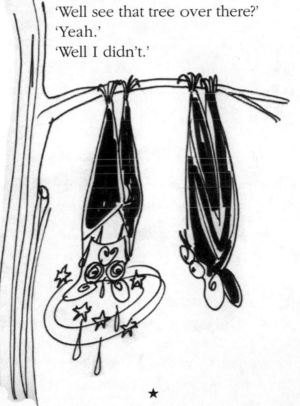

★

A blonde was suffering from constipation, so her doctor prescribed suppositories. A week later she went back to the doctor, still suffering the same problem. 'Have you been taking them regularly?' asked the doctor.
'What do you think I've been doing,' replied the blonde. 'Shoving them up my butt?'

★

Two blondes were walking along the railroad one morning after spending all night at a nightcub. 'Wow, these stairs are killing me,' said the first blonde. The second blonde groaned back. 'The stairs don't bother me as much as the low handrail.'

★

Diamonds are a girl's best friend.
Dogs are a man's best friend.
So which is the dumber sex?

★

Three unemployed blondes were out shopping one day when they found an oil lamp in an antique store. Together they began rubbing it and miraculously, a genie appeared. 'I will grant you all as much intelligence as you desire,' said the genie. 'Wow,' said the first blonde. 'I'd like to be ten times smarter than I am now,' and in a flash the genie granted her the wish. The next day the blonde got a job as a teacher. 'Hmmm,' said the second blonde. 'I'd like to be twenty times smarter.'

'Your wish is my command,' said the genie, as he blinked his eyes and granted her the wish. The next day she found a job as a nuclear physicist. 'Well,' said the third blonde. 'I like things the way they are. I don't have to go to a job and think all the time... if anything I'd rather be ten times dumber!'

'Allright,' said the genie, and granted her the wish. The next day she woke up and found she was a man.

DOH!

★

What's the definition of a blonde German?
Someone who thinks Einstein is a glass of beer.

★

How do blondes get pregnant?
And I thought blondes were dumb.

★

The blonde's husband said his wife was obsessed with shopping. 'She's bonkers, she'll buy anything that's marked down. Yesterday she came home with an escalator.'

★

What's the difference between a blonde and
a brick?
*When you lay a brick it doesn't follow you
around for three weeks whining.*

★

Why did the blonde stay up all night studying?
She had a urine test in the morning.

★

Have you heard about the blonde who had an
average IQ?
Neither has anyone else.

★

Tired of being called dumb, a blonde spent
weeks and weeks learning all the capitals for
every state of America. The next time someone
started telling a blonde joke she said
indignantly, 'Hey, not all blondes are stupid
you know. Let me prove it. Tell me the name
of any state in America and I'll tell you its
capital.'
'Montana,' someone suggested.
'M,' was her triumphant response.

★

One day Carl went out scuba diving. He was 15 feet below sea-level when he noticed a guy at the same depth he was, but without any scuba gear. Carl went another further 15 feet down, and the guy joined him a few minutes later. Carl was really puzzled by this, but continued further down yet another 15 feet. The guy caught up with him once again. By this stage Carl couldn't believe his eyes. He took out his waterproof blackboard and chalked on it, 'How on earth are you able to stay under this deep without any scuba equipment?' The guy took the board and chalk, scribbled over what Carl had written, and wrote, 'I'M DROWNING, YOU IDIOT!'

★

A nuclear scientist and a blonde are sitting on a bus together. The scientist leans over and asks if she would like to play a game. He says, 'I'll ask you a question, and if you don't know the answer, you pay me $10 and vice versa.' She's tired, so says no, but he keeps persisting. 'Look, then, you pay me $10 if you don't know the answer, and I'll pay you $100 if I don't know the answer.' He thinks that since she's a blonde he's sure to win the game. So she agrees. The scientist asks, 'How big is the Great Wall of China?' The blonde says nothing, but simply reaches into her purse and hands over $10. 'My turn now,' she says. 'What flies to the moon on Monday and returns on Thursday?' The scientist looks puzzled, and whips out his laptop computer and searches his CD encyclopedias. He rings up all his scientific buddies and puts the word out to find an answer. Meanwhile, the blonde has fallen asleep. Some time later, when he has exhausted all his contacts and can not find the answer he nudges her awake and hands her $100. 'Well, what is the answer?' he asks her in frustration. In silence, she reaches into her bag and hands him $10.

★

A psychologist, a minister, and a scientist are walking in the forest when they come upon a little hut. As it is getting late, they go into the hut and ask the man there if they can spend the night. The man obliges. 'You must be hungry,' says the hospitable man, and takes them in the kitchen, where they find a dining table standing eight feet high. They all have to jump like crazy to reach the food on the table, and are very tired by the end of the meal. 'Hmm,' says the psychologist. 'This man has obviously designed this table to act as a protective mechanism against overeating.'

'No,' disagrees the minister. 'He is obviously making a statement about the nature of God, the source of All Things Good. He is showing appreciation for the food by jumping for it... in a way it's a little like saying grace before eating.'

'You're both wrong,' says the scientist. 'He obviously created this table with advanced rules of thermodynamics in mind. Heat rises, therefore the heat in this room will rise to the ceiling, keeping the food on the table warmer for longer.' After some argument, the men finally ask why the man has such a tall dining table. 'Hmmm,' he says, 'Seems as I recall, I had a lot of wood and no saw to cut it with.'

★

How do you sink a submarine full of blondes?
Knock on the door.

★

How are men and carpet alike?
If you lay them right the first time, you can walk all over them for years to come!

★

Confucius say...
He who run behind bus get exhausted.

★

If at first you succeed, try not to look too astonished.

★

Ever stop to think, and forget to start again?

★

A blonde stopped at a Coke machine and put in a dollar. When a Coke came out she put it on top of the machine. She then put another dollar in the machine and got another Coke, and put it also on top. She did this about ten times, then a man behind her said, 'Do you mind if I put my dollar in and get one?' The blonde replied, 'Yes I do mind — can't you see, I'M WINNING!'

★

A blonde was coming home from work. As she turned into her street she noticed smoke coming out of her house. She started yelling, 'Fire! Fire! My place is on fire, come quick!' Then she called the fire department. She said, 'My house is on fire, my house is on fire, come quick.' The guy asked her how to get there and she said, 'In your big red truck, of course!'

★

Male Chauvinist Pigs!

How many male chauvinists does it take to change a light bulb in the kitchen?
Who cares? Let the bitch cook in the dark.

★

Why did the woman cross the road?
More to the point, what was she doing out of the kitchen?

★

Why do women have periods?
Because they deserve them.

★

What do you do when your washing-machine stops working?
Slap the bitch until she starts again.

★

The time had come. Aliens were going to blow up Earth in five minutes. A group of friends were forlornly sharing a meal together, knowing it was the last time they would ever see each other. The only woman of the group suddenly said, 'Is there one last chance for me to be a real woman?' One of the guys answered, 'Sure, honey,' and taking off his shirt he said, 'Iron this.'

★

Why do men die before their wives?
They want to.

★

Why do men pass more gas than women?
*Because women won't shut up long enough to
build up pressure.*

★

Bigamy is having one wife too many. Some
say monogamy is the same.

★

One day an inquisitive little boy went to his mother and asked, 'Mommy, what's a pussy?' The mother took him out to the neighbor's house and showed her son their kitten. The next day the boy pulled on his mother's apron and asked, 'Mommy, what's a bitch?' The mother took him to the park, and walked around until she found a dog. 'There you go,' she said, pointing to it. 'This is a dog. A female dog is called a bitch.' The next day the boy sought confirmation from his father. 'Dad, what's a pussy?' His father knelt down beside the bed, pulled out an issue of Playboy and drew a circle around the middle section of one of the naked women. 'Son, that is a pussy.'
'Oh,' said the boy. 'What's a bitch then?'
'Everything outside of the circle,' replied his father.

What do you say to a feminist that has no arms or legs?
Nice tits.

★

If your wife keeps coming out of the kitchen to nag at you, what have you done wrong?
Made her chain too long.

★

Why do cavemen drag their women by the hair?
Because if they dragged them by the feet, they would fill up with mud.

★

How can you tell if your wife is dead?
The sex is the same, but the dishes keep piling up.

★

How do you turn a fox into an elephant?
Marry it!

★

Why do brides wear white?
Because that's the colour of all kitchen appliances!

★

WHY IS FRUIT SALAD BETTER THAN A WOMAN?

Fruit salad may be cold, but at least that's the way it's meant to be.

Fruit salad always looks good in the morning.

Fruit salad doesn't care if you fall asleep afterwards.

Fruit salad is cheaper.

Your friends aren't interested in stealing your fruit salad.

You can make fruit salad as sweet as you want.

You can look at girly pictures while having fruit salad.

If you put icecream in your fruit salad, it doesn't put on weight.

Fruit salad doesn't nag.

Fruit salad is ready in 15 minutes or less.

Fruit salad doesn't have a time of the month... it's good all the time.

Fruit salad doesn't steal the sheets.

Fruit salad doesn't mind if you wake up at 3 a.m. and decide to have some.

You can have an intelligent conversation with fruit salad.

No matter how ugly you are, you can always get a bowl of fruit salad.

★

What's the difference between a woman and a tornado?
Nothing. They both start with a blowjob and you end up losing your house.

★

Josh (just an ordinary guy) and gorgeous contortionist named Eva walk into an exclusive Beverly Hills furrier. 'Show the girl your finest mink!' exclaims Josh. As Eva tries it on, the salesman discreetly whispers to Josh, 'Sir, that particular fur goes for $10,000.' 'No problem! I'll write you a check,' replies Josh. 'Certainly,' bows the salesman. 'Today is Saturday. You may come by on Monday to collect the coat, once your check has cleared.'
So Eva and Josh leave the furrier in raptures, headed for the nearest hotel room. First thing Monday morning, Josh returns to the furrier. The salesman is outraged. 'How dare you show your face here? There wasn't a single penny in your account!' he fumed. 'Never mind that,' grinned Josh. 'Just wanted to thank you for the best weekend of my life!'

★

What do you call a man who's been lucky in love?
A bachelor.

★

A man comes home from a hard day of work. After a relaxing dinner with his wife, they decide to have an early night. As the man lies in bed, his wife is brushing her teeth in the bathroom.

The man calls to his wife, 'My little boopey-boo, I'm lonely.'

So the woman comes out of the bathroom and crosses the room to the husband. On the way she trips on the carpet and falls on her face.

The husband, with a concerned look on his face says, 'Oh, did my little honey-woney fall on her little nosey-wosey?'

The woman picks herself up and gets into bed. The two have passionate sex and afterwards the woman gets up to go to the bathroom. On the way she catches her foot on the same bit of carpet and falls flat on her face.

The man looks at his wife lying on the floor and snorts, 'Clumsy cow, aren't we?'

★

Heaven, Hell and Other Biblical Stuff

One Friday night three men were standing in line at the Pearly Gates of Heaven. St Peter told the first man, 'I'm only admitting people in today who have had a really horrible death. How did you die?'

The first man replied, 'Well, I got home from work early today, and my wife was acting really strange, so I figured she was cheating on me. I could hear noises coming from somewhere but couldn't see anyone. I went outside and, sure enough, there was this guy hanging off the balcony. I started bashing his fingers until he let go and fell. He landed in the bushes, still alive, so I rushed into the kitchen, grabbed the fridge and threw it at him. All of this caused a blood vessel in my brain to burst, killing me.'

'That sounds like a pretty bad death to me,' said St Peter as he let the man in. The second man then recounted his story. 'Every day I exercise on the balcony of my apartment. This morning as I was exercising I slipped and fell over the edge. Luckily I caught the railing of the balcony on the floor below me. But this maniac appears, and bashes my fingers until I have to let go. I get lucky again, and land in some bushes, not too badly hurt. Then, before I know it, a fridge falls out of the sky and crushes me to death.' Once again, St Peter conceded it was a horrible death. Then the third man told his story.

'Picture this,' he began. 'I'm lying naked inside a fridge...'

★

The two directors of a large business knew their office building was unsafe, but were too cheap to make the necessary changes. As a result, the entire building burnt down to the ground, killing almost one hundred innocent people. Satan told the directors that they had two choices. They could spend the rest of eternity in the Cold Room, where their blood would freeze and their extremities would drop off, or they could spend it in the Hot Room, where their skin would blister and peel off slowly and painfully, layer after layer. Both choices sounded pretty bad to the directors. Suddenly one of them noticed the Sex Room, and with a huge smile he leapt toward it. Opening the door, he revealed a room full of directors getting blowjobs from the best looking secretaries he had ever seen. He turned to Satan and said with a wink, 'Hey, I think we want this room!' Satan shook his head and said, 'You can't go there... that's secretary Hell!'

★

A priest, a baptist minister and a rabbi in the same town all traded in their cars on nice new ones around the same time. Feeling the need to celebrate, the priest sprinkled water on his car's hood. Not to be outdone, the baptist minister drove his car into the lake. The rabbi thought for a while and then brought a hacksaw over to his car and carefully sawed off a half-inch of tailpipe.

★

In the beginning there was nothing, then God said 'Let there be light.'
And there was light. There was still nothing, but you could see it a lot better.

★

Jesus, hanging from the cross, sees Peter in the throng of people at the bottom of the hill. 'Peter!' he calls. Peter hears and says, 'I hear you, my Lord. I'm coming.' As he begins the climb a guard blocks his way and says, 'Stop, or I'll have to cut off your leg.' But Peter replies, 'I mustn't stop, my Lord is calling for me.' So he holds out his leg for the guard to cut off, then continues on, bleeding badly. Jesus continues to call, 'Peter, Peter!' Peter, in terrible pain, hops on up the hill, gasping, 'I'm coming, my Lord, I'm coming.' Just then he is stopped by another guard who says, 'I'll cut your arm off if you try to get past me,' so Peter holds his arm out and says, 'As you will. I must go to the Lord.' So the guard chops off his arm and Peter continues on, growing pale from the blood loss. Now crawling along up the hill, Peter hears Jesus calling again. 'I'll be there soon, my Lord!' promises Peter. Another guard blocks his way. 'Stop, or I will cut off your other arm,' said the guard. Weak and in pain, Peter holds out his arm to be chopped off. He says, 'Our Lord is beckoning me. I must go to him.' Now, armless and with only one leg, he somehow makes it to the top of the hill, dragging his bloody body to Jesus' feet. 'Lord, I have answered your call.' Jesus looks down at him and says, 'Hey, guess what Peter! I can see your house from here!'

★

What do you call an Atheist Insomniac Dyslexic? *Someone who stays up all night wondering if there is a dog.*

★

There was a Pope who was loved by all men, and when he died and went to Heaven Saint Peter met him with a warm embrace.

'Welcome your holiness, we are honoured to have you here. Your dedication in serving your fellow man has earned you great respect here, and for this we grant you free access to all parts of heaven. You may go anywhere and speak to anyone. Now, is there anything which your holiness desires?'

'Well, yes,' the Pope replied. 'I have spent many years trying to work out the mysteries of the Universe. I have spent hours pondering questions that have confounded philosophers through the ages. I would dearly love to read any transcripts which recorded the actual conversations between God and the prophets of old. I would love to see what was actually said, first-hand.'

Saint Peter immediately ushered the Pope to the Heavenly library. The Pope sat down and began to read the true history of the Earth. Some time later a scream of heart-chilling anguish rang out from the bookshelves of the library. Angels came running. There they found the Pope, with a look of complete horror on his face, pointing to a single word on an old parchment, saying, 'There's an "R" — it's "celibrate!"'

Two nuns are bicycling down a cobblestone street. The first one says to the other, 'I haven't come this way before.' The second one says, 'It's the cobbles.'

How do you get a nun pregnant?
Dress her up as an altar boy.

★

An American called Jay arrived in Hell, and
was told he had a choice to make. He could
go to Capitalist Hell or to Communist Hell.
Naturally, Jay wanted to compare the two, so
he strolled on over to Capitalist Hell. There,
outside the door, was a demon, looking bored.
'What's it like in there?' asked Jay. 'Well,' the
demon replied, 'in Capitalist Hell, they cut your
fingers off, boil you in oil, chain you to a tree,
tear your kidneys out, then cut you up into
small pieces with sharp knives.'
'That's terrible!' gasped Jay. 'I'm going to check
out Communist Hell!' He wandered over to
Communist Hell, where he discovered a huge
line of people waiting to get in. Jay pushed his
way through to the head of the line, where he
asked one of the demons what Communist
Hell was like. 'In Communist Hell,' the demon
replied impatiently, 'they cut your fingers off,
boil you in oil, chain you to a tree, tear your
kidneys out, then cut you up into small pieces
with sharp knives.'
'But that's the same as Capitalist Hell!'
protested Jay.
'True,' sighed the demon, 'but sometimes
we don't have oil, sometimes we don't
have knives...'

★

A guy dies and goes to Hell. At the gates the Devil explains, 'You must choose one of the following rooms, and from this day forward, you will remain in that room for all eternity.' The Devil then takes him to the first room and opens the door. Inside, a circle of damned people with bowling balls strapped to their heads and feet walk around barefoot on hot coals. 'Oh, I don't think I want to live in this room,' says the man, so the Devil takes him to the second room. In this room, the damned are walking around on burning hot broken glass, listening to Mariah Carey. 'I don't think I could bear this room either,' says the man. So they walk on. In the last room, the damned are standing around up to their armpits in shit, drinking coffee. 'This doesn't look too bad!' says the man. 'I think I'll stay here for eternity.' 'Very well,' said the Devil, closing the door behind him. 'Hmm, nice coffee,' thinks the man, as a demon hands him a cup. Suddenly the room supervisor calls out on his megaphone, 'Okay everybody, coffee break's over! Back on your heads!'

★

A scruffy man wandered into a bar and sat down next to a priest. The man's clothes were dirty, he had lipstick smudges on his face, and a half-empty bottle of gin was sticking out of his pocket. He opened his newspaper and began listening to his headphones. After a few seconds he took the headphones off and turned to the priest. 'Hey, Father, what causes arthritis?'

The priest, eyeing the guy up and down in a disapproving manner, said, 'Arthritis is caused by loose living, running around with cheap, vulgar hussies, too much drink, and a contempt for fellow man.'

'Well I'll be damned,' muttered the drunk, putting his headphones back on. After a moment, the priest began to feel guilty about his unkind outburst. 'I'm very sorry, I was out of line. I really do apologize for my rudeness,' he said. 'How long have you had arthritis?'

'I don't have it, Father. I just heard here on the radio that the Pope does.'

★

Three guys die and are lined up at the Pearly Gates. St Peter asks them, 'Were you faithful to your wives?' The first guy answers, 'Yes. Never even thought about another woman.' St Peter says, 'Good man. See that Rolls Royce over there? That's yours to drive in Heaven.' The second guy says, 'Well, I had one short affair, but I confessed to my wife and we eventually sorted it out.' St Peter says, 'That was decent of you. Okay, see that small BMW over there? That's yours to drive around Heaven.' The third guy says, 'I hate to say this, but I cheated on my wife on our wedding night and continued doing so all my life.' St Peter says, 'That's okay. You can have that Buick over there.' The three guys get into their cars and start cruising around Heaven. A few weeks later, the second and third guys come across the first guy, sitting in his Rolls Royce and looking very depressed. 'Hey buddy, what's wrong? You're driving a Rolls, you're in Heaven... what's the matter with you?' He says glumly, 'I saw my wife here yesterday.' The other two reply, 'But that's great! What's the problem?'

'She was driving a beat-up 70s Toyota.'

★

Two men in black were both eating their lunch in a sunny park one day. After the normal small talk about the wonderful weather, one said to the other, 'So I assume you're a Catholic priest?'

'That's right. And I guess you're a rabbi?'

'Yes, that's true.' The two munched on their sandwiches for a minute. After a while the rabbi leaned over and whispered, 'Have you ever broken a commandment?'

The priest nodded bashfully. 'I slept with a woman once.' He then said to the rabbi, 'Have you ever eaten pork?' The rabbi looked around to make sure no one passing by was listening.

'Yes,' he whispered. There was a short silence, which was broken by the priest.

'Sex is much better than pork isn't it!'

★

As Father Alan was aware that many of those in his parish were heavy drinkers, he decided to preach a sermon to show that animals did not fall prey to the follies of alcohol as men did. He began the story of the peasant who traveled throughout the world with his trusty dog. One hot day, as a special treat, the peasant bought a bucket of beer for the dog, but the dog refused it. The peasant then gave the dog a bucket of water instead, which the dog drank thirstily. 'Tell me why the dog would drink the water and not the beer?' Father Alan asked. From the back of the church someone yelled, 'Because it was a Goddamn dog, that's why.'

★

For six years, Father Frank had read sermons every Sunday morning at the small-town church. Feeling it was time he moved on to a bigger church, Father Frank had taken up a position in a faraway town. A morning tea party was held to say goodbye. Presenting him with a going-away present, one young woman said, 'We don't know what we will do without you Father. Until you came we didn't know what sin was.'

★

There was a priest and a choir boy who both wanted to study medicine at the local university. One day the choir boy went to take an entrance exam. He returned to the church the next day looking very down in the dumps. 'How was the exam?' asked his priest, hoping to get some tips, as his entrance exam was that afternoon. 'They asked quite a lot of "fill in the missing letter" questions about first aid and stuff. I got a score of 65%. It wasn't good enough to get in,' said the choir boy. The priest looked worried, but went to take the test anyway. The next day at church the choir boy asked the priest how the exam went. 'I went very badly. I think I got all wrong but one.'
'Which question was that?'
'It was... "What do you do when you come across an unconscious lady? You feel her pu_s_?"'
'Yeah, that's easy,' said the boy. 'The answer is "pulse".'
'Damn,' said the priest. 'Got that one wrong too.'

★

As it was such a nice day, the priest called the church to say he was too sick to take morning service that Sunday. He loaded up his fishing gear and went down to the beach. God, watching from up above, didn't think the priest should get away with this. He called one of the angels over to watch what he was going to do. The priest cast his line and immediately caught a 200 pound fish, the biggest he had ever seen in his entire life, let alone caught.

'I thought you were going to punish him,' said the angel, disappointed.

'I have,' replied God. 'Who is he going to tell?'

A man accidentally falls over a cliff, and in the panicked moments on the way down he manages to grab onto the only branch within reach or sight. In a few moments, he summons enough strength to move again, and he yells, 'Help! Is there anyone up there who can help me?'

A moment passes without event, and he again cries, 'Help! Can anyone hear me? I need help!' After another moment a booming voice answers, 'This is the voice of God. Believe in me. Have faith. Say a prayer and let go of the branch. You will float gently to the ground, unharmed. Just let go.'

Looking down at the jagged rocks and the pounding surf, the man thinks for a second, and then calls up, 'Is there anyone ELSE up there?'

★

A faith healer is addressing his audience, convincing them of the benefits of faith and prayer as a means of curing the sick. He asks for volunteers from the audience so that he can demonstrate his powers. Two young men come forward.

'What ails you, son?' says the healer to the first man, named Robbie.

'I h-have a b-b-bad s-s-s-stam-m-m-m-mer,' is the reply.

'And you?' the healer says to Ken, the second man, who leans unsteadily on wooden crutches.

'I've been a partial cripple since birth.'

'Now,' says the healer, 'I will show you how the power of our Lord will help you overcome your illness.' He lays one hand across Robbie's mouth, and the other on Ken's leg, and encourages his audience to pray together. Then he says to the two men, 'Do you have faith in God, do you believe in the power?'

'YES!' says Ken.

'Y-Y-YES,' says Robbie.

'Now I want you to go behind that screen and do exactly as I say.' So Ken and Robbie go behind the screen and the healer says, 'Ken, if you truly believe, then throw out your crutches,' and, to everyone's amazement, Ken's crutches come sailing over the top of the screen. Then the healer says, 'Now Robbie, if you truly believe, say something!' and after a hushed silence, a voice rings out, 'Ke-e-en's f-f-f-fallen over.'

★

What's the definition of a masochist?
A celibate priest. They give up their sex lives, only to have people come in and tell them the highlights.

★

One Tuesday morning a guy arrives at the pearly gates. He waits there for ages until he has reached the front of the queue. St Peter is leafing through the Big Book to see if the guy is worthy of entering Heaven. After several minutes, St Peter closes the book, furrows his brow, and says, 'You haven't done anything really spectacularly good in your life, but you also haven't done anything bad. Tell you what, if you can tell me one really good deed that you did in your life, I'll let you in.'

The guy thinks for a moment and says, 'Okay, well there was this one time when I was out driving and I saw a gang assaulting this poor girl. There were about 20 of them. So I slowed down, got out of my car, grabbed the jack out of the trunk, and walked straight up to the leader of the gang. He was a huge guy with a studded leather jacket and a chain running from his nose to his ear. As I walked up to the leader, the gang members formed a circle around me. So, I ripped the leader's chain out of his face and smashed him over the head with the jack,' the guy says. Then I turned around and yelled at the rest of them, "Leave this poor, innocent girl alone! You're all a bunch of sick, deranged animals! Go home before I kill the lot of you!"'

St Peter, very impressed, says, 'Wow! When did this happen?'

'About ten minutes ago.'

★

An Amish boy and his father were in a mall. They were amazed by almost everything they saw, but especially by two shiny, silver walls that could move apart and back together again. The boy asked his father, 'What is this, Father?' The father responded, 'Son, I have never seen anything like this in my life. I don't know what it is.' While the boy and his father were watching wide-eyed, an old lady in a wheelchair rolled up to the moving walls and pressed a button. The walls opened and the lady rolled between them into a small room. The walls closed and the boy and his father watched small circles of lights with numbers above the walls light up. They continued to watch as the circles began to light up in the reverse direction. The walls opened up again and a beautiful young woman stepped out, smiling seductively. The father turned to his son and said, 'Quick... go get your mother.'

★

It's a sunny day, and a priest decides to take a walk to the pier. He greets a fisherman along the way and the two begin talking. The fisherman asks if the priest has ever fished before, to which the priest answers no. So the fisherman says, 'Well, give this a go, Father.' And what do you know, the priest immediately catches a big one, a huge one in fact.

'Wow, look at that sonofabitch!' exclaims the fisherman in admiration.

Priest: 'Uh, sir, can you please mind your language?'

Fisherman: (a quick thinker, this one) 'I do apologize, Father, but that's what the fish is called: a sonofabitch.'

Priest: 'Oh, I'm sorry, I'm not normally a seafood eater, I am not aware of the terminology.'

After the trip, the priest takes his prize catch to the bishop.

Priest: 'Look at this big sonofabitch!'

Bishop (shocked): 'Please, mind your language, we are in church!'

Priest: 'No, it's alright! That's what the fish is called and I caught it. I caught this sonofabitch!'

Bishop: 'Oh. Well, I could clean this sonofabitch and have it for dinner.'

So the bishop takes the fish, cleans it and takes it to the Head Mother.

Bishop: 'Could you cook this sonofabitch for dinner tonight?'

Head Mother: 'Goodness, what language!'

Bishop: 'No, that's what this fish is called, a sonofabitch! Father caught it, I cleaned it, and we want you to cook it.'

Head Mother: 'Oh okay, I'll cook the sonofabitch tonight.'

That night the Pope stops by for dinner. He thinks the fish is great and asks where they got it.

Priest: 'I caught the sonofabitch.'

Bishop: 'And I cleaned the sonofabitch.'

Head Mother: 'And I cooked the sonofabitch.'

The Pope stares at them for a minute with a steely gaze, pours a whisky, pops a cigar into his mouth, puts his feet up on the table and chuckles, 'You know, you sonofabitches are alright!'

★

'Okay, listen!' commanded Noah. 'On my ark there will be absolutely no sex. No kissing, no fondling, no nothing. Now, all you males, take off your penis and hand them to my sons. I'll give you a receipt for your penis, and once we see land I'll return each penis to its rightful owner.

After a few days Mr Rabbit hopped into his wife's cage. 'Quick!' he said in excitement. 'Get on my shoulders and look out the window to see if there is any land there yet!'

Mrs Rabbit got onto his shoulders and looked out at the ocean.

'No sir,' she said. 'No land yet.'

'Darn!' yelled Mr Rabbit. This went on every day until Mrs Rabbit got fed up with him.

'What is the matter with you? You know it will rain for forty days and nights. Only after the water has drained will we be able to see land. Why are you acting so excited all the time?'

'Look!' said Mr Rabbit with a crazy, joyous look on his face as he held out a piece of paper. 'I GOT THE DONKEY'S RECEIPT!!'

★

A couple of politicians, very much in love, were both killed in a car crash. When they got to Heaven they wanted to continue practising politics so they requested an election. They drew up election speeches and worked out policies, but it took St Peter an awfully long time to find another politician to run against them in the election. After a long struggle, they became the winning candidates, and decided they performed so well together as a political entity that they should also get married. So they trundled off to St Peter to ask him to supply a priest to perform the wedding ceremony. 'Are you kidding?' said St Peter. 'It took me 100 years to find another politician in Heaven to run against you in the election. I'll never be able to find a priest in Heaven to marry you!'

★

There was a man who had only ten days left to live. He told his family to sell all he had and trade in his money for gold and bury it with him in a suitcase, as he wanted to take it to the next world. After he had passed away, he approached St Peter at the pearly gates. When St Peter asked him to explain what he was doing with a suitcase, the man replied, 'I brought the most important thing to me in the world, the most valuable possession I have.' Curious, St Peter asked what it was. The man excitedly opened his suitcase for him to see, and upon viewing what was inside, St Peter drew a perplexed face and asked, 'Pavement?'

★

Three priests, all traveling by train into the city for a religious convention, happened to be sitting in the same carriage. Becoming familiar with one another, they began to confess their sins. 'I can't resist women,' said the first priest. 'I have succumbed to temptation time and time again.'

'I can't keep off the booze,' said the second. 'At least once a week I end up lying naked in a drunken stupor on the dining table.' The third priest was quiet.

'So what's your vice?' asked the first priest. 'Gambling? Stealing from the collection plate?'

'No,' replied the third priest. 'My sin is a bad one. I gossip, and I can hardly wait to get to that convention.'

★

An elderly priest visited a ranch one day to sell his horse. A farmer for years, Chuck knew a good horse when he saw one and agreed to buy it. But when Chuck jumped on the horse, rearing to go, it would not move an inch. 'Oh, sorry,' said the priest. 'The horse is religious. He'll only go when you say "Jesus Christ", and will only stop when you say "Amen".' Chuck thanked the priest, said 'Jesus Christ,' and was off sprinting around the countryside. After riding for only an hour they suddenly found themselves in a shooting range. BANG! A gun fired right next to them, sending the horse into a galloping frenzy. As Chuck was taken at full bolt through the woods he closed his eyes, trying desperately to think of the word to make it stop, finally yelling, 'Amen!' The horse skidded to a halt and when Chuck's heart had stopped racing, he opened up his eyes and saw that they had stopped right on the edge of a terrifying mountain chasm. 'Jesus Christ,' he said.

★

What's a catch-22 situation for a Jew?
Free pork!

★

Two very devout Catholics, who had been
dating for several years, were out driving in a
desolate area in the country one day when
their car broke down. As the only mechanic
within 100 miles of the town was busy with
another job, the two decided they would have
to spend the night at a motel. There was only
one motel within walking distance, and there
was only one room available, with only one
bed. 'Well,' said the boyfriend to the girlfriend,
'it looks like we are going to have to sleep in
the same room tonight. I don't think the Good

Lord or our parents will mind if we share the same bed, just this once.'

'Okay,' replied the girlfriend. They got ready for bed, and each took their agreed place at either extreme of the bed. Ten minutes later the girlfriend said, 'I'm really cold.'

'Okay, I'll get you a blanket,' said the boyfriend, and he got out of bed and found a blanket in the cupboard. Ten minutes later the girlfriend said, 'I'm still really, really cold.'

'Okay, then, I'll get you another blanket,' said the boyfriend, getting up once more to fetch a blanket from the closet. Ten minutes later the girlfriend said, 'Look, I'm still freezing. I don't think the Lord would mind if we acted as man and wife for just this one night.'

'You're probably right,' said the boyfriend. 'Get up and get your own damn blanket.'

★

A priest decides it's time to pay a visit to a nearby convent that is in an undesirable part of town. As he looks for the convent he is approached by several prostitutes who proposition him. 'Thirty bucks a trick!' Not knowing exactly what this meant, the embarrassed priest hurries on to the convent. Inside he asks Mother Superior, 'What's a trick?' She answers, 'Thirty bucks, just like out on the street!'

★

A man was caught in a flash flood and had only a thin tree branch to hang onto to prevent him from being washed into the water. As the water became stronger and he began to tire, a motorboat appeared out of nowhere.

'Come on buddy, get in,' yelled the boatman. 'It's okay,' the man said. 'I have faith in Jesus. He will save me.' So the boat continued on and the water began to rise. When it was up to his neck another boat appeared. 'Better get in or you'll drown,' shouted the boatman.

'No, it's okay,' said the man. 'I have faith in Jesus. He will save me.' The boatman shrugged and rowed away. By this time the water had reached the man's chin. A third boat appeared. 'This is your last chance, get in!' yelled the boatman. 'No, Jesus will save me.' The boat went off and seconds later, the man drowned. Arriving in Heaven he was greeted by Jesus. 'Hey, Jesus, I trusted in you and you let me drown! I don't believe it!'

'Neither do I. I sent three damned boats to save you.'

★

'You're not a hypnotist, are you?' asked the doorman of the jazz club. 'No, I'm a singer,' the fellow replied. 'Come right this way then,' said the doorman, taking the singer to see the Manager. 'You'd better not tell me you're a hypnotist!' said the Manager grimly.

'No! I'm a singer,' said the fellow. So the Manager took him over to Madeleine, the pianist. They began to rehearse and at the end of the first song Madeleine asked, slightly worried, 'You're not going to do anything else in your act are you? No hypnotism or anything?' The singer shook his head in frustration. 'Look, I keep telling everyone I'm a singer. What's all this crap about hypnotism?'

'Well,' said Madeleine. 'Last week we hosted a convention for priests and nuns. We thought we'd better not hire a comedian because, well, you know what innocent folk those of the calling are. So we brought in a hypnotist instead. The convention filled the whole audience — that's over 200 people! The hypnotist was pretty damn good, too, got them all in a trance!'

'Well, so what was the problem?'

'Well,' said Madeleine, 'Halfway through the act he slipped on something on the floor and tumbled off the stage. He landed on his nose and broke it, and yelled, "F***!" You can just imagine what God's thinking of us now!'

★

One day Jesus comes across an angry, stone-clenching mob encircling a screaming woman. 'What's going on?' he demands. 'She's an adulteress,' cries a voice. 'She must be stoned to death.'

'Let he who is without sin cast the first stone,' replies Jesus, staring back at the crowd. At this, they fall silent, and one by one they shuffle off, ashamed. Except for one little old woman who staggers up to the adulteress with a monster of a rock in her arms. She smashes it down on the other woman, killing her instantly. Jesus lets out a huge sigh and then says, 'You know, Mom, sometimes you really piss me off.'

★

One day Adam thought it was time to ask God a question or two.

Adam: 'Lord, why did you make Eve so beautiful? Her beauty baffles me.'

God: 'So you will always want to look at her.'

Adam: 'And why, Lord, is Eve's skin is so soft?"

God: 'So you will always awant to touch her.'

Adam: 'That's wonderful, Lord. But why oh why, did you make that girl so darned stupid?'

God: 'Why, that's simple Adam. It was so she would love you.'

A Jewish man meets his non-Jewish friend one Friday for lunch.

Non-Jew: 'So, you can't eat shellfish, anything with a split hoof or any animal that chews its cud?'

Jew: 'Right.'

Non-Jew: 'Well, what if a horse's hooves were magically unsplit? Could you eat a horse then?'

Jew: 'Hmm, I guess so.'

Non-Jew: 'You mean you could eat a WHOLE horse?'

★

Early one morning a nun is walking through the city. She sees a drunk lying in the gutter outside a bar with his head resting on an empty beer bottle. She stops and says to him, 'You poor man. Don't you know that alcohol will ruin your life? Come to the Catholic mission with me and I'll help you stop drinking.'

The drunk opens one eye, looks up and says, 'Sister, you don't know what you're talking about. A little drink now and then won't hurt anyone. But if you come inside and have a drink with me, I will go with you to your mission.'

The nun thinks it was worth doing in order to get him to the mission so she agrees, but she says, 'Can you bring it out here? I don't want to be seen drinking in a bar.'

'Sure, no problem,' says the drunk.

'Oh, and another thing,' says the nun. 'Can you put my drink in a coffee mug?'

'Okay,' agrees the drunk, and he goes into the bar and says to the barman, 'Gimme a double bourbon, and put it in a coffee mug!'

The barman says, 'So, is that nun out there again?'

★

Turn On the Lights!

How many men does it take to change a light bulb?
Four. One to actually change it, and three friends to brag to about how he screwed it.

★

How many real men does it take to change a light bulb?
None. Real men aren't afraid of the dark.

★

How many feminists does it take to change a light bulb?
Five, one to screw it in and four to host a women-only seminar on how the bulb is exploiting the socket.

★

How many road workers does it take to change a light bulb?
You're kidding aren't you?

★

How many Miss Americas does it take to change a light bulb?
Just one. She holds the bulb and the world revolves around her.

★

How many hippies does it take to change a light bulb?
Six. One to screw it in, and five to share the experience.

★

How many civil libertarians does it take to change a light bulb?
None. If you want to sit in the dark, that's your business.

★

How many social workers does it take to change a light bulb?
Only one. But the light bulb has to want to change.

★

How many cafeteria staff does it take to change a light bulb?
Sorry, we closed 12 seconds ago and I've already counted the till.

★

How many politicians does it take to change a light bulb?
Two. One to screw it in and one to screw it up.

★

How many fishermen does it take to change a light bulb?
One. And you should have seen it. It was this big!

★

How many pro-lifers does it take to change a light bulb?
Five. Two to screw in the bulb, two to testify that it was lit from the moment they began screwing, and one to shoot them all, just in case they are pro-choice.

★

How many psychotherapists does it take to change a light bulb?
Just one, but it takes 30 visits at $90 a session.

★

How many motor mechanics does it take to change a light bulb?
Five. One to force it with a hammer, one to tell you it's no longer in warranty, and three to go out for more bulbs.

★

How many PhD students does it take to change a light bulb?
'You'll find out when I present my thesis on it in five years.'

★

How many actors does it take to change a light bulb?
Ten. One to climb the ladder, and nine to stand around grumbling, 'That should be me up there.'

★

How many models does it take to change a light bulb?
A whole room full, but they're all too busy doing their hair.

★

How many actresses does it take to change a light bulb?
One. But you should have seen the line outside the producer's hotel room.

★

How many movie directors does it take to change a light bulb?
Just one, and when it's finished, everyone thinks that his first light bulb was much better.

★

How many women with PMS does it take to change a light bulb?
Three. Why three? It just does, that's why.

★

How many scriptwriters does it take to change a light bulb?
Why do we have to change it?

★

How many art gallery visitors does it take to change a light bulb?
Two — one to do it and the other to say any four year old could do it better.

★

How many technical writers does it take to change a light bulb?
Just one, provided there is a programer around to explain how to do it.

★

How many actresses does it take to change a light bulb?
Just one. They don't like sharing the spotlight.

★

How many Microsoft executives does it take to screw in a light bulb?
None. They just redefine 'darkness' as the industry standard.

★

How many sound men does it take to change a light bulb?
One, two, three. One, two, three.

★

How many mystery writers does it take to change a light bulb?
Two. One to screw it in almost all the way and another to give it a surprise twist at the end.

★

Politicians and Other Crooks

How long does it take for a female politician to
have a shit?
Nine months.

★

A scientist, a salesman and a politician are driving along the countryside, and decide to spend the night in a small inn. 'I only have two free beds, so one of you will have to sleep in the barn,' says the innkeeper. The scientist volunteers to do so and makes his way out to the yard. A short time later, when the others have settled into their beds, the scientist knocks on the door. 'There's a cow in the barn. I'm Hindu and it is against my religion to sleep next to a sacred animal.' So the salesman says, 'Okay, I'll sleep out there then.' He gathers up his blankets and heads to the shed. A few seconds later he is back, saying, 'There's a pig in the barn. I'm Jewish and it would offend me to sleep next to an unclean animal.' So the politician is sent to the barn. A minute later there is knocking again, only this time much louder. The scientist and salesman open the door and see that it's the cow and the pig.

★

A sign outside the Free Range Lion Safari Park: Adults, $10. Children $5. Politicians, free.

★

If a politician or a tax inspector were both about to be burnt to death in a fire, and you could only save one of them, would you make a cup of coffee or take a nap?

★

What do you call a cross between a politician and a boomerang?
A nasty smell you can't get rid of.

★

What do you do if you run over a politician?
Reverse.

★

What's the difference between a dead dog on the road and a dead politician on the road?
Skid marks in front of the dog.

★

How do you stop a politician from drowning?
Take your foot off his head!

★

What's black and brown and looks good on a politician?
A doberman.

★

What do you have when a lawyer is buried up to his neck in sand?
Not enough sand.

★

Father Christmas, the Tooth Fairy, a smart blonde, an honest politician and a homeless old man are walking down the street together when they simultaneously spot a $100 bill. Who gets it? The homeless old man, of course. The other four are mythological creatures.

★

A customer goes into a brain store.
'How much for engineer brain?'
'$3 a pound.'
'How much for doctor brain?'
'$5 a pound.'
'How much for politician brain?'
'$500 a pound.'
'Why is politician brain so much more expensive?'
'Do you know how many politicians you need to kill to get a pound of brain?'

★

In a biological science tutorial, one student commented to another, 'Hey, did you know that in our lab we're using politicians now instead of rats?'
'Really?' the other replied. 'How come?'
'Well, for three reasons: first, there are more politicians in alleys and back streets than rats; second, the lab assistants don't get attached to them; and third, there are some things that even a rat won't do. The only problem with using politicians, however, is that it's far more difficult to apply our findings to real human beings.'

★

What happens to a politician who takes Viagra?
He grows taller.

★

Lord, give me the ability to accept the things I cannot change, the strength of will to change the things that need changing, and the wisdom to hide the bodies of those people I had to kill because they really pissed me off.

★

Why did the post office have to recall the new 'politician' stamps?
Because people couldn't tell which side to spit on.

★

A politician and a librarian were holidaying in an expensive resort in Tahiti. The politician said, 'I'm here with my insurance money, because my house burnt down and everything I owned was destroyed by fire.'
'That's a bit of a coincidence,' said the librarian. 'I'm here because my house and all my belongings were destroyed by flood, and my insurance also paid for everything.'
The politician looked puzzled. 'How do you start a flood?'

★

A politician was approached by the Devil, who promised him that he could arrange it so that the politician would win every election and be ruler of the world before he turned 50. All he had to do was sell his soul, his wife's soul, his child's soul, and the souls of all his ancestors. The politician looked puzzled for a minute and asked, 'So what's the catch?'

★

Why won't snakes attack politicians?
Professional loyalty.

★

The homework assignment for third grade required each child to draw a picture of their parents, showing what they did for a living. The teacher looked at everyone's homework the next day in class. 'Josh, that's a nice picture of a laboratory. Is your mother a scientist?' asked the teacher.

'Yes,' he answered proudly. 'Claire, I'm guessing from your picture of sausages that your daddy is a butcher.'

'Yes, he is,' replied Claire. But the teacher looked puzzled when she came to Benny's picture of a house, decorated with red fairy lights.

'Benny, that's a nice picture, but what exactly does your dad do?'

Benny announced, 'My dad's a pimp in a whorehouse.' The teacher was shocked, and promptly changed the subject. That night she phoned Benny's father. She told him about Benny's picture and demanded an explanation. Benny's father said, 'Well, actually, I'm a politician, but how do I explain a thing like that to an eight-year-old kid?'

★

Why do they always bury politicians 12 feet deep?
Because deep down, politicians are okay.

★

On visiting a seriously-ill lawyer in the hospital, his friend found him sitting up in bed, frantically leafing through the Bible.
"What are you doing?" asked the friend.
"Just looking for loopholes," replied the lawyer.

★

A lawyer opened the door of his BMW when suddenly a car came along and hit the door, ripping it off the car completely. When the police arrived at the scene, the lawyer was complaining bitterly about the damage to his precious BMW.
"Officer, look at what they've done to my Beee-mer," he whined.
"You lawyers are so materialistic, you make me sick!" retorted the officer. "You're so worried about your stupid BMW, that you didn't even notice that your left arm was ripped off in the accident!" he chided.
"Oh my GOD, I'm going to faint!" replied the lawyer, finally noticing the bloody left shoulder where his left arm once was, "Where in the hell is my Rolex?"

★

The Mafia newsletter began a Letters to the Editor column in which Mafia members were invited to freely express any grievance or political opinion they cared to. The only stipulation was that letters were to be signed with name, address and next of kin.

★

Join the Army, meet interesting people, kill them.

★

It's easy to distinguish the Mafia from the musicians. The musicians are the ones without the violin cases.

★

What's the ideal weight for a lawyer?
About five pounds, including the urn.

★

Judge: 'Did you stab the victim
                to death?'
Defendant: 'No I didn't.'
Judge: 'Do you realise what the
                penalties are for perjury?'
Defendant: 'Yes, and they're a damn lot
                better than the penalty for
                murder.'

★

The Italian crookster was returning to Rome.
He had arranged two appointments; the first
with the Pope, the second with the Mafia boss.
'Who should I see first?' He asked his adviser.
'The Pope,' was the response. 'You've only got
to kiss his hand.'

★

Staking out a notoriously bad street for drunk drivers, a policeman watched from his car as a guy lurched through a bar door, tripped on the pavement and stumbled into a car, falling asleep on the front seat. One by one, the drivers of the other cars drove off. Finally, the sleeper woke up, started his car and began to leave. The cop pulled him over and administered a Breathalyzer test. When the results showed a 0.0 blood-alcohol level, the puzzled policeman asked him how that was possible. 'Easy,' came the reply. 'Tonight was my turn to be the decoy.'

★

The FBI was hiring new recruits. Three men were called in for an interview. The interviewer, a thick-set, nasty looking man, told the first of the interviewees, 'One of the selection criteria for this position is undying loyalty to this organisation. We expect you to do everything you are told, no questions asked. We want you to take this gun, go into the other room and shoot your wife.' The first interviewee refused. 'Sorry, it's against my principles to do that.' He was promptly asked to leave and never again apply for a position there. The second applicant was then called in and given the same instruction. 'I can't do that,' he protested. 'It's our tenth anniversary tomorrow.' The interviewer thanked him for his time, but told him to leave and never again apply for a position there. The last interviewee was then shown in, and given the same instruction. 'Okay, no problem, I'll go do it now.' And he went into the other room where his wife was waiting. Shots were fired. Then all sorts of noises were heard ... grunting and groaning, a shriek here and there, a thud or two. Finally the third applicant returned and was asked what had happened. He replied, 'Some moron put blanks in the gun. So I had to strangle her.'

★

The three bears returned home from an early morning walk to find the door of their house wide open. Cautiously they went inside. 'Someone's been eating my porridge,' Papa Bear said. 'And someone's been eating my porridge,' Mama Bear said. Baby Bear rushed in. 'Who cares about the porridge? Someone's taken the video!'

★

One day a man is at a casino playing the one-arm bandits when he notices a frog sitting next to him. 'Ribbit,' says the frog, 'use this machine.' A little weirded out, the man nevertheless swaps machines, and what do you know, his first go and he lands the jackpot. 'Jeepers!' he thinks. The frog then says, 'Ribbit, now use that machine over there.' So the man goes over to the machine and sits down, and straight away the coins are pouring out all over him. 'I'm on a really good thing here,' he thinks to himself, and decides to take the frog to Las Vegas where the big money is at. So that night the man and the frog board a plane and arrive there the following day.

After playing the tables for only ten minutes the man is a millionaire, thanks entirely to the frog and his strange lucky ways.

He says, 'Frog, I don't know how to repay you.

What can I do to show my appreciation?'
The frog replies, 'Ribbit, ribbit, kiss me.' The
man figures, well, why not, if that would make
the frog happy, so be it. So he gives the frog a
big sloppy kiss and the frog magically turns in
to a gorgeous 15 year old girl.
'And that, your honor, is how the girl ended up
in my room.'

★

A police officer pulls over this guy who had been weaving in and out of the lanes. He goes up to the guy's window and says, 'Sir, I need you to blow into this Breathalyzer tube.' The man says, 'Sorry officer, I can't do that. I am an asthmatic. If I do that I'll have a really bad asthma attack.'

'Okay, fine. I need you to give a blood sample.'

'I can't do that either. I am a haemophiliac. If I do that, I'll bleed to death.'

'Well, then we need a urine sample.'

'I'm sorry, officer, no can do. I'm also a diabetic. If I do that I'll get really low blood sugar.'

'Okay then. I need you to come out here and walk this white line.'

'I can't do that, officer.'

'Why not?'

'Because I'm drunk.'

★

Irishmen and Other Funny Folks...

A Russian, an American and an Israeli are waiting to order in a restaurant. The waiter says, 'Excuse me, but I've got bad news. There's a shortage of meat.'
The American asks, 'What's a shortage?'
The Russian asks, 'What's meat?'
The Israeli asks, 'What's excuse me?'

★

A wealthy Frenchman, touring the south, stopped his Porsche for lunch in a one-horse town. After eating a ham sandwich, he was presented with a bill for $40.
'Oohlala!' he exclaimed.
'Is ham that rare out here?'
'Nope,' said the owner. 'But rich Frogs are.'

★

The Russian woman went into the store and said to the storekeeper, 'Don't you have any bread?' The storekeeper replies, 'Oh, you've got the wrong store. The store next door is the bakery and they have no bread. This is the grocers, and we have no groceries.'

Polva was in Moscow doing her weekly shopping. She went to the bakery, but as there was such a long queue she decided to walk on. The queue at the butcher store was even longer so instead she tried the grocery store, where the queue was longer than the bakery and butcher queues put together. 'I've had enough of this,' she said in frustration. Grabbing her husband's gun, she decided to march down to the Kremlin and do away with the Secretary General. But when she got there she found 200 people in line before her.

★

A couple of hillbillies were honeymooning. As they got into bed, the wife looked over to her new husband and said, 'Cletus, I ain't never done this before — please be gentle.' A scared look instantly appeared on Cletus's face and he leapt out of bed and to the telephone. 'Pa, she's a virgin, what do I do?' 'Come home, son. If she ain't good enough for her own family, she ain't good enough for ours.'

★

An Irishman and a Scottish lass were having sex. 'Cor, Jimmy! That wasn't very good,' remarked the Scot. 'Aren't Irish men supposed to be thick?' He replied, 'Aren't Scots supposed to be tight?'

★

An Irishman walks into a bar and says, 'Barman, give me three pints of Guinness, please'

So the barman gives him three pints. The Irishman proceeds to alternately sip one, then the other, then the third until they're all gone. He then orders three more Guinness', and the barman says, 'Sir, I know you like them cold, so you can start with one and I'll bring you a fresh one as soon as you're low.'

The Irishman replies, 'You don't understand. I have two brothers, one over in Australia and another at home in Ireland. We made a vow to each other that every Saturday night we'd still drink together. So right now, my brothers have three pints of Guinness in their parts of the world, and we're all enjoying a drink together.'

The barman thinks this is a wonderful tradition, and every week, he sets up the guy's three pints of Guinness as soon as he enters the bar. One week, the man orders only two pints. He drinks them, then orders two more. The barman sadly shakes his head, 'Knowing your tradition, I'd just like to say that I'm sorry one of your brothers died.'

The man looks confused and then laughs, 'Oh my brothers are fine... I just quit drinking!'

★

The Japanese tourist gave a traveler's check to the bank teller. When he counted his money he said, 'Why do I get less money today?' 'Fluctuations,' said the teller.

'And fluck you, too,' said the tourist.

★

Two Irish hunters were driving through the country to go deer hunting. They came upon a fork in the road where a sign read 'DEER LEFT' so they went home.

★

A couple of English lads were buying some
groceries at the supermarket when a
Catholic priest, wearing his left arm in a sling,
asked them to reach up and get him down
some dishwashing detergent from the top shelf.
'What happened to your arm?' asked one of
the lads.
'Oh, I broke it. I slipped as I was getting out of
the bath.' There was a silence until the priest
disappeared into the next aisle.
'What's a bath?' said one lad to the other.
'I dunno,' he replied. 'I'm not Catholic.'

★

An Irishman had been chugging down whisky
all night when the bartender called out, 'Okay,
people, bar's closing.' So the Irishman slurped
down the last of his drink, stood up to leave
and fell flat on his face. He tried to stand one
more time; same result. He figured he'd crawl
outside — hopefully the fresh air would sober
him up. Once outside he stood up and fell flat
on his face again. So he began to crawl home.
When he finally arrived at the door he stood
up and again fell flat on his face. He crawled
through the door and into his bedroom. When
he reached his bed he tried one more time to
stand up. This time he managed to pull himself
upright, but he quickly fell right into bed and

was sound asleep as soon as his head hit the pillow. The next morning his wife prodded him awake and said, 'So, you've been out drinking again, huh?'

'What makes you say that?' he asked, putting on an innocent look.

'The barman called — you left your wheelchair there again.'

★

What was written on the walls of an English brothel?

Please tell the girls when you're finished.

★

An Irish couple were cleaning out their garage when the husband accidentally kicked over a bottle and broke it. Instantly a genie appeared, and said to them both, 'Thank you so much for freeing me from that ghastly bottle. To show my gratitude, I will grant you two wishes. The third I will keep for myself.'

The husband asked for a promotion at work, and the wife asked for a multi-million dollar annual salary. The genie obliged.

'Now for my wish,' began the genie. 'Sir, I wish to have my way with your wife. After all, I've made you successful,' he said to the husband, 'and you rich,' he said to the woman.

The husband and wife agreed that this was fair enough, and she went off to the bedroom with the genie, whereupon he proceeded to have his way with her. After they had finished doing the deed, the genie asked the wife if she would mind if he asked her a few questions.

'No, I don't mind,' she said.

'How long have you been married?'

She replied, 'Six years.'

The genie then asked, 'How old is your husband?'

To which she answered, '36'.

Then the genie asked, 'So, how long has he believed in this genie stuff?'

★

An Irish couple went to the family planning clinic. 'We've been married for over ten years and still have no children. Our friends think it's because we're stupid.'

'Rubbish,' said the doctor. 'It's most likely to do with the timing. How often do you do it?'

'Do what?' asked the wife.

★

An Italian boy and a Jewish boy come of age at the same time. The Italian boy's father presents him with a brand new pistol. On the other side of town, at his Bar Mitzvah, the Jewish boy receives a beautiful gold watch. The next day when the two boys see each other at school they show each other what they got. It turns out that each boy likes the other's present better, and so they trade. That night, when the Italian boy is at home, his father sees him looking at the watch.

'Where you getta thatta watch?' asks the father. The boy explains that he and his Jewish friend had traded. The father blows his top. 'Whatta you? Stupidda boy? Whatsa matta you? Somma day, you maybe gonna getta married. Then maybe somma day you gonna comma home and finda you wife inna bed with another man. Whatta you gonna do then? Looka atta you watch and say, "How longa you gonna be?"'

★

Sick, Dirty, and Downright Disgusting

What's the difference between snot
and brussel sprouts?
You can't get a kid to eat brussel sprouts.

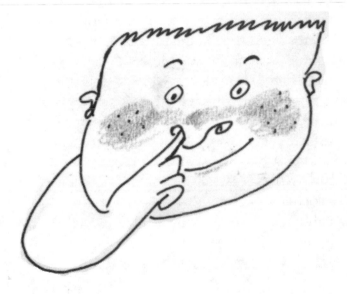

★

An old man and old woman met in a retirement home. After dating for a month, the old man said to the woman, 'I know we're old and can't do much sexually anymore. But would you please hold my penis?' The woman obliged, so every day for the next two months the couple would sit in the park by the lake and the old woman would hold the man's penis. One day the man didn't show up at their regular meeting place. The woman became concerned and set out searching for him. She soon spotted him sitting on a bench, with another woman beside him. She walked up to the bench to find his penis in the other woman's hand. She felt terribly distraught at this and sobbed, 'We've been together for three months now. I thought we were getting along just fine. Now I find you here with this other woman. What does she have that I don't?'

'Parkinson's!' replied the old man gleefully.

★

Out on the bowling green one day, a man finds a lamp. He rubs the lamp, and a genie appears to grant him one wish. The bowler does not hesitate to think — he says, 'I'd like to be the best lawn bowler in my club.'

'No problem,' says the genie, 'but your sex life will be reduced as a side effect.' The genie blinks twice, and the deed is done. A few months later the genie reappears and asks the man how his bowling is going. 'Great,' says the man. 'I'm now the best in the club.'

'And how's your sex life now?'

'It's okay. I'm still getting a bit a few times a month.'

'Is that all?' exclaimed the genie.

'Well,' says the bowler. 'I don't think it's too bad for an aging scout leader with a very small troop.'

★

There was a young woman who lived with her grandmother. One night, the granddaughter came bouncing down the stairs dressed to go out to a party wearing a see-through blouse without a bra. Her grandmother was shocked, 'Listen here, Missy,' she chided 'Now I don't want to see you dressed like that. You go right back upstairs and put on a nice dress and act like a lady, not some doggone hussy!'

'Grandma, you are so darned backward!' whined the granddaughter. 'I want to show off my rosebuds, and you can't stop me!' she spat, turning on her heel and stalking out the door. The next day, the granddaughter came outside to find her grandmother seated in her rocking chair on the porch. She too was wearing a see-through blouse without a bra.

'Grandma! What are you doing? I have some friends coming around any time now. Please go change your blouse, you are so embarrassing!' the young woman shrieked.

'You listen to me, young lady' said her grandmother sternly, 'If you can show off them rosebuds, then I can certainly show off these here hanging baskets.'

★

A guy goes into a car carrying a briefcase. Being curious, the bartender says, 'Hey buddy, what's in the case?'

Without a word, the guy opens the case and a little man, only a foot high, leaps out. He runs to the piano, tunes it, and begins to play. He is a wonderful musician, and pretty soon the bar is full of people. The bartender sells more beer than he has for the entire previous month.

'Hey, your little man is fantastic!' he says to the guy with the case. 'Where did you get him?'

'Well I came across a genie bottle one day in the Amazon forest, and the genie granted me just one wish.'

'Wow,' says the bartender. 'I wouldn't mind having a wish from a genie. Do you think I could find the bottle?'

'Oh sure,' says the guy, 'but I have to warn you that when you make your wish you'll have to speak very slowly and pronounce everything very clearly.'

'Well, it works, doesn't it? asks the bartender. 'You got your wish didn't you?'

'Tell me,' replies the guy wearily, 'do you really think I would wish for a twelve-inch pianist?'

★

FUN THINGS TO DO WHILE WAITING FOR A FREE TOILET CUBICLE

1. Start crossing your legs and squirm desperately, while edging your way closer to the person next to you.

2. Go to the hand towel dispenser and yank a whole heap out and distribute them around, charging a dollar per wad.

3. Get down on your hands and knees and start peering under the cubicle doors, calling out gleefully, 'I can see you!'

4. Shake hands with everyone in line and tell them this is your fourth visit today.

5. Frown, sigh, and mutter, 'Gotta go, gotta go!' Then pause, grimace, and say, 'Oops!'

6. Talk about the new brand of toilet paper you have discovered.

7. Get out your lunch and start eating.

★

Joel: 'What's the difference between a shower curtain and toilet paper?'
Adrian: 'I don't know.'
Joel: 'Oh, so it was you!'

★

Three men checked into a hotel. The clerk at the counter told them there was only one room left so the men decided to all share the bed. Next morning, the man that slept on the right side of the bed said, 'I had a really weird dream. I dreamt that someone jerked me off.' 'That's weird,' said the guy on the left side of the bed, 'I also dreamt that someone jerked me off.'

The man in the middle said, 'I had a different dream, I dreamt that I went skiing.'

★

For many months Jim wished that he and Jen would 'get down to business', but he felt a bit shy about broaching the subject. One evening, however, he and Jen were enjoying a romantic dinner down on her parents' farm. The mood seemed right — even the silhouette of a bull humping a cow in the distance seemed to be telling Jim that this was the right moment to finally bring up the subject. He took her hand gently and whispered in her ear, 'I'd sure like to be doing what that bull is doing.'
'Well, why don't you,' she whispered back. 'Dad's been away, so I'm sure the cow would be happy to.'

★

What did the leper say to the prostitute?
You can keep the tip.

★

How can you tell which is the head nurse?
She's the one with the dirty knees.

★

Big Hawk the Indian was with the park ranger one day when they got lost. The park ranger says to Big Hawk, 'Use your tracking ability to get us out of this mess.' Big Hawk bends down and puts his ear to the ground. 'Buffalo come.' The park ranger replies, 'How do you know?' Big Hawk says, 'Ear sticky.'

★

Some crooks break their way into a bank vault and find hundreds of safes. They open the first safe and the only thing they find in there is a vanilla pudding. The head crook says, 'I'm hungry.' So they eat the pudding. They open up the second safe and there's another vanilla pudding. So they devour it too. Safe after safe, no money, only pudding. After all the safes had been opened, they were starting to feel ill from all that pudding. 'Well,' they say, 'we didn't get any money, but at least we won't have to buy dinner tonight!' The next day on the news they hear: 'Yesterday the biggest sperm bank in the world was robbed...'

★

Three sons left the mountains to make their fortunes, and they all did very well for themselves. They got together recently and were discussing what they each had done to benefit their elderly mother.

'Well,' said Cletus, 'I bought Mom a huge house in Beverly Hills.'

'You think that's impressive. I bought Mom a stretch Rolls Royce and hired her a full time driver.' snorted Luther.

'I've got you both beat,' smiled Jim Bob. 'I bought Mom a miraculous parrot that can recite any Bible verse you tell it to.'

A little later, the mother sent out a thank you note to all three sons. It read: 'Cletus, the house you bought was too big. I only live in one room, but have to clean the entire house. Luther, the car is useless. I don't go anywhere because I'm too old, and have seen it all before. But Jim Bob, you know exactly what I like. That chicken you got me, it was purely delicious.'

★

Tali and Foley were having dinner at a restaurant one night when Tali noticed a spoon in their waiter's apron. Tali didn't think too much of this until another waiter came over with glasses of water. He, too, sported a spoon in his apron. Tali told Foley of her observation, and as they both looked around the room, they could see that all the waiters had spoons in their aprons. When the first waiter returned to take their order, Tali asked, 'What's with the spoons, waiter?' 'Well,' explained the waiter, 'this place is under new management, and our new boss has all these fantastic ideas about how to improve efficiency. Apparently he read some study about how patrons drop spoons on the floor 80 percent more often than any other utensil. So now we all carry a spoon with us to cut down our trips to the kitchen and save time.' Just as he concluded, a 'ch-ching' came from the table behind him, and he quickly replaced the fallen spoon with the one from his pocket. 'I'll grab another spoon the next time I'm in the kitchen instead of making a special trip,' he proudly explained. Tali and Foley were both impressed, and sat back to wait for their meal. When the waiter came over again to bring them their steaks, Foley noticed a black plastic cord protruding from the waiter's fly. A quick look around the room revealed that a similar piece of cord dangled out of each waiter's fly.

'Excuse me,' said Foley to their waiter, a little embarrassed. 'What's the deal with the cord hanging out of your fly?'

'Oh, that,' smiled the waiter. 'That's another good idea the new boss came up with to save time in the bathroom.'

'How's that?'

'You see, we use the cord to pull out our penises at the urinals and thereby eliminate the need to wash our hands, cutting time spent in the bathroom by over 95 percent!'

'Oh, that makes sense,' said Foley, thinking through the process. 'Hey, wait a minute. If the cord helps you pull it out, how do you get it back in?'

'Well,' the waiter whispered, 'I don't know about the other guys, but I use my spoon.'

★

Did you hear about the cross-eyed circumciser?
He got the sack.

★

Did you hear about the male prostitute who contracted leprosy?
He did okay for a while, and then his business dropped off.

A ventriloquist walked into an Kansas town and saw a farmer with his dog.

Ventriloquist: 'Hey, cool dog. Mind if I speak to him?'

Farmer: 'Dogs don't talk!'

Ventriloquist: 'Hey dog, how's it going?'

Dog: 'Not bad, not bad.'

Farmer: (Look of disbelief)

Ventriloquist: 'Is this your owner?' (pointing at the farmer)

Dog: 'Yep.'

Ventriloquist: 'Does he treat you well?'

Dog: 'Yeah, great. He walks me every day, feeds me great food, couldn't be better.'

Farmer: (Look of disbelief)

Ventriloquist: 'Mind if I talk to your horse?'

Farmer: 'Horses don't talk!'

Ventriloquist: 'Hey horse, how's it going?'

Horse: 'Not bad, not bad.'

Farmer: (Look of disbelief)

Ventriloquist: 'Is this your owner?'
(Pointing at the farmer)

Horse: 'Yep.'

Ventriloquist: 'How's he treat you?'

Horse: 'Really well. Lots of fresh hay and oats, he rides me every day, and the water is always clean.'

Farmer: (Look of disbelief)

Ventriloquist: 'Mind if I talk to your SHEEP?'

Farmer: (Stuttering, and hardly able to talk)....
'Th-th-them sheep ain't nothing but liars!'

★

A tourist dining in a five star restaurant noticed that the waiter had his thumb in every dish he served. When the chicken soup came out, the waiter's thumb was resting in it, when the lamb casserole was brought to the table, the waiter's thumb was in it, and when the hot apple pie for dessert was brought out, again, the waiter's thumb was in it.

'What's going on here?' demanded the tourist. 'You've had your thumb in every dish I've been brought. It's disgusting.' The waiter said, 'I have arthritis in my thumb and must keep it warm.'

The tourist was furious. 'I don't care, you filthy bastard, putting your thumb in my food. Why don't you stick it up your ass!'

'I do,' replied the waiter. 'In the kitchen.'

★

Is a castrated pig disgruntled?

★

Why aren't hemorrhoids called 'asteroids'?

★

What did one lesbian frog say to the other?
Gee, we really do taste like chicken.

★

A guy walks into a club and sits down. He starts dialling numbers on his hand, as if using a telephone, then holds an animated discussion with his fingers. The club owner notices and walks up to him. 'Listen, buddy. This is a rough club. I don't want any fights breaking out here, so you better stop that funny business of yours.'
The guy says, 'Look, pal. I'm not trying to start anything. I'm just a hi-tech guy. I've had a phone inserted into my hand so I can always be contacted. Whenever my wife or agent want to call me, they can, without the batteries dying. By the way, where's the bathroom?' The

club owner points the way and the guy walks off. After 20 minutes go by and the guy hasn't emerged from the bathroom, the club owner starts to get a little worried. After all, the club attracted some rather nasty people sometimes. Fearing the worst, he goes into the bathroom. He finds the guy leaning towards the wall, spread-eagled. His pants are pulled down and he has a roll of toilet paper sticking out of his butt.

'Oh shit!' said the club owner. 'Did they rob you? Are you hurt?'

The guy turns and says, 'Oh, I'm fine. I'm just waiting for a fax.'

★

Two unemployed men are bumming
around town when Man #1 says, 'I'd
really like a night on the booze, but I don't
think $2 is gonna stretch that far.'
Man #2 replies, 'Alright. I've got a plan.
We start with buying a hotdog.'
Man #1 asks quizzically, 'And how
is that going to help?'
Man #2 replies, 'Well, we get the
hotdog and throw away the roll. Then I'll
take the sausage and put it down my pants
and we go to a bar. We order some drinks,
and when the bartender asks for his money,
I'll pull down my zipper. You drop to
your knees and act like you're having a
real good time down there, and the
barkeeper will throw us out, and we won't
have to pay.'
Man #1 agrees. So they go into a bar, order
some drinks, and gulp them down.
When the bartender says, 'That'll be $8.50,'
Man #2 drops his pants and pulls out the
sausage. Man #1 drops to his knees. The
bartender immediately throws them out of his
bar.
The two then visit several more bars, pulling
off the same trick. After the seventh bar

Man #1 finally says, 'Buddy, we've gotta stop this. My knees are killing me!'
Man #2 replies, 'You think that's bad, I lost the sausage after the third bar.'

★

A male and female whale were out for a romantic swim one sunny day when they saw a whaling ship. The male whale said to the female: 'Let's go and blow out our air holes at the same time so the ship will sink.' So they went over and did it. Sure enough, the ship capsized and sank. But the sailors found their way out and were swimming to shore. Furious, the male whale said to the female, 'Let's chase them and eat them before they get to shore!' But this time his companion was not so keen. 'Look,' she said. 'I went along with the blowjob, but I absolutely refuse to swallow the seamen.'

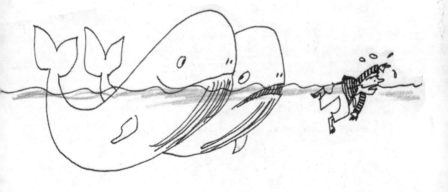

★

If a male hillbilly and a female hillbilly get married in the hills, but move to Washington DC, are they still brother and sister?

★

One night a bartender notices this hideous guy at the far end of the bar with several hot women around him. The bartender says to him, 'Please don't get offended when I tell you this, but I couldn't help noticing you have several beautiful women hanging all over you. Forgive my honesty, but you are not exactly the most handsome person I've ever seen. In fact, you're quite ugly. Now, normally, I would think these ladies are attracted to you because of your money, but I can tell by the way you're dressed and the fact that they are buying YOU drinks, it's not the money. Tell me, sir, what is it about you that attracts all these babes?'

The man paused a moment, licked his eyebrows, and said, 'I haven't the faintest idea.'

★

Three couples visited the local minister to see how to become members of his church. The minister said that they would have to go without sex for two weeks and then come back and tell him how they went.

The first couple was retired, the second couple was middle aged, and the third couple was newlywed.

Two weeks went by and the couples returned to the minister. The retired couple said that it was no problem at all. The middle-aged couple said that it was tough for the first week, but it was no problem after that. The newlyweds said that it was fine until she dropped the can of paint.

'Can of PAINT?' exclaimed the minister. 'Yeah,' said the newlywed man. 'She dropped the can and bent over to pick it up. I'm sorry to say that I had to have her right there and then. Lust took over. We were out of control.'

The minister just shook his head, and said that they were no longer welcome in the church. 'Oh, that's okay,' sighed the man. 'We're no longer welcome in the hardwore store, either.'

★

One day, a farmer was tending to his livestock when he noticed that one of the cows was completely cross-eyed. He called up a veterinarian friend of his who told him to bring in the cow. The vet took one look at the cow, stuck a tube up the cow's butt, and blew into the tube until the cow's eyes straightened out. The vet charged the farmer a hundred bucks, and the farmer went home happy. About one week later, the cow's eyes were cross-eyed again, but this time the farmer figured he could probably take care of it himself. So he called his hired hand over, and together they put a tube up the cow's butt. The farmer put his lips to the tube and started to blow. Strangely, nothing happened, so he asked his hired hand to give it a try. The hired hand removed the tube, turned it around, put it back into the cow's butt and started to blow.

'What are you doing?!' asked the farmer, horrified.

'Heck, I wasn't gonna use the side that you'd put your lips on,' came the reply.

★

The Hospital Director was showing a nun around his hospital in the hope of receiving a donation from the church. 'And this is B wing,' said the director, as they passed a room where they could see a man masturbating wildly. Naturally the nun was very shocked by this and demanded an explanation as to why these activities were allowed in the hospital. 'Ah,' said the director. 'That poor patient is suffering from quite a horrible disease. He produces so much sperm that unless he gets rid of it five times a day his testicles will explode.'

'Oh,' said the nun. 'Well I guess I can understand.' They continued through B wing and opened the door to C wing. The nun peeked into the first room they passed and saw a nurse, on her knees, giving a patient a blowjob. 'Oh, my God!' she shrieked. 'I demand an explanation for this!'

The doctor said. 'Same problem, better health insurance.'

★

A businessman returns from the Far East. After a few days, he notices a strange growth on his penis. He is very concerned about the growth that has appeared, and promptly visits one doctor after another. However, they all offer him the same unwanted advice. 'It seems that you've been screwing around in the Far East. But I'm afraid there's no cure. There is nothing I can do but cut it off.'

The man panics, but figures that if it is a common affliction in the East they must know how to cure it there. So he goes back to India and visits a doctor in Bombay.

The doctor examines him and says, 'You've been fooling around in my country, haven't you? This is a very common problem here. Did you see any other doctors about the growth?'

The man replied, 'Yes, a few back home.'

The doctor says, 'And they told you it had to be cut off?'

The man answers, 'Yes, I couldn't believe it!'

The doctor smiles knowingly, shaking his head 'Well, their advice is incorrect and most unnecessary. After all, your penis will fall off all by itself.'

★

A man and his wife were sitting in church one Sunday. The man was having a little snooze, and his wife was knitting. The priest implored them, 'Who created the Earth and Man, my congregation?'

The woman poked her husband with a knitting needle, and he screamed, suddenly jolting awake, 'GOD!'.

The priest looked at the man and, admiring his enthusiasm, nodded, 'That is correct'

Then the priest asked, 'Who, my congregation, is the son of God?'.

Once more, the woman poked her husband with the knitting needle. The man woke up startled, and screamed, 'Jesus Christ!'

Again, the priest said, 'That is correct.'

Finally the priest asked, 'Tell me, my congregation, what did Eve say to Adam when she didn't want to have any more children?'

The knitter poked her husband again. This time he awoke absolutely furious, and screamed at his wife, 'Poke me with that damned thing one more time, and I'm going to rip it off you!'

The priest smiled and said, 'That is correct'.

★

Sammy was a session performer hired to play guitar for a movie score. He couldn't wait to see the finished film and hear his music. After he was paid for the job, he asked the producer where he could catch the film. The producer explained that the music was for a porno flick, and told Sammy the addresses of some seedy movie houses where it was showing. Sammy was a bit embarrassed that this is what his 'art' was going to, but thought to himself, 'Well, it is a movie all the same. And I did get paid a lot'. So, in disguise, Sammy went to see the film. Hoping no one would recognize him, he slunk to the back of the cinema and sat next to an elderly couple who also appeared to be in disguise. The movie started, and it was the filthiest, most perverse porno flick ever. The lead character was an attractive woman who was into group sex, S & M, the works.

Very embarrassed and blushing, Sammy turned to the old couple beside him and whispered, 'I'm really not into the sick stuff. I'm just here for the music.'

The woman turned to Sammy and whispered back, 'That's okay, we're just here to see our daughter.'

★

An almost blind guy walked into a sexy lingerie shop to purchase their most see-through item for his wife. After receiving some help from the store clerk, he bought a lace teddy for $200, and brought it home for his wife. She took it upstairs and realized that it didn't quite fit. But, she figured, since it's supposed to be see-through, and since her husband was almost blind, she might as well wear nothing at all. So, she came downstairs completely naked.

'Huh?' said the old man, giving her a squeeze. 'For the amount of money I paid, they could have at least ironed the damned thing.'

★

Now there's this guy who owns a stud farm, and one day a midget calls in, hoping to buy a horse. He walks up, and the owner asks him if he wants a male or female horse.

'A female horth,' the midget says. *That's quite a speech impediment*, the farm owner thinks. So anyway, the owner shows him one of his best fillies.

'Nithe horth, can I thee into her mouth?' the midget asks. So the owner picks up the midget and shows him the horse's mouth.

'Nithe mouth. Can I thee her eyeth?'

So the owner picks up the midget and shows

him her eyes.

'What about the ear-th?' Now the owner is a bit fed up, but he picks up the midget one more time and shows him the horse's ears.

'Okay, finally, I'd like to thee her twat.' With that, the owner picks up the midget and shoves his head up the horse's twat, then pulls him out.

Feeling totally disgusted and sick, the midget says, 'Perhapth I thould thay it diffwently. I'd like to thee her run!'

★

One cold and bleak morning, a man is driving through the country. Suddenly, from out of nowhere, a massive bald man steps on the road. He's seven foot tall, and his muscles ripple in every inch of his body. At the roadside there also stands a young woman. She is absolutely beautiful — slim, shapely, fair complexion, golden hair ... heart-stopping. The driver stops and stares, and his attention is only distracted from the lovely girl when the monster opens the car door and drags him from his seat with a fist resembling a raw ham.

'Right,' he shouts, 'Masturbate!'

'But...' stammers the driver.

'Do it now or I'll kill yer!'

So the driver turns his back, drops his trousers

and jerks off. Thinking of the girl on the roadside, this doesn't take him long. 'Right,' snarls Mr Tough. 'Do it again!'

So the driver does it again.

'Right buddy, do it again,' demands Mr Tough. This goes on for nearly two hours. The hapless driver is in agony, and has collapsed in a sweating, jibbering heap on the ground.

'Do it again,' says Mr Tough.

'I can't — you'll just have to kill me,' whimpers the man.

Mr Tough looks down at the pathetic soul slumped on the roadside.

'Okay, *now* you can drive my daughter to the next town.'

A little girl runs out to the garage where her father is working on his car, and asks him, 'Daddy, what's sex?' So her father sits her down, and tells her all about the birds and the bees. He tells her about conception, sexual intercourse, sperm and eggs. He tells her about puberty, menstruation, erections, wet dreams. He thinks, what the hell, and goes on to tell her the works. He describes masturbation, anal and oral sex, group sex, bondage and discipline, homosexuality, sex toys ... you name it. The girl is somewhat awestruck with this sudden influx of bizarre new knowledge, and her father finally asks, 'So, why did you want to know about sex?' 'Oh, Mommy said lunch would be ready in a couple of secs...'

★

Confucius say...
He who walk through airport door sideways, going to Bangkok.

★

Confucius say...
Boy who sleep with stiff problem wake up with solution in hand.

★

Confucius say...
Girl who sits on Judge's lap gets honorable discharge.

★

Confucius say...
Lady who go camping must beware of evil intent.

★

Confucius say...
Man who keep feet firmly on ground have trouble putting on pants.

★

Confucius say...
Man who stand on street corner with hands in pockets, not feeling crazy, feeling nuts.

★

Confucius say...
Man with tight trousers is pressing his luck.

★

One day, Pinocchio and his girlfriend were in bed doing what girls and wooden boys do. As they were cuddling later, Pinocchio could tell that something was bothering his girlfriend. So, he asked her, 'What's the matter, honey?' Pinocchio's girlfriend gave a big sigh and replied, 'You're probably the best guy I've ever met, but every time we make love you give me splinters.' This remark bothered Pinocchio a great deal, so the next day he went to seek advice from his creator, Gepetto. After listening to the problem, Gepetto handed over a square of sandpaper and said, 'Now this should smooth out the problem!' Gratefully, Pinocchio took the sandpaper and went off to try it. Now, a few weeks passed by and Gepetto was in town to have some blades sharpened at the hardware store when he ran into Pinocchio. Pinocchio was buying up ALL of the sandpaper in the hardware store, so Gepetto remarked, 'So, Pinocchio, things must be going pretty damn well with you and the girls.'
Pinocchio replied, 'Girls? Who needs girls?'

★

A guy, his dog, and a pig are the only survivors of a terrible shipwreck, and they find themselves stranded on a desert island. A few slow weeks pass by. Every evening they'd lie out on the beach and watch the stars. One night, the guy was feeling a little amorous and really wanted some feminine company. The pig started to look like not such a bad prospect. So the guy rolled toward the pig and put his arm around it, giving it a bit of a cuddle. However, the dog was quite jealous about this and growled and barked until the guy took his arm away.

A few weeks passed by, and lo and behold, there was another shipwreck. The only survivor was a beautiful young woman, with a perfect hourglass figure and golden suntan. Luckily the young woman was uninjured. She got along well with the others and went to the beach with them every evening to watch the stars. One balmy night the guy began getting 'those' ideas again, and this time, darn it, he was going to give in. He'd been alone for such a long time. So, he shyly leaned across to the girl and whispered, 'Umm, would you mind taking the dog for a walk?'

★

It being the noughties and all, a middle-aged man decided he would have a facelift for his birthday. It costs him $5000, and he is ecstatic about the result. He looks fantastic! On the way home he stops at a drugstore to buy some candy and says to the girl serving him, 'How old do you think I am?'

'Hmm, about 33,' was the reply.

'I'm actually 45!' the man says, feeling really happy. After that he goes into McDonalds for lunch, and asks the cashier there the same question. Her reply is even better... 'Oh, you look about 30.' The man is now feeling very pleased with himself. While standing at the bus stop he asks an old bag lady the same question. She croaks, 'I am 90 years old, and my eyesight is not what it once was, but when I was young there was a sure way of telling how old a man is. If I put my hand down your pants and play with your balls for ten minutes I will be able to tell your exact age.' As there was no one around, the man thought what the hell and let her slip her wrinkled hand down his pants and have a good rummage around. Ten minutes later the old lady says, 'Okay, it's done. You are 45.'

Stunned, the man says, 'That was brilliant! How did you do that?' The old lady replies, 'I was behind you in McDonalds.'

★

A doctor had the reputation of helping couples increase the joy in their sex life, but always promised not to take a case if he felt he could not help them. Mr and Mrs Adams went to see the doctor, and he gave them thorough physical exams, psychological exams, and various tests and then concluded, 'Yes, I am happy to say that I believe I can help you. On your way home from my office stop at the supermarket and buy some grapes and some donuts. Go home, take off your clothes, and you, sir, roll the grapes across the floor until you make a bullseye in your wife's love canal. Then on hands and knees you must crawl to her like a leopard and retrieve the grape using only your tongue. Then next, ma'am, you must take the donuts and from across the room, toss them at your husband until you make a ringer around his love pole. Then like a lioness, you must crawl to him and eat a donut.'

The couple went home and their sex life improved out of sight. They told their friends, Mr and Mrs Rainard, that they should see the good doctor. The doctor greeted the Rainards and warned he would not take the case unless he felt that he could help them; so he conducted the physical exams and the same battery of tests.

Then he told the Rainards the bad news. 'I can't help you, so I will not take your money.

I believe your sex life is as good as it will ever be. I'm sorry.'

The Rainards pleaded with him, and said, 'You helped our friends, now please, please help us.'

'Well, okay,' the doctor said. 'On your way home from the office, stop at the supermarket and buy some apples and a box of Froot Loops...'

★

An old man and an old lady are getting ready for bed one night when all of a sudden the woman bursts out of the bathroom, flings open her robe and yells: 'Super Pussy!'

The old man says: 'I'll have the soup.'

★

Modern Technology

Who is General Failure and why is he reading my hard disk?

★

Bill Gates dies and is ready to enter the afterlife. He meets St Peter at the Pearly Gates, who looks a little confused. 'I don't know if I should let you in here, Bill. I mean, sure, you helped bring computers to the world, but then, you also created that Windows crap. I can't decide where I should put you. I know this is against procedure and all, but I think maybe I'll let YOU choose. I'll let you check out both places for a couple of minutes so you can make up your mind.'
'Okay then,' said Bill, 'I'll try Hell first.' So off Bill went to Hell. Hell was beautiful. The weather was warm, the sun was shining, and there were lots of bikini-clad women frolicking about. He was ecstatic. 'This is great!' he told St Peter. 'I love it here! But I guess I should have a look at Heaven, though I doubt it could be any better.' The two flew up in the sky to Heaven, where angels drifted about, singing beautiful songs and smiling at everyone. It was a very peaceful and serene place. Still, it wasn't

as enticing as Hell, and Bill didn't need to think long. 'I think I'd prefer Hell,' he said. 'Fine,' replied St Peter. So Bill Gates went to Hell. Two weeks later, St Peter decided to check on the late billionaire to see how he was doing. When he entered the gates of Hell he found Bill shackled to a wall, screaming in pain as hot flames licked his body and demons prodded him with sharp knives.

'How's everything going?' St Peter asked. Bill gasped in anguish, 'This is awful! This is nothing like the Hell I visited two weeks ago! I can't believe this is happening! What happened to that other place, with the beautiful beaches and the scantily clad women playing in the water?'

'That was a demo version,' replied St Peter.

★

How many Tech Support people does it take to change a light bulb?

Have you looked at the user manual? I'm not going to help you until you've looked at the user manual. Damned light bulb users ... shouldn't be allowed to have one if they don't know how to use them!

★

COMPUTER VIRUSES

Bulimia Virus — eats up all your files then spews them out all mixed up.

Pro-Life Virus — won't let you delete a file no matter how unwanted it is.

Pro-Choice Virus — gives you a choice about whether or not to delete a file, even when it knows you definitely want to delete it.

Gynaecologist Virus — invades your system where you don't want it to.

Elvis Virus — your computer gets slow and lazy, and makes horrible sounds.

Alien Virus — invades your system in places where no virus has ever been before.

Consultant Virus — tests your system then sends you a bill for $2500.

★

How many programers does it take to change a light bulb?
That's impossible, it's a hardware problem.

★

How many database programmers does it take to change a light bulb?
Three. One to write the dead light bulb removal script, one to write the new light bulb insertion script, and one to act as a light bulb administrator to make sure nobody else tries to change the light bulb at the same time.

★

TOP 10 REASONS COMPUTERS MUST BE FEMALE

1. They sometimes just sit there, blinking dumbly at you.

2. No one but their creator understands their internal logic.

3. Even your smallest mistakes are immediately committed to memory for future reference.

4. The message, 'There is a General Application Error,' is about as informative as, 'If you don't know why I'm mad at you, then I'm certainly not going to tell you.'

5. They frustrate the hell out of you when you give a command and they don't, won't, or can't follow it.

6. Sometimes, try as you might, you can't turn them on, particularly if you already have a floppy in.

7. If your floppy disk has a virus, you can be damn sure your computer will get it.

8. They sometimes suffer communication problems. They won't talk to the printer, won't acknowledge the modem's presence, and won't write to the hard disk.

9. You continually have to talk to the supplier, which you really don't want to do.

10. If you write a program wrong it can start an endless loop and just go on and on and on and on...

★

TOP 10 REASONS COMPUTERS MUST BE MALE

1. They have a lot of data, but are still clueless.

2. A better model is always just around the corner.

3. They look nice and shiny until you bring them home.

4. It is always necessary to have a backup.

5. They'll do whatever you say if you push the right buttons.

6. The best part of having one is the games you can play.

7. In order to get their attention, you have to turn them on.

8. The lights are on, but nobody's home.

9. Big power surges knock them out for the night.

10. Size does matter.

★

REASONS WHY E-MAIL IS LIKE A PENIS

1. Those who have it would be devastated if it were ever cut off.

2. Many of those who don't have it would like to try having it (e-mail envy).

3. If you're not careful, it can spread viruses.

4. If you use it too much, you'll find it becomes more and more difficult to think coherently.

5. Everyone thinks it's far more important than it actually is.

6. If you're not careful, it has a way of getting you into lots of trouble.

7. When the system is down, no one is happy.

8. If an e-mail comes with a virus, it can wreak havoc with the whole system and make you wary of using it again.

★

It is the year 2087. The United Nations have finally finished designing a super intelligent computer that can deal with any problem. Military leaders are huddled around the new machine. They describe the latest happenings and the strategic plans they have engineered in order to beat the enemy. They ask the computer, 'Shall we attack now? Or retreat?' The computer computes for the next day and a half and comes up with the answer, 'Yes!' 'Yes, what?' asks one of the generals, stupefied. After another half a day, the computer replies, 'Yes, sir!'

A tourist is looking around a pet shop, when a guy walks in and says to the shopkeeper, 'I'll have a C monkey, thanks.' The shopkeeper takes a monkey out of a cage and says, 'That's $2000, pal.' The customer hands over the money and walks out with the monkey. Curious, the tourist says to the shopkeeper, 'I had no idea monkeys were so expensive!' The shopkeeper replies, 'Well, that monkey can progam in C, so he's well worth the money.' The tourist points to another monkey. 'What about that one, then? He's $5000 — what does he do?'

'Oh, he's a C++ monkey. He can do some amazingly useful stuff.'

The tourist nods, and then notices yet another monkey — this one with a $50,000 price tag. He gasps, 'Oh my God, that one costs a fortune! What does he do?'

'Well, I haven't actually seen him do anything yet,' replies the shopkeeper, 'but he says he's a contractor.'

★

Just imagine what would happen if people behaved the same way with their cars as they do with computers?

HELPLINE: Motoring Helpline, how can I help you?

CUSTOMER: I got in my car and closed the door, and nothing happened!

HELPLINE: Did you put the key in the ignition and turn it?

CUSTOMER: What's an ignition?

HELPLINE: It's a starter motor that draws current from your battery and turns over the engine.

CUSTOMER: Ignition? Motor? Battery? Engine? How come I have to know all of these technical terms just to use my car?

HELPLINE: Motoring Helpline, how can I help you?

CUSTOMER: My car ran fine for a week, and now it won't go anywhere!

HELPLINE: Is the gas tank empty?

CUSTOMER: Huh? How do I know!?

HELPLINE: There's a little gauge on the front panel, with a needle, and markings from 'E' to 'F.' Where is the needle pointing?

CUSTOMER: It's pointing to 'E.' What does that mean?

HELPLINE: It means that you have to go to the gas station, and buy some more gas. You can install it yourself, or pay the man to install it for you.

CUSTOMER: What!? I paid $20,000 for this car! Now you tell me that I have to keep buying more components? I want a car that comes with everything built in!

HELPLINE: Motoring Helpline, how can I help you?

CUSTOMER: Your cars suck!

HELPLINE: What's wrong?

CUSTOMER: It crashed, that's what went wrong!

HELPLINE: What were you doing?

CUSTOMER: I wanted to run faster, so I pushed the accelerator pedal all the way to the floor. It worked for a while, and then it crashed – and now it won't start!

HELPLINE: It's your responsibility if you misuse the product. What do you expect us to do about it?

CUSTOMER: I want you to send me one of the latest versions that doesn't crash anymore!

HELPLINE: Motoring Helpline, how can I help you?

CUSTOMER: Hi! I just bought my first car, and I chose your car because it has automatic transmission, cruise control, power steering, power brakes, and power door locks.

HELPLINE: Thanks for buying our car. How can I help you?

CUSTOMER: How do I work it?

HELPLINE: Do you know how to drive?

CUSTOMER: Do I know how to what?

HELPLINE: Do you know how to DRIVE?

CUSTOMER: I'm not a technical person! I just want to go places in my car!

★

YOU KNOW YOU ARE AN
E-MAIL JUNKIE IF ....

1. You get a tattoo reading 'best viewed with Netscape Navigator 1.1 or higher.'

2. You turn off your modem and get this awful empty feeling, like you just pulled the plug on a loved one.

3. You decide to stay at college for an additional year or two, just for the free Internet access.

4. You laugh at people with 9600-baud modems.

5. You start using smileys in your snail mail.

6. You suffer anxiety when you don't have access to your computer. You start to twitch. You pick up the phone and manually dial your ISP's access number. You try to hum to communicate with the modem... And you succeed.

7. You start introducing yourself adding 'dot.com'

8. All of your friends have an @ in their names.

9. Your cat has its own home page.

10. You can't call your mother... she doesn't have a modem.

11. You check your mail. It says 'no new messages.' So you check it again.

12. You start tilting your head sideways to smile.

13. You don't know what sex three of your closest friends are, because they have neutral user names and you never bothered to find out.

14. You move into a new house and decide to Netscape before you landscape.

15. You tell the cab driver you live at 'http://www.365.big.house/rendered.html.'

★

15 THINGS YOU LEARN ABOUT COMPUTERS FROM THE MOVIES

1. You never have to use the spacebar when typing long sentences.

2. All monitors are readable from six feet away.

3. You can gain access to any information you want by simply typing ACCESS ALL SECRET FILES on any keyboard.

4. Likewise, you can infect a computer with a destructive virus by simply typing UPLOAD VIRUS.

5. Computer operators never make typos at crucial moments.

6. All computers, in every lab and office, are connected. You can access the information on the villain's desktop computer, even if it's turned off.

7. Powerful computers beep whenever you press a key or the screen changes. Some computers also slow down the output on the screen so that it doesn't go faster than you can read.

8. People typing away on a computer will turn it off without saving the data.

9. A hacker can get into the most sensitive computer in the world, and guess the secret password in two tries.

10. Any PERMISSION DENIED has an OVERRIDE function.

11. Complex calculations and loading of huge amounts of data will be accomplished in under three seconds.

12. When the power plant/missile site/computer lab overheats, all the control panels will explode, as will the entire building.

13. No matter what kind of computer disk it is, it'll be readable by any system you put it into.

14. Computers never crash during key, high-intensity activities.

15. The more high-tech the equipment, the more buttons it has. However, everyone must have been highly trained, because the buttons aren't labelled.

★

HOW TO BE REALLY ANNOYING AT AN INTERNET CAFE

1. Log on, wait a second, then get a frightened look on your face and scream, 'Oh my God! They've found me!'

2. Laugh uncontrollably for about three minutes. Stop and look suspiciously at anyone who looks at you.

3. Type frantically often stopping to shoot an evil glance at the person sitting next to you.

4. Sit normally for a while. Suddenly look startled by something on the screen and crawl underneath the desk.

5. Sing a sea shanty. And then another.

6. Ask the person next to you if they know how to tap into top secret Pentagon files.

7. Bring a chainsaw. If anyone asks why you have it, mysteriously whisper, 'Just in case...'

8. Light candles in a pentagram around your terminal before logging on.

9. Make out with the person sitting next to you, whether you know them or not.

10. Put a straw in your mouth and your hands in your pockets. Type by hitting the keys with the straw.

11. Draw a picture of a woman (or man) and tape it to your monitor. Try to seduce it. Then act like it hates you and complain loudly that women (or men) are worthless.

12. Print out the complete works of Shakespeare. When, two days later, it is all done, slap your forehead and exclaim, 'Doggone it! All I wanted was a line or two'.

13.   Put a large gold-framed portrait of Queen Elizabeth and Prince Phillip on your desk. Loudly proclaim that you sure miss the folks back home.

14.   Attempt to eat your computer mouse. Season it first.

15.   Borrow someone else's keyboard. Simply reach over and say 'Excuse me, mind if I borrow this a sec'. Then smugly sing 'Finder's keepers' when they ask for it back.

16.   Keep looking at invisible bugs and try to swat them.

17.   Make absurd gurgling and choking noises. Pretend it's the computer and look really lost.

18.   Pull out a pencil. Start writing on the screen. Complain that the lead doesn't work properly.

★

Rip-snorting Goodies

The weekly sales meeting of the encyclopedia company is in progress and the sales director is annoyed because they aren't selling well. 'Wilbur, how many encyclopedias have you sold this week?'

'Uhh, three, boss.'

'WHAT? THREE! YOU'RE FIRED, NOW! GET OUT OF MY SIGHT! What about you Clay?'

'Umm, four, boss.'

'WHAT? FOUR! YOU'RE FIRED, NOW! GET OUT OF MY SIGHT!'

He then spotted Tim, a new employee.

The director, expecting the worst, said, 'Okay, since it's only your first week, what have you been able to sell?'

'Th-th-th-three th-th-th-thousand, s-s-s-sir.'

The director was flabbergasted. 'How on earth did you achieve such an incredible figure?'

'S-s-s-sir, I usually j-j-j-just walk up to th-th-th-the house and when th-th-th-the owner asks me wh-wh-wh-what I want, I t-t-t-tell them: 'H-h-h-hi, my name is T-T-Tim and I s-s-s-sell en-en-en-encyclopedias, now d-d-d-do you w-w-w-wish to b-b-b-buy one or shall I j-j-just r-r-r-read it to you?'

★

THE 10 TELLTALE SIGNS OF
ADVANCED PARENTHOOD

1. You find yourself singing nursery rhymes to your kid on the bus without feeling silly.

2. You become addicted to Barney.

3. You buy toys for your child and play with them before he does.

4. You buy matching clothes for you and your three year old.

5. You find yourself watching family movies — and loving them.

6. You want to point a gun at the kid that bullied your son at creche and made him cry.

7. You warn everyone that they can't give your kids any presents that make noise.

8. You hope fish fingers are healthy because it's the only thing your child will eat.

9. You manage not to laugh when your five year old daughter asks for a willy like her brother.

10. You fast-forward through the scene where the Lion King's father dies.

★

THE WORLD'S 10 SHORTEST BOOKS

1. All in a Day's Work — Diary of a Road Worker

2. Exciting Confessions of a Bank Clerk

3. Great English Lovers

4. Focus — Meditation for Sufferers of Attention Deficit Disorder

5. A Journey Through the Mind of a Blonde

6. Logic and Reason — Why Vegetarians Eat Fish and Chicken

7. Career Opportunities for History Majors

8. The Joys of Celibacy

9. Everything Men Know About Women

10. Everything Women Know About Men

★

A photographer from an environmental magazine was assigned to cover a fire that had broken out in a large national park. The magazine wanted to show the havoc the fire was creating and the damage it was doing to the trees.

By the time the photographer had taken an interstate plane and hired a car to take him close to the area, it was quite late and he knew he'd better move fast or he wouldn't be able to shoot anything. He hurried to the small strip runway where a small plane had been arranged to take him over the burning area. He got to the airport, saw a plane warming up, and grabbing his bag, he rushed on to it, shouting, 'Okay, let's go.'

The pilot swung the little plane into the wind, and within minutes they were in the air.

The photographer said, 'Fly over the park and make two or three low passes so I can take some pictures.'

'Why?' asked the pilot.

'Because I am a photographer,' he responded, 'and photographers take photographs.'

The pilot was silent for a moment; finally he stammered, 'You mean you're not the flight instructor?'

★

The boss was annoyed because, for the third day running, his secretary was late. Finally, when she arrived, an hour late, he said, fuming, 'You should have been here at nine!'

'Why?' she asked. 'What happened?'

★

Why do mice have such small balls?
*Because so very few of them know
how to dance.*

★

What do road workers and sperm have in common?
Only one in two million does any work.

★

The new employee needed a cup of coffee.
So he dialled the number of his secretary but
got the wrong one. When someone picked up
the phone he said, 'Get me a coffee, will ya?'
'Do you know whom you are talking to?' the
other side asked. 'No,' he replied. 'You are
talking to the director of this company,' the
other side replied. The employee asked, 'Do
you know who is talking on this side?'
'No,' the other side replied.
'Good.' And he put the phone down.

★

A customer walks in to Tony's Barber Shop for
a haircut. As he snips away, Tony asks, 'So,
any gossip?' The man tells him he's off for a
long-awaited trip to London.
'London?!' Tony says, 'Why would you want to
go there? It's full of English people and is
freezing! Well, how are you getting there?'

'We're flying with FGA,' the man replies.
'FGA?!' yells Tony. 'They're awful. Their planes are old, their flight attendants are ugly and they never run on schedule! So where you staying?'
'We'll be at the downtown QE International.'
'That DUMP?!' says Tony. 'That's the worst hotel in all of England! No heating in the rooms, grotty carpets, way overpriced! What are you gonna do in London?'
The man says, 'We're going to visit the Queen.'
'HA! That's rich!' laughs Tony. 'You and a million others! Bet you don't even catch a glimpse of her.' A month later, the man comes in for a visit. Tony asks, 'Well, how did that trip to London turn out? Betcha FGA gave you the worst flight of your life!'
'No,' answered the man. 'The flight was excellent. Had a gorgeous air hostess and the food was better than anything I have ever eaten.'
'Hmmm,' Tony says, 'Well, I bet the hotel was just like I described.'
'No, quite the opposite! They'd just finished refurbishing. It's the finest hotel in London, now. They gave us the Royal suite for no extra charge!'
'Well,' Tony mumbles, 'I KNOW you didn't get to see the Queen!'
'Actually, we were quite lucky. As we toured Buckingham Palace, a guard tapped me on the

shoulder and explained that the Queen likes to
personally meet some of her visitors, and if I'd
be so kind as to wait, the Queen would come
out and say hello. Sure enough, after five
minutes the Queen walked through the door
and shook my hand. I knelt down as she
spoke a few words to me.'

Impressed, Tony asks, 'Tell me, please! What
did she say?'

'Oh, not much really. Just, 'Where'd you get
that TERRIBLE haircut?'

★

THE 10 THINGS THAT WE WANTED TO HAPPEN IN THE BRADY BUNCH

1. Marsha gets syphilis.

2. Greg gets incurable acne.

3. Jan gets pregnant.

4. Cindy's hair falls out from over bleaching.

5. Sam is caught in bed with Bobby.

6. Cindy loses her lisp.

7. Alice is convicted of child molestation.

8. Peter stops looking like a girl.

9. Tiger is put down for mauling a baby to death.

10. Carol and Mike partner-swap with the next-door neighbors.

★

The new travel agency in town was running a competition to draw in more customers. The prize, for the one hundredth customer to walk in the store, was a return trip for two to Hawaii. Julian, the only travel agent not out to lunch one Friday, noticed an old man and an old woman peering wistfully through the travel agency window at a poster of Hawaii on the wall. Knowing that if they walked in they would be the winners, Julian beckoned them in. They came in a little reluctantly as they were pensioners and had no money for a holiday. 'Yes?' asked the elderly woman. A big grin burst out on Julian's face as he said, 'Congratulations! You've just won a trip to Hawaii!' Well you should have seen the look of amazement on their faces! Julian presented them with the airline tickets and they left, over the moon.

A couple of months later Julian saw the little old lady as he was on his way home from work. 'How was Hawaii?' he asked her. 'Did you have a good time?'

'Oh, it was lovely. The weather was beautifully warm, the food sumptuous and the beach was just perfect. But tell me, who was that old codger I had to share the room with?'

★

Two missionaries in Africa were captured by a tribe of very hostile cannibals who put them in a large pot of water, built a huge fire under it, and left them there. As the water boiled and the heat grew more and more intense, one of the missionaries started to laugh hysterically. The other missionary couldn't believe it! He said, 'What's wrong with you? We're being boiled alive! They're gonna eat us! What could possibly be funny at a time like this?' The other missionary said with a gleeful smile, 'I just pissed in the soup!'

Two marble statues, one a sculpture of a muscly, attractive hunk, and the other a sculpture of a beautiful and shapely princess, had been standing in the city square for several years. They were positioned face to face, in a just-about-to-kiss pose, but the nature of their existence meant that they couldn't move to complete the kiss, or indeed, get up to any other mischief. One summer morning God spoke to them. 'You have been such patient statues, I am going to reward you with half an hour of human life, to do whatever you wish.' Brought to life, the statues shook themselves a bit and then said to each other excitedly, 'Shall we?' They then disappeared into some bushes. Curious passers-by heard a lot of rustling, but were too polite to investigate. After a while they emerged from the bushes hot, flustered and happy. God, feeling glad that things had obviously gone very well between the two, decided to grant them another 15 minutes. 'Why not start all over again?' giggled the marble woman. 'Yes,' agreed the marble man. 'Let's do it again. Only this time I'll hold down the pigeon and you can poop on it!'

★

A blind man was walking down the street when his guide dog stopped and peed on his leg. Reaching into his pocket, he took out a cookie and gave it to the dog. A passer-by who had seen everything was impressed with the man's kindness. 'That's a nice thing to do after what your dog just did.'

'Not really,' replied the blind man. 'I just needed to find out where his mouth is so I can kick him in the balls.'

★

There were two people walking down the street. One was an artist. The other one didn't have a job either.

★

A man sitting by himself in a restaurant asked a waitress passing by for a glass of water. 'How dare you say that to me!' screamed the woman angrily. 'You filthy disgusting pig!' The man, terribly embarrassed by all the stares he was receiving, said softly, 'I was only asking for a drink.' The woman, incensed, shrieked at the top of her lungs, 'Another word and I am calling the police!' Slinking down in his seat, the man hid behind the menu, waiting for a less conspicuous time to sneak out of the restaurant. A few moments later the waitress came to his table and whisperered apologetically, 'Sir, I'm terribly sorry about what I did before. I'm training to be a psychologist and I'm conducting a study on public embarrassment.' The man stared at her for a moment and looking around the restaurant, bellowed, 'Wow! You'd do all that for me for just $2? And you'd do it to every other guy in the restaurant for another $10?'

★

A solo hiker was asked in a newspaper interview what the most important thing to take on a hiking trip was. 'Well,' he replied. 'When I passed my wilderness training certificate, I was given a first aid box containing a martini-making kit, a mixer, a stirrer, some gin, vermouth and olives. I didn't quite understand its relevance to bushwalking, so one of the guys took me aside and said, 'Never, ever go hiking alone without it. You might be lost out in the wilderness for days or weeks, perhaps a month. Soon, alone and thirsty, you'll remember your martini kit and begin making yourself a martini. Within ten seconds there will be someone at your side saying, "That's not the way to make a martini..."'

★

Three cool cowboys are sitting around a campfire, telling tall stories. The first says, 'I must be the meanest, toughest cowboy there is. Why, just the other day, a bull got loose and trampled six men before I wrestled it to the ground, by the horns, and killed it with my bare hands.' The second can't stand to be bested. 'Why that's nothing. I was walking down the trail yesterday and an elephant charged right at me. I grabbed it, bit its trunk and tied it up, all with one hand.' The third cowboy remained silent, slowly stirring the coals with his penis.

★

It's 100 degrees in the desert and a man lies exhausted and dying of thirst. He has stripped all his clothes off except his shorts, but is still sweating badly from the heat. From out behind a sand dune a salesman appears, staggering under the weight of a load of clean, new, white shirts. Smiling winningly, the salesman tries to sell the dying man a shirt. 'Jesus,' said the man. 'I'm dying of thirst and boiling to death. The last thing I need is a shirt!' The salesman shrugs, bids him farewell, and disappears behind the sand dune. The parched man crawls along the ground, desperately trying to reach a bar he can see in the distance. As he gets closer he can see that there are all types of cool, refreshing drinks to choose from. Mustering up the last of his strength he goes up to the door. 'Sorry,' said the doorman, barring the way. 'You can't come in without a shirt.'

★

A tourist in Vienna visits a graveyard one morning (as you do) and suddenly he hears music. Wondering where it could be coming from, he follows the sound until he locates the origin: the grave of Beethoven. As he reads the headstone, he realises that the music is in fact the famous Ninth Symphony — being played backward! Puzzled, he persuades a friend to return with him that afternoon. By the time they arrive back at the grave, the music has changed. This time it is the Seventh Symphony, and it is also being played backward. Curious, the two friends later return with a music scholar. By this time the Fifth Symphony is playing, yes, backward. The expert points out that the symphonies are being played in the reverse order in which they were composed — first the Ninth, then the Seventh, then the Fifth. Very, very strange. By the next day the word has spread and dozens of people have gathered around the grave, all listening to the Second Symphony being played — you guessed it — backward. Just then a gravedigger walks by, and someone in the crowd asks him if he has an explanation for the music.

'Well it's pretty obvious isn't it?' the gravedigger says incredulously. 'He's decomposing!'

★

The bishop of a large cathedral sent word through the streets that he was after a new bellringer. A day or so later, the applicants came filing in, and the bishop took each of them up to the belfry to begin the screening process. After interviewing several of them he became tired and was about to call it a day when an armless man approached him and announced he was there to apply for the bellringer's job. The bishop was incredulous. 'But you have no arms!'

'That hinders me not,' said the man. 'Watch!' He then began striking the bells with his face, producing a most beautiful melody. The bishop listened in astonishment, convinced he had found his man. The bellringer rang the bells again, but this time he slipped on something and plunged headlong out of the window and to his death below. The stunned bishop rushed down to the fallen figure, where a crowd had already gathered. As they parted to let the bishop through, one of them asked, 'Bishop, who was this man?'

'I'm not quite sure,' the bishop sadly replied, 'but his face rang a bell.'

(But wait, there's more...)

Although very sad, the following day the bishop continued the interviews. The first man to approach him said, 'Your excellency, I am the brother of the poor, armless wretch who

fell to his death
from this very belfry
yesterday. I pray
that you pay due
homage to his life
by allowing me to
replace him.' The bishop
agreed to give the man an audition, and as the
armless man's brother stooped to pick up a
mallet to strike the first bell, he groaned,
clutched at his chest and died on the spot. Two
monks, hearing the bishop's cries of grief at
this second tragedy, rushed up the stairs to his
side. 'What has happened?' the first asked
breathlessly. 'Who is this man?'
'I don't know his name,' sighed the distraught
bishop, 'but he's a dead ringer for his brother.'

★

Toby was given a parrot for his birthday. Unfortunately, this parrot was one bad-mouthed bird. Every second word was an expletive. Toby tried very hard to change the parrot's ways — he played soft music, read aloud chapters on etiquette, and he never, ever, swore. But nothing worked. One day, the parrot was so rude to one of Toby's friends that Toby went beserk. He shook the bird, getting madder and madder, and when the bird wouldn't shut up, he finally threw it into the freezer for a bit of peace and quiet. For a few moments the parrot squawked and screamed, but then it became silent. Toby, being the good-natured boy that he was, was worried that he may have hurt the parrot, so he quickly opened the freezer door. The parrot gracefully stepped out onto Toby's arm and said very softly, 'I apologize for my offensive language. I will try very, very hard in the future to watch my behavior and to wash my mouth out with soap if I even think of swearing again.'
Toby was completely amazed at this change of heart. He was just about to ask him what had made the parrot 'see the light' when the parrot spoke again.
'May I ask what the chicken did?'

★

The manager of an old folks home was collecting the mail one day when two poor guys show up, looking for work. Feeling sorry for them, the manager asks if they'd like to chop some firewood in return for some money. They enthusiastically agree, and the manager goes to the toolshed and finds a couple of axes for them. Some time later, as the manager is in his office, he looks out the window and notices one of the guys doing some amazing acrobatics on the back lawn. He's jumping in the air, doing cartwheels and swinging from branch to branch. He watches in awe as the old guy swings from a branch, does a flip mid-air, and lands with another cartwheel.

He calls the other guy over to the window and says, 'That friend of yours is marvellous. I'd like him to perform for the senior citizens here — it might pep them up a bit. Do you think he would accept $100?'

'Well,' responds the guy, 'I'll have to go ask him.'

'HEY NORM! For $100 WOULD YOU CHOP OFF ANOTHER TOE?'

★

Toe: a device for finding furniture in the dark.

★

You might be a redneck if...
You think the stockmarket has a fence.

You might be a redneck if...
You've been involved in a custody battle over a hunting dog.

You might be a redneck if...
Your grandpa died and left everything to his widow. Problem is she can't touch a thing till she's fourteen.

You might be a redneck if...
Your pickup lines start with 'Nice tooth, baby!'

You might be a redneck if...
You think the last four words of the national anthem are 'Gentlemen, start your engines'

You might be a redneck if...
Fifth grade was the best six years of your life.

You might be a redneck if...
One of your kids was born on a pool table.

You might be a redneck if...
The figurines on top of your wedding cake were wearing overalls.

You might be a redneck if...
Your favorite restaurant has a sawdust floor.

You might be a redneck if...
You've ever burped and killed a fly.

You might be a redneck if...
There were dogs in the church on your
wedding day.

You might be a redneck if...
You've ever had to tow your car out of a
pothole in your driveway.

You might be a redneck if...
Your wedding cake was made by Sara Lee.

You might be a redneck if...
You're driving a vehicle with no original body
parts.

You might be a redneck if...
You take a load to the town dump and come
back with more than you took.

You might be a redneck if...
You refer to sixth grade as 'your senior year'.

You might be a redneck if...
You've ever had a dream about beef jerky.

You might be a redneck if...
There are twelve pillows on your bed. One for you, your wife and your ten dogs.

★

I didn't fight my way to the top of the food chain to be a vegetarian.

SHIT

Amish: Old shit is good for the soil, but this modern shit is worthless.

Atheist: I don't believe this shit.

Bureaucrat: I'm sorry, but we can't do this shit until you fill out the form.

Capitalist: Can I sell you some shit?

Catholic: I'm not doing this shit now because it's the wrong time of the month and I don't want any little shits running around.

Christian: When shit happens, pray.

Communist: It's survival of the shittiest.

Evangelist: Send us all your shit.

Existentialist: What is shit anyway?

Jehovah's Witness: Knock Knock, I know you shits are home.

Jew: Why does this shit always happen to us?

Mysticist: This is really weird shit. For $300, we can help you get in touch with your inner shit.

Quality Control Inspector: This shit ain't good enough.

Seventh Day Adventist: No shit on Saturdays.

Statistician: There is an 83.7% chance that shit will happen.

★

Any small object when dropped will hide under another object.

★

Confucius say...
Man who wants pretty nurse, must be patient.

★

There once was a man who had a severe digestive problem. Every time he drank malted milk, which unfortunately happened to be his favorite drink, he would suffer malt-scented farts for the rest of the day. Now, because of this problem, he normally abstained from drinking malted milk, but because it was his birthday, he thought, 'Hey, what the hell', and indulged in two big shakes at lunchtime, with extra malt in each. As he walked home from work, the tirade of bad smells began. He hoped like crazy that they would all be out of his system by the time he reached home. Naturally, his wife very much disapproved of smelly things. So he farted and fluffed and mockered all the way home. When he arrived there his wife opened the door and said, 'Put on this blindfold. I have a lovely surprise for you,' and he obliged. She led him though the house and sat him down at the table, and just as she was about to remove the blindfold the phone rang. 'Don't move,' she said, and off she went. When she was gone, he seized the opportunity and let go. It was not only loud, but so smelly he had a hard time breathing, so he felt for his napkin and fanned the air about him. As he was wondering if that was the last one, he felt another well of gas build up inside him. He raised his leg and 'rrriiiipppp!' It sounded like a diesel engine revving, and smelled a helluva lot worse. To keep from gagging, he tried waving his arms, hoping to move the smell away from him. Things had just about returned to normal when he felt another urge coming. He shifted his weight to his other leg and let go. This was a real blue ribbon winner; the dishes on the table shook and a couple of pictures fell down from the wall. For the next ten minutes, while he listened to his wife on the phone, he kept up a mega farting session, following each one with a mad fanning of the arms and grunts of disgust at the smell. When he heard his wife returning from the hallway, he folded his hands on top of his napkin and tried to regain some composure. Smiling contentedly, he was the picture of innocence when his wife walked in. Apologizing for taking so long, she asked if he had peeked at the dinner. After assuring her he had not, she removed the blindfold and yelled, 'Surprise!!' To his extreme and utter horror, there were ten dinner guests seated around the table for his surprise birthday party.

★

The owner of a market research company was interviewing people for a position which involved going around to houses and talking to people about their opinion on certain products. He was particularly keen to hire one applicant who had a great deal of experience and was very well spoken. The only problem was a disconcerting mannerism: the man seemed to have a nervous tic. Every few seconds his head would shake wildly from side to side. The sales manager decided to be frank. 'You've got all the qualifications for the job and I'd really like to hire you, but I'm afraid that tic of yours might be a problem.'

'No problem,' said the candidate. 'All I need to make it go away is a couple of cough drops. Look. I'll take some now.' And he began emptying his pockets on the desk. The prospective employer was startled to see dozens of packages of condoms piling up: edible ones, lubricated ones, multicolored ones, every variety imaginable. 'Aha,' cried the young man happily, 'Here they are.' He brandished two lozenges, swallowed them, and sure enough, the head shaking stopped immediately. 'So much for the tic,' said the sales manager sternly, gesturing at the mountain of rubbers, 'But what about all these condoms? I don't want you screwing around on the job.'

'No fear. I'm a happily married man.'

'So how can you account for the contents of your pockets?'

'It's simple, sir. Did you ever go into a drugstore, shaking your head like crazy, and ask for a packet of cough drops?'

★

A man takes his Saint Bernard to the vet.
'He's been behaving funny lately, and his nose
isn't wet anymore.'
The vet picked the dog up and looked at its
nose. 'I'm going to have to put him down,'
said the vet.
'Why, just because his nose is dry?' asked
the man in disbelief.
'No, because he's too heavy!'

★

A pig snuffles into a bar and orders a beer.
Barman says, 'Hey, you're a pig.'
'Well, you got me there!' says the pig.
'You know what I mean,' says the barman.
'You can talk — that's pretty unusual for a pig.'
'Yeah, well, freaks of nature do happen
sometimes,' replies the pig. 'Now gimme a
beer will ya?'
The barman serves him up one and asks if he
lives in the area.
'Nah, I just work around here — over on the
building site actually.' The barman nods and
they chat a bit more. Each day after that, the
pig snuffles and snorts his way into the bar
during his lunchbreaks. About a week or so
after the pig and the barman first began
talking, a circus comes to town. The circus
owner comes in for a pint at midday one day,
just as the pig is ordering a beer. After the initial

shock of seeing a talking pig, the circus owner approaches him and says, 'Hey, you should join my circus. You'd make a lot of money.'

'Hang on,' says the pig. 'You work in a circus right?'

'Yeah.'

'That's like one of those tent things, isn't it? With a big pole in the middle?'

'That's right.'

'The tent's made out of canvas, right?'

'Of course,' replies the circus owner. 'One hundred percent canvas.'

The pig gives the circus owner a very puzzled look.

'So why in hell would you want a bricklayer?'

★

A snail crawls into a bar just on closing time. He knocks on the door until the barman finally opens the door, and looks around. When he sees the snail he says, 'Go away. We're closed, and besides, we don't serve snails here.' He then slams the door in the snail's face. The snail again pounds on the door until the bartender gets so frustrated that he opens the door and kicks the snail away. A year later as the bartender is closing up for the night, he hears a pounding on the door. He opens the door, and who is there but the same snail from a year previous. The snail looks up and says, 'What did you do that for?'

★

A man walks into a psychiatrist's office and says, 'Doctor, I need your help. I think I'm a dog.'
The psychiatrist replies, 'Well get up on the couch and we'll talk about it.'
The guy says, 'Can't. I'm not allowed on the couch.'

★

KIDS' ADVICE TO OTHER KIDS

'Never trust a dog to watch your food.'
Tyler, age 9

'When your dad is mad and asks you, "Do I look stupid?" don't answer.'
Tabitha, age 6

'Never tell your mom her diet's not working.'
Nathaniel, age 13

'Puppies still have bad breath, even after eating a Tic-Tac.'
Caleb, age 9

'Never hold a dust-buster and a cat at the same time.'
Madeleine, age 9

'You can't hide a piece of broccoli in a glass of milk.'
Ezra, age 9

'Don't wear polka-dot underwear under white shorts.'
Charlotte, age 11

'If you want a kitten, start out by asking for a horse.'
Elizabeth, age 15

'Felt markers are not good to use as lipstick.'
Annabelle, age 9

'Don't pick on your sister when she's holding a baseball bat.'
Skeet, age 10

'When you get a bad grade in school, show it to your mom when she's on the phone.'
Jakob, age 10

'Never try to baptize a kitten.'
Caitlin, age 8

★

What are the three best things about having Alzheimer's disease?
1. You can play hide and seek by yourself.
2. You can play hide and seek by yourself.
3. You can play hide and seek by yourself.

★

A man wants a pet that can do anything so he goes to the pet shop and asks the owner if he has any ideas. The shop owner suggests a dog. But the man shakes his head. The owner says, 'How about a cat then?'

The man replies, 'No way! Cats are useless. I want a pet that can do everything!'

The shop owner thinks for a minute, then says, 'I've got it! A centipede!'

The man says, 'A centipede? Hmmm, I've never considered a centipede. Yeah, why not?' So he takes the centipede home.

'Wash the floor,' he tells the centipede and twenty minutes later, the floor is immaculate! He is absolutely amazed.

'Clean the bedroom,' he says next. Twenty minutes later the room is spotless.

The man thinks to himself, 'This is the most amazing thing I've ever seen. This really is a pet that can do everything!' Next he says, 'Run down to the corner store and get me a newspaper.'

The centipede walks out the door. Ten minutes later... no centipede. Twenty minutes later... no centipede. Thirty minutes later... still no centipede. The man is wondering what's going on. He can't imagine what could have happened. Did the centipede run away? Did it get run over? Where is that centipede?

So he goes to the front door, opens it... and

there's the centipede sitting right outside.
The man says, 'Hey! I sent you down to the
corner store half an hour ago to get me a
newspaper. What's the matter?'
The centipede says, 'I'm going! I'm going! I'm
just putting on my shoes, okay?'

★

A woman went to her doctor, concerned about
the testosterone he had prescribed on her last
visit. 'Doc, I think I've been taking too much.
I'm growing hair in all sorts of weird places.'
The doctor said, 'That's normal. Testosterone
causes hair growth. Just where is it occurring?'
'On my dick.'

★

275

A man had been suffering from terrible head-aches for years and years. Finally he decided he couldn't stand the pain anymore.

'Doctor, you gotta do something!' he pleaded. 'Well, the latest cure for this type of thing is pretty severe, but we know it works,' replied the doctor gravely. 'It's castration.'

The man was horrified, but could put up with his headaches for no longer. The next week, he underwent the operation. The headaches disappeared as the doctor had promised, and the man landed himself an interview with an important finance company. Needing a new suit for the interview, the man went shopping.

'Looks like you take a size 38,' said the sales-man as he pulled some suits off a rack. 'That's pretty good,' said the man. 'How did you know that?'

'Mate, when you've been in this business as long as I have, you get to know this sort of thing.' He then pulled out some underwear. 'Hmm, I guess a 36 for these,' he said. 'Well, you're wrong there,' said the man. 'I've been a 34 for years.'

'No, you're definitely a 36,' insisted the salesman.

'Look, I should know. I always wear 34.'

'Well, okay,' said the salesman. 'But they're going to pinch your balls and give you headaches.'

★

On the top of a tall building in a large city, there was a bar. In this bar, a man was drinking heavily. He would ask the bartender for vodka, then walk out to the balcony and jump off. Minutes later he would be back again and repeat the whole process. This one guy watched this happen a number of times until curiosity got the better of him. Finally he went up to the man and asked, 'Hey, you keep drinking, then jumping off the balcony. And yet, minutes later, you're back up here again, completely fine. How do you do it?'

'Well, that new brand of vodka provides buoyancy so that when I get near the ground, I slow down and land gently. It's fun. You should try it.'

The guy, who was also quite plastered, thought to himself, 'Hey, why not? If he can do it, I guess I can too.' So he went out to the balcony, jumped off, and splat. The guy is dead. The bartender looked over to the other guy and says, 'Superman, you're a real asshole when you're drunk.'

★

Little Red Riding Hood is skipping merrily
home when she sees the Big Bad Wolf
crouched down behind a log. 'My, what big
eyes you have, Mr Wolf,' says Little Red Riding
Hood. The wolf jumps up and runs away!
Further down the road Little Red Riding Hood
sees the wolf again. This time he is crouched
behind a tree stump. 'My, what big ears you
have Mr Wolf,' says Little Red Riding Hood.
Again the wolf jumps up and runs away. Just
near the driveway of her home, Little Red
Riding Hood sees the wolf again, this time
crouched down behind her letter box. 'My,
what big teeth you have Mr Wolf,' taunts Little
Red Riding Hood. With that the Big Bad Wolf
jumps up and yells furiously, 'Will you f*** off,
I'm trying to take a shit!'

★

A guy walks into a bar, carrying three ducks. He puts them down on the bar, and begins chatting with the barman. The barman is experienced and, several hundred jokes later, has learned not to ask people about the animals that they bring into the bar, so he doesn't mention the ducks. After a couple of drinks, the guy goes to the bathroom, leaving the ducks alone with the barman. There is a bit of an awkward silence, so the barman tries to make some conversation.

'What's your name?' He says to the first duck.

'Greg,' says the duck.

'How's your day been?'

'I've been in and out of puddles all day. Had an excellent time.'

'Oh. That's nice,' says the barman. Then he says to the second duck, 'Hi. And what's your name?'

'Dean,' is the answer.

'So how's your day been?'

'Great. Had a ball. Been in and out of puddles all day.'

So the barman turns to the third duck and says 'So, what's your name?'

'My name is Puddles. And don't bother asking about my day.'

★

TEN THINGS A WOMAN WILL NEVER SAY

1. Don't worry about it. I don't mind you forgetting our anniversary.

2. Are you sure you've had enough to drink?

3. I'm bored. Let's have a threesome!

4. Shouldn't you be down at the bar with your buddies?

5. That was a great fart! Do another one!

6. I've decided to stop wearing clothes in the house.

7. You're so sexy with a beer gut.

8. I'd rather watch the game than go shopping.

9. Let's look at a girlie magazine.

10. Let's tape ourselves in bed tonight and show the guys tomorrow!

★

Three friends were traveling in the country when their car broke down in the middle of nowhere. After realizing that there was nothing they could do to fix it themselves, they decided to walk until they found somewhere to stay for the night. Eventually, after walking several miles, they came across a little house. After knocking for quite a few minutes, a man appeared at the door. The three friends asked if they could stay the night because their car had broken down. 'I'll let you stay here on one condition,' said the man reluctantly. 'Don't draw any attention to my son. He was born with no ears, and is extremely sensitive about it. I mean it, do not even look at the sides of his head!'

After agreeing to this, the three friends were taken into the house and showed the room where they would sleep. The next morning at the breakfast table the son was munching away on toast, and the three friends found they could not help staring at the sides of his head where his ears had been.

'What are you looking at?' demanded the earless boy.

The first of the friends replied, 'I was just admiring your teeth — they are so clean and sharp. Make sure you look after them so you don't ever have to get dentures.'

The second friend said, 'And I was just

admiring your thick head of hair. Make sure you look after it, for you wouldn't want to go bald and have to wear a wig.'
The third said, 'I was just looking at your clear blue eyes. Make sure you take care of them... Lord knows you can't wear glasses.'

★

A woman got caught in a burning house one day and suffered severe burns to her face. Her husband, sweet man that he was, decided to donate his own skin from his butt so that she could have a skin graft. They agreed to tell no one about where the skin came from, it being rather a delicate matter. After the surgery was completed, everyone was amazed at how well it turned out. The wife looked more beautiful than ever before! (The husband, meanwhile, couldn't sit down for a week.) One day the wife was just so overcome with emotion at her husband's sacrifice she said, 'Darling, you don't know how much I appreciate what you have done for me. There is no way I could ever repay you.' To which he replied, 'My love, think nothing of it. I get thanks enough whenever I see your mother kiss you on the cheek.'

★

EMPLOYEE TIPS TO MANAGERS

1. If I've done something wrong, tell me first thing Monday morning, as soon as I get in. It's bound to make it a good week for me.

2. If you have an extremely urgent job for me, run in and ask for a progress report every 10 minutes, stressing that you need it done quickly. That helps a lot. Even better, hover behind me as I work — that's sure to produce a good result.

3. Always leave without telling anyone where you are going. It's good for the soul to have a panic attack when a decision has to be made and you're not there to approve it.

4. Never give me urgent work in the morning. Always wait until 4 p.m. and then bring it in to me. The challenge of a deadline is refreshing.

5. Keep me working until 8 p.m. every night. I have no life, no family to go home to. Please realize this and keep me busy every waking second so I don't dwell on it.

6. If I do a job well, don't tell anyone. It'll be our little secret. On the other hand, if I do a terrible job, please tell everyone. It's important that we all know our worth in the office environment.

7. If you have special instructions for a job, don't tell me what they are. The best thing is to wait until the job is completed, and then tell me what I should have done. No use confusing me with useful information.

8. Don't give me my annual leave when I want it. Instead, dish it out one day at a time, so I'm not tempted to take an exciting overseas holiday.

9. When you show clients around the building and into our private offices, never bother to introduce me to the people you are with. You and I both know I mean nothing to the company, so don't even glance in my direction as you stand in front of my desk talking with them.

10. Confide in me about your financial woes. I especially like hearing about all the tax you have to pay on that 10K bonus you got at Christmas last year.

★

It was Cam's eighth birthday and he was playing with his new train set on the porch. His mother walked past and heard him say, 'Toot toot! Any f***ing moron who wants to get off the f***ing train better do so now. Any f***ing losers who want to get on, haul your f***ing asses on now!'

Cam's mother was mortified that her son was using such foul language. 'Listen here, young man,' she said sternly. 'We don't use that language in this house. Birthday or not, you go to your room now and stay there for two hours. When you come out, you can play with your new train set, but only if you use nice language.'

Cam sulkily went to his room. Two hours later he came out and began playing with his train set again. Soon the train pulled up at a station and Cam's mother tiptoed out of the kitchen to eavesdop on her son. She heard him say, 'All passengers who are getting off the train, please make sure you leave nothing behind. Thank you for traveling with us today and we hope your trip was a pleasant one.'

She hears her son continue, 'For those of you getting on the train, refreshments will be served in 30 minutes in the dining car. We hope you will have a pleasant and relaxing journey with us today.'

The mother smiled. Then Cam added, 'And for

those of you who are bothered about the TWO HOUR delay, go take it out on the f***ing bitch in the kitchen.'

★

A health and safety inspector is being shown the workings of a latex factory by the manager. The first thing the manager takes him to see is a machine that makes baby bottle teats. 'Hiss... pop' goes the machine, and the director explains, 'The hissing sound is caused when the rubber is injected into the mould. The popping sound comes from the needle piercing a hole in the end of the teat.'

The manager then takes the inspector to where the condoms are being manufactured. The machine makes a 'hiss, hiss, hiss, hiss-pop' noise. 'Wait a minute!' says the inspector. 'I know what the 'hiss, hiss' is, but why does this machine have a 'pop' sound too?'

'Oh, well, it's just the same as the baby bottle teat machine,' says the manager. 'It pokes a hole in every fourth condom.'

'Well, that can't be good for the condoms!'

'Yeah, but it's great for the baby bottle business!'

★

Santa is getting ready to take his annual vacation, but as usual, more and more problems kept coming up. Four of the elves get food poisioning, the trainee elves start showing their disgruntlement with their low wages by going on a 'work slow' strike, and the toy-producing business falls further and further behind schedule. Then his wife tells him her mother is coming to visit. When Santa goes outside to harness the reindeer he finds that half of them have sauntered off to the bar for the afternoon because they don't feel appreciated. More stress. Then, when Santa begins loading the sleigh, one of the boards cracks and his sack of toys falls off, slipping and sliding all across the snow. Frustrated, Santa trudges into the house for a long glass of bourbon. But the elves have hit the liquor cabinet and there is nothing to drink, not even any girly drinks left. In disgust he throws his empty glass down and it explodes into bits all over the floor. Just then the doorbell rings and the cursing, grumbling Santa throws open the door. A little angel is standing on his doorstep, with a great big Christmas tree. And the angel asks ever so sweetly, 'Santa, where would you like me to put this?'

And that, my friend, is how the little angel came to be on top of the Christmas tree...

★

A keen country boy applied for a salesman's job at a city department store. In fact it was the biggest store in the area — you could get anything there. The boss asked him, 'Have you ever been a salesman before?'

'Yes, I was a salesman in the country,' said the lad. The boss thought he'd give the boy a chance and said, 'You can start now. I'll come by at five o'clock and see how you are doing.' The day was long and arduous for the young man, but finally 5 o'clock came around. The boss arrived and asked, 'How many sales did you make today?'

'One,' said the young salesman.

'Only one?' blurted the boss. 'Most of my staff usually make over 30 sales a day. How much was the sale worth?'

'Forty-one thousand, two hundred and sixty-eight dollars,' said the young man.

'How did you manage that?' asked the flabbergasted boss.

'Well,' said the young salesman, 'this man came in and I sold him a small fish hook, then a medium hook and finally a really large hook. Then I sold him a small fishing line, a medium one and a huge one. I asked him where he was going fishing and he said down the coast. I said he would probably need a boat, so I took him down to the boat department and sold him that twenty foot schooner with the twin engines. Then he said

289

his little hatchback probably wouldn't be able to pull it, so I took him to the car department and sold him a new car.'

The boss took two steps back and asked in astonishment, 'You sold all that to a guy who came in for a fish hook?'

'No,' answered the salesman. 'Actually, he came in to buy a box of tampons for his wife and I said to him, "Your weekend's shot, you may as well go fishing."'

★

A man flew to Las Vegas to gamble, but he lost all his money. All he had left was his plane ticket home, and he had to get to the airport somehow. So he went out to where there was a taxi waiting and explained his situation to the cabby. He promised to send the taxi fare money from home, but to no avail. The cabby said, 'If you don't have fifteen dollars, get the hell out of my cab!'

So the man was forced to hitchhike to the airport and only just made it in time. A few months later the man returned to Las Vegas and this time he won big. Again he went to get a taxi back to the airport. Well who should he see out there, at the end of a long line of taxis, but the cabby who had refused to give him a ride when he was down on his luck. The man

thought for a moment about how he could make the guy pay for his lack of charity, and he hit on a plan. He asked the first taxi driver in line how much the fare was to the airport.
'Fifteen bucks,' came the reply.
'And how much for you to give me a blowjob on the way?' he asked.
'What?! Get the hell out of my taxi.'
The man asked each taxi driver in the line the same questions, with the same results. When he got to his old friend at the back of the line, he got in and said, 'Take me to the airport.' Then, as they drove past the long line of cabs he gave a big smile and thumbs up sign to each driver.

★

The truck broke down in the country and there was no alternative for the trucker but to walk the ten miles to the nearest farmhouse. He explained his predicament to the farmer and asked if he could spend the night. 'Sure,' replied the farmer, 'But I must warn you that I don't have any daughters. I don't even have a spare room so you'll have to share my bed.'
'Damn,' said the trucker. 'I'm in the wrong joke.'

★

World's Best

Humor

Compiled by Oliver Roydhouse

Cartoon Laws of Physics

Cartoon Law I

Any body suspended in space will remain in space until made aware of the situation.

A duck steps off a cliff, expecting further pastureland. He loiters in midair, soliloquizing flippantly, until he looks down.

Cartoon Law II

Any body in motion will tend to remain in motion until solid matter intervenes suddenly.

Whether shot from a cannon or in hot pursuit on foot, cartoon characters are so absolute in their momentum that only a telephone pole or an oversized boulder retards their forward motion absolutely.

Cartoon Law III

Any body passing through solid matter will leave a perforation conforming to its perimeter.

Also called the 'silhouette of passage', this phenomenon is the speciality of victims of directed-pressure explosions and of reckless cowards who are so eager to escape that they exit directly through the wall of a house. The threat of skunks or matrimony often catalyses this reaction.

Cartoon Law IV

The time required for an object to fall 20 stories is greater than or equal to the time it takes for whoever knocked it off the ledge to spiral down 20 flights to attempt to capture it unbroken.

Such an object is inevitably priceless, the attempt to capture it inevitably unsuccessful.

Cartoon Law V

All principles of gravity are negated by fear.

Psychic forces are sufficient in most bodies for a shock to propel them directly away from the Earth's surface. A spooky noise or an adversary's signature sound will induce motion upward, usually to the cradle of a chandelier, a treetop, or the crest of a flagpole. The feet of a character who is running, or wheels of a speeding auto need never touch the ground, especially when in flight.

Cartoon Law VI

As speed increases, objects can be in several places at once.

This is particularly true of tooth-and-claw fights, in which a character's head may be glimpsed emerging from the cloud of altercation at several places simultaneously. This effect is common as well among bodies that are spinning or being throttled. A 'wacky' character has the option of self-replication only at manic high speeds and may ricochet off walls to achieve the velocity required.

Cartoon Law VII

Certain bodies can pass through solid walls painted to resemble tunnel entrances; others cannot.

This inconsistency has baffled generations, but at least it is known that whoever paints an entrance on a wall's surface to trick an opponent will be unable to pursue him into this theoretical space. The painter is flattened against the wall when he attempts to follow into the painting. This is ultimately a problem of art, not of science.

Cartoon Law VIII

Any violent rearrangement of feline matter is impermanent.

Cartoon cats possess even more deaths than the traditional nine lives might comfortably afford. They can be decimated, spliced, splayed, accordion-pleated, spindled or disassembled, but they cannot be destroyed. After a few moments of blinking self-pity, the cartoon cats will re-inflate, elongate, snap back or solidify.

Corollary: a cat will assume the shape of its container.

Cartoon Law IX

Everything falls faster than an anvil.

Cartoon Law X

For every vengeance there is an equal and opposite revengeance.

This is the one law of animated cartoon motion that also applies to the physical world at large. For that reason, we need the relief of watching it happen to a duck instead.

Cartoon Law Amendment A

A sharp object will always propel a character upward. When poked (usually in the buttocks) with a sharp object (usually a pin), a character will defy gravity by shooting straight up, with great velocity.

Cartoon Law Amendment B

The laws of object permanence are nullified for 'cool' characters.

Characters who are 'cool' can make previously non-existent objects appear from behind their backs at will. For instance, the Road Runner can materialize signs to express himself without speaking.

Cartoon Law Amendment C

Explosive weapons cannot cause fatal injuries. They merely turn characters temporarily black and smoky.

Cartoon Law Amendment D

Gravity is transmitted by slow-moving waves of large wavelengths.

Their operation can be witnessed by observing the behavior of a canine suspended over a large vertical drop. Its feet will begin to fall first, causing its legs to stretch. As the wave reaches its torso, that part will begin to fall, causing the neck to stretch. As the head begins to fall, tension is released and canine will resume its regular proportions until such time as it strikes the ground.

Cartoon Law Amendment E

Dynamite is spontaneously generated in 'C-spaces' (spaces in which cartoon laws hold).

The process is analogous to steady-state theories of the tensions involved which postulated that the tensions involved in maintaining a space would cause the creation of hydrogen from nothing. Dynamite quanta are quite large (stick sized) and unstable (lit). Such quanta are attracted to psychic forces generated by feelings of distress in 'cool' characters (see Amendment B, which may be a special case of this law), who are able to use said quanta to their advantage. One may imagine C-spaces where all matter and energy result from primal masses of dynamite exploding. A big bang indeed.

Famous Last Words

I'll get a world record for this.

Let me reach in and get your watch out of the printing press.

Gee, that's a cute tattoo.

It's fireproof.

He's probably just hibernating.

What does this button do?

I'm making a citizen's arrest.

So, you're a cannibal.

It's probably just a rash.

Why am I standing on a plastic sheet?

Are you sure the power is off?

The odds of that happening have to be a million to one!

Pull the pin and count to what?

Which wire am I supposed to cut?

I wonder where the mother bear is.

I've seen this done on TV.

These are a good kind of mushroom.

I'll hold it and you light the fuse.

Real Headlines

Something Went Wrong in Jet Crash, Experts Say

Panda Mating Fails; Veterinarian Takes Over

Police Begin Campaign to Run Down Jaywalkers

Safety Experts Say School Bus Passengers Should Be Belted

Drunk Gets Nine Months in Violin Case

Survivor of Siamese Twins Joins Parents

Iraqi Head Seeks Arms

Prostitutes Appeal to Pope

Including Your Children When Baking Cookies

Lung Cancer in Women Mushrooms

Eye Drops Off Shelf

Teachers Strike Idle Kids

Clinton Wins on Budget, But More Lies Ahead

Enraged Cow Injures Farmer With Axe

Plane Too Close to Ground, Crash Probe Told

Miners Refuse to Work After Death

Juvenile Court to Try Shooting Defendant

Stolen Painting Found by Tree

Two Sisters Reunited After 18 Years in Checkout Counter

Killer Sentenced to Die for Second Time in 10 Years

Never Withhold Herpes Infection from Loved One

War Dims Hope for Peace

If Strike Isn't Settled Quickly, It May Last a While

Cold Wave Linked To Temperatures

Deer Killed 17,000

Couple Slain; Police Suspect Homicide

Red Tape Holds Up New Bridges

Typhoon Rips Through Cemetery; Hundreds Dead

Man Struck by Lightning Faces Battery Charge

New Study of Obesity Looks for Larger Test Group

Astronaut Takes Blame for Gas in Spacecraft

Kids make Nutritious Snacks

Chef Throws His Heart into Helping Feed Needy

Arson Suspect Held in Massachusetts Fire

Ban on Soliciting Dead in Trotwood

Local High School Dropouts Cut in Half

New Vaccine May Contain Rabies

Hospitals Are Sued By 7 Foot Doctors

Things You Would Never Know Without the Movies

During all police investigations, it will be necessary to visit a strip club at least once.

When they are alone, all foreigners prefer to speak English to each other.

If being chased through town, you can usually take cover in a passing St Patrick's Day parade — at any time of year.

All beds have special L-shaped cover sheets which reach up to the armpit level on a woman, but only to the waist level on the man lying beside her.

The chief of police will almost always suspend his star detective — or give him 48 hours to finish the job.

All grocery bags contain at least one French bread.

The ventilation system of any building is the perfect hiding place — no one will ever think of looking for you in there, and you can travel to any other part of the building undetected.

Police departments give their officers personality tests to make sure they are deliberately assigned to a partner who is their polar opposite.

The Eiffel Tower can be seen from any window in Paris.

All bombs are fitted with electronic timing devices with large red readouts so you know exactly when they are going to go off.

You are very likely to survive any battle in any war unless you make the mistake of showing someone a picture of your sweetheart back home.

Should you wish to pass yourself off as a German officer, it will not be necessary to speak the language — simply having a German accent will do.

A man will show no pain while taking the most ferocious beating, but will wince when a woman tries to clean his wounds.

Kitchens don't have light switches. When entering a kitchen at night, you should open the fridge door and use that light instead.

If staying in a haunted house, women should investigate any strange noises in their most revealing underwear.

Cars that crash will almost always burst into flames.

Mediaeval peasants had perfect teeth.

Any person waking from a nightmare will sit bolt upright and pant.

Even when driving down a perfectly straight road, it is necessary to turn the wheel vigorously from left to right every few moments.

It is always possible to park directly outside the building you are visiting.

A detective can only solve a case once he has been suspended from duty.

It does not matter if you are heavily outnumbered in a fight involving martial arts — your enemies will patiently attack you one by one by dancing around in a threatening manner until you have knocked out their predecessors.

No one ever involved in a car chase, hijacking, explosion, volcanic eruption or alien invasion will ever go into shock.

Any lock can be picked by a credit card or a paper clip in seconds — unless it's the door to a burning building with a child tapped inside.

Television news bulletins usually contain a story that affects you personally at the precise moment that it is aired.

★ ★ ★ ★

Make it idiot-proof and someone will make a better idiot.

Creative Ways to Say Someone is Stupid

He is depriving a village somewhere of its idiot.

Not the brightest bulb on the Christmas tree.

A few peas short of a casserole.

Fell out of the stupid tree and hit every branch on the way down.

An intellect rivalled only by garden tools.

Chimney's clogged.

Doesn't have all his dogs on one leash.

Elevator doesn't go all the way to the top floor.

Forgot to pay her brain bill.

Her sewing machine's out of thread.

His antenna doesn't pick up all the channels.

His belt doesn't go through all the loops.

Missing a few buttons on his remote control.

Not the sharpest knife in the drawer.

The wheel's spinning, but the hamster's dead.

She doesn't have all the chairs around the table.

She's not the brightest crayon in the box.

About as sharp as a marble.

The gates are down, the lights are flashing but the train isn't coming.

Fell out of the family tree.

Got into the gene pool while the lifeguard wasn't watching.

Insurance Claims

The following excuses are from actual insurance claim forms that are intended to concisely summarize the accident.

Coming home, I drove into the wrong house and collided with a tree I don't have.

The other car collided with mine without giving warning of its intentions.

I thought my window was down, but I found out it was up when I put my hand through it.

I collided with a stationary truck coming the other way.

A truck backed through my windshield into my wife's face.

A pedestrian hit me and went under my car.

The guy was all over the road, I had to swerve a number of times before I hit him.

I pulled away from the side of the road, glanced at my mother-in-law and headed over the embankment.

In my attempt to kill a fly, I drove into a telephone pole.

I had been shopping for plants all day and was on my way home. As I reached an intersection, a hedge sprang up, obscuring my vision.

I had been driving for 40 years when I fell asleep at the wheel and had an accident.

I was on my way to the doctor's with rear end trouble, when my universal joints gave way, causing me to have an accident.

As I approached the intersection, a stop sign suddenly appeared. It was too late to stop in time to avoid the accident.

To avoid hitting the bumper of my car in front, I struck a pedestrian.

My car was legally parked as it backed into the other vehicle.

An invisible car came out of nowhere, struck my car and vanished.

I told the police that I was not injured, but on removing my hat, I found that I had a skull fracture.

I was sure the old fellow would not make it to the other side of the street when I struck him.

The pedestrian had no idea which way to go, so I ran over him.

I saw the slow-moving, sad-faced gentleman as he bounced off the hood of my car.

I was thrown from my car as it left the road and I was later found in a ditch by some stray cows.

The telephone pole was approaching fast. I tried to swerve out of its way, when it struck the front of my car.

Warning Signs of Insanity

Your friends tell you that you have been acting strange lately, and then you hit them several times with a sledgehammer.

Everyone you meet appears to have tentacles growing out of places you wouldn't expect tentacles to be grown from.

You start out each morning with a 30-minute jog around the bathroom.

Every commercial you hear on the radio reminds you of death.

People stay away from you whenever they hear you howl.

You laugh out loud during funerals.

Nobody listens to you anymore, because they can't understand you through that hockey mask.

You begin to stop and consider all of the blades of grass you've stepped on as a child, and worry that their descendants are going to one day seek revenge.

You have meaningful conversations with your toaster.

Your father pretends you don't exist, just to play along with your little illusion.

You collect dead windowsill flies.

Whenever you listen to the radio, the music sounds backwards.

You have a predominant fear of fabric softener.

You wake up each morning and find yourself sitting on your head in the middle of your front lawn.

You tend to agree with everything your mother's dead uncle tells you.

You call up random people and ask if you can borrow their dog, just for a few minutes.

You argue with yourself about which is better: to be eaten by a koala or to be loved by an infectious disease.

You think that exploding wouldn't be so bad, once you got used to it.

People offer you help, but you unfortunately interpret this as a violation of your rights as a boysenberry.

You try to make a list of the Warning Signs of Insanity (cough).

Mathematics of Relationships

Smart man + smart woman = romance
Smart man + dumb woman = pregnancy
Dumb man + smart woman = affair
Dumb man + dumb woman = marriage
Smart boss + smart employee = profits
Smart boss + dumb employee = production
Dumb boss + smart employee = promotion
Dumb boss + dumb employee = overtime

★ ★ ★ ★

Jesus is coming — quick, everybody look busy.

Woman – A Chemical Analysis

Health and Safety Executive Hazardous Materials Report

ELEMENT: Woman

SYMBOL: Wo

DISCOVERER: Adam

ATOMIC MASS: Accepted as 110lb but can range from 90lb—300lb.

OCCURRENCE: Copious quantities in all urban areas.

Physical Properties

Boils at nothing, freezes with no known reason.

Melts if given special treatment.

Bitter if incorrectly used.

Found in various states, ranging from virgin metal to common ore.

Yields to pressure applied at correct points.

Chemical Properties

Has great affinity for precious metals and stones.

Absorbs great quantities of expensive substances.

May explode without warning, and with no known reason.

Insoluble in liquids, but activity greatly increases with saturation in alcohol.

Most powerful money-reducing agent known to man.

Common Uses

Highly ornamental — especially in the sun or a sports car.

Can be a great aid to relaxation.

Very effective cleaning agent.

Tests

Pure specimen turns rosy-pink when discovered in natural state.

Turns green when placed beside a better specimen.

Potential Hazards

Highly dangerous, even in experienced hands.

Illegal to possess more than one, although several can be maintained in different locations so long as they do not come into direct contact with each other.

General Advice

Avoid contact wherever possible as cures can be expensive.

How to Be a Real Man

Don't call, ever.

If you don't like a girl, don't tell her. It's more fun to let her figure it out by herself.

Lie.

Name your penis. Be sure it is something narcissistic and unoriginal, such as 'Spike'.

Use this pick-up line: 'My girlfriend's pregnant, will you go out with me?'

Play with yourself. Talk about it.

Be as ambiguous as possible. If you don't want to answer, a nice grunt will do.

Always remember: you are a man. Therefore, no matter what, it isn't your fault.

Lie.

Girls find it attractive if a man has had more woman than baths.

Never ask for help. Even if you really, really need help — don't ask. People will think you have no penis.

Women like it when you ignore them. It arouses them.

Vanity is the most important trait for a man to have. Use reflective surfaces at every opportunity.

If, God forbid, you have to talk to a girl on the phone, use only monosyllabic words and noises. Bodily noises are permissible.

Hack and spit.

Everyone finds a man more attractive if he can write his name in urine.

One sure way to make a girl like you is to go after her best friend. She will then see what she's missing and love you for not giving up on her.

Tell her you will call. Then, refer back to rule #1.

Say things like 'What?'

Don't wear matching clothes. People will think your girlfriend picked them out, and it will cramp your style when picking up chicks.

Lie.

Deny everything. Everything.

Use this break-up line: 'It's not me, it's you.'

If you like a girl, tell all your female friends about her.

Because if any of your female friends like you, they'll really want to know.

Don't have a clue.

If you get a clue, pretend you didn't and disregard it.

No means yes.

Yes means no.

If you don't get sex whenever you want, your testicles will shrivel. Enforce this myth at all times.

If anyone asks, you have had sex in all possible positions and locations. Improvise.

Much like an orgasm signifies the end of a sexual peak, sex often signifies the end of a relationship.

Feelings? What feelings?

Life is one big competition. If someone is better than you at anything, either pretend it's not true or kick some ass.

Do not make decisions about relationships. If you are backed into a corner and must make a decision, stall.

If you still must come up with an answer, leave yourself a loophole for escape.

Every sentence that anyone says can be contorted to have sexual meaning. Do so.

At any given opportunity, point out how things look like various genitalia. If, by chance, you have Play-Doh, make sure you make an exact replica of your penis. Measure to make sure it's right.

Lie.

'Love' is not in your vocabulary. Don't even think about saying it.

A general rule: if whatever you're doing does not satisfy you completely in five minutes, it's really not worth it.

Dump your girlfriend. Beg and plead until you get her back. Dump her again. Repeat cycle.

Lie.

Always apologize. Never mean it.

If you hurt someone, pretend you care. Don't.

Try to have a good memory, but it's okay if you forget trivial things. You know, like your girlfriend's birthday and eye color.

Ignorance solves problems. If you can't see them, they can't see you.

It is never your duty to take responsibility for your actions.

Create new words and phrases to describe genitalia, sex, semen etc.

Lie.

If people express extreme disgust at whatever you are doing, don't stop! This is the desired reaction.

You are male, therefore you are superior.

Agenda for a boring evening: get beer. Drink beer. Have sex. Drink more beer. Pass out.

Females do not care what you do to them as long as they get to please you.

Don't ever notice anything.

If you're going out with someone but you love someone else, don't say anything. Wait until the girl you are going out with falls in love with you, and then tell her.

Basic fundamental rule of dating: quantity, not quality.

Basic fundamental rule of sex: quantity *is* quality.

Lie.

If you cheat on a girl, but no one finds out, then technically you've done nothing wrong.

Crying is not manly. Then again, if you are a man, what do you have to cry about, anyway?

If the question begins with 'why?' the answer is 'I don't know'.

Remember, every virgin girl is saving herself for you.

If you ever find yourself in a position where you have been proven wrong, blame others. Come up with creative and believable excuses why they are at fault — not you.

Don't ever let anyone say 'I told you so.' If you hear this phrase and it didn't come out of your mouth, go ballistic.

If your woman makes you go shopping with her, drive around until a parking spot right near the door opens up. If this takes hours, so be it. You will have the coveted 'door spot' and others will worship your skills.

Keep track of how many seconds in your life you have thought about sex. Compare with others.

If you do something really mean to a girl, and she doesn't want to talk to you, pretend nothing happened. If she still doesn't talk to you, casually ask, 'Is something wrong?'

Three words: let's be friends. Translation: I never want to speak to you again, but it's bad for my nice-guy image if you are mad at me, so I'll pretend I want to be your friend.

Lie.

If you're on a date, and there is a lull in the conversation, tell the girl how many different dorms you've been laid in.

The best sex position is you, lying face up... and twenty girls on top.

Practise your blank stare.

Spend your spare time thinking of excuses and shove them up your ass. Then, whenever you need one, you can pull it out of your ass.

If you are ever forced to show emotion, just pick random emotions like rage and lust and insanity and display them at random, inconvenient times. You won't be asked to do it again.

If you are asked to do something you really don't want to do, first try your manly best to get out of it. If that doesn't work, go ahead and do what you were asked to do, but complain that you don't know how to do it and continuously ask questions on how to do each little part. If still no one rushes in to do it for you, finish the job in the most half-assed way you possibly can and then say, 'See? I told you I couldn't do it. Eventually, people will stop asking you to do things.

Work out day and night to make your body even more beautiful than it already is. When people ask if you've been working out, say things like, 'No, baby, I was born like this!'

Beer. Then more beer.

Dump your girlfriend for an occasional night or five out with 'the gang'.

Lie.

The Singles Bar

A collection of some of the worst pick-up lines of all time.

I may not be Fred Flintstone, but I bet I can make your Bed Rock.

I may not be the best-looking guy here, but I'm the only one talking to you.

If you're going to regret this in the morning, we can sleep until the afternoon.

Oh. I'm sorry, I thought that was a braille name tag.

Excuse me, do you have your phone number? I seem to have lost mine.

I'm new in town, could I have directions to your house?

You look like a girl that has heard every line in the book, so what's one more going to hurt?

Screw me if I'm wrong, but is your name Ursula?

You might not be the most attractive girl here, but beauty is only a light switch away.

I lost my bed, can I borrow yours?

Your must be Jamaican, because Jamaican me crazy.

Are your legs tired? Because you've been running through my mind all night long.

Hey baby, I'm like American Express, you don't want to leave home without me.

Do you have change? My mother told me to call home when I met the girl of my dreams.

I can't find my puppy, can you help me find him? I think he went into this cheap motel room.

The fact that I'm missing my teeth just means that there's more room for your tongue.

Hi, my name is Pogo, want to jump on my stick?

★ ★ ★ ★

Hard work has a future pay-off, Laziness pays off now.

Government Health Warnings

Due to increasing product liability litigation, wine, beer and spirit manufacturers have accepted the Medical Association's suggestion that the following warning labels be placed immediately on all containers ...

Warning: consumption of alcohol may make you think you're whispering when you're not.

Warning: consumption of alcohol is a major factor in dancing like an idiot.

Warning: consumption of alcohol may cause you to tell the same boring story over and over again until your friends want to smash your head in.

Warning: consumption of alcohol may cause you to thay shings like thish.

Warning: consumption of alcohol may lead you to believe that ex-lovers are really dying for you to telephone them at four in the morning.

Warning: consumption of alcohol may leave you wondering what happened to your trousers.

Warning: consumption of alcohol may make you think that you can converse logically with members of the opposite sex without drooling.

Warning: consumption of alcohol may make you think that you have mystical Kung Fu powers.

Warning: consumption of alcohol may cause you to roll over in the morning and see something really scary (whose species and/or name you can't remember).

Warning: consumption of alcohol is the leading cause of inexplicable rug burns on the forehead.

Warning: consumption of alcohol may lead you to believe that you are invisible.

Warning: consumption of alcohol may lead you to believe that people are laughing *with* you.

Warning: consumption of alcohol may cause an influx in the time-space continuum, whereby small (and sometimes large) gaps of time may seem to literally disappear.

Warning: consumption of alcohol may cause pregnancy.

★ ★ ★ ★

I considered atheism but there weren't enough holidays.

★ ★ ★ ★

Learn from your parents' mistakes — use birth control.

English Subtitles to Hong Kong Movies

I am damn unsatisfied to be killed this way.

Fatty, you with your think face have hurt my instep.

Gun wounds again?

Same old rules: no eyes, no groin.

A normal person wouldn't steal pituitaries.

Damn, I'll burn you into a BBQ chicken!

Take my advice, or I'll spank you without pants.

Who gave you the nerve to get killed here?

Quiet you I'll blow your throat up.

You always use violence, I shouldn't have ordered the glutinous rice chicken.

I'll fire aimlessly if you don't come out!

You daring lousy guy.

Beat him out of recognizable shape!

I got knife scars more than the number of your leg's hair!

Beware! Your bones are going to be disconnected.

How can you use my intestines as a gift?

The bullets inside are very hot. Why do I feel so cold?

Personal Ad Translations

A list of abbreviations in the 'Women Seeking Men' classifieds. The first word is the code word; the second is the real meaning.

Adventurous = Has had more partners than you ever will

Artist = Unreliable

Athletic = Flat-chested

Beautiful = Pathological liar

Contagious smile = Bring your own penicillin

Emotionally secure = Medicated

Enjoys art and opera = Snob

Exotic beauty = Would frighten a Martian

Feminist = Fat; ball buster

Free spirit = Substance user

Friendship first = Trying to live down reputation as slut

Fun = Annoying

Gentle = Comatose

In transition = Needs new sugar-daddy to pay bills

Looks younger = If viewed from far away in bad light

Loves travel = If you're paying

Loves animals = Cat lady

Mature = Will not let you treat her like a farm animal in bed, like last boyfriend did

New-age = Hair all over

Old-fashioned = Lights out, missionary position only

Open-minded = Desperate

Poet = Depressive schizophrenic

Professional = Bitch

Redhead = Uses hair dye

Reubenesque = Hugely fat

Romantic = Looks better in candlelight

Self-employed = Jobless

Special = Took the short school bus

Spiritual = Involved with a cult

Tall, thin = Anorexic

Tanned = Wrinkled

Voluptuous = fat

Widow = Nagged first husband to death

Writer = Pompous

Young at heart = Toothless old fogey

Sniglets

Carperpetuation (kar' pur pet u a shun) n. The act, when vacuuming, of running over a string or a piece of lint at least a dozen times, reaching over and picking it up, examining it, then putting it back down to give the vacuum one more chance.

Disconfect (dis kon fekt') v. To sterilize the candy you dropped on the floor by blowing on it, somehow assuming this will 'remove' all the germs.

Elbonics (el bon' iks) n. The actions of two people maneuvring for one armrest in a movie theatre.

Elecelleration (el a cel er ay' shun) n. The mistaken notion that the more you press an elevator button the faster it will arrive.

Frust (frust) n. The small line of debris that refuses to be swept onto the dust pan. Finally the person gives up and sweeps it under the rug.

Lactomangulation (lak' to man gyu lay' shun) n. Manhandling the 'open here' spout on a milk container so badly that one has to resort to the 'illegal' side.

Peppier (peh pee ay') n. The waiter at a fancy restaurant whose sole purpose seems to be walking around asking diners if they want ground pepper.

Phoneesia (fo nee' zhuh) n. The affliction of dialling a phone number and forgetting whom you were calling just as they answer.

Pupkus (pup' kus) n. The moist residue left on a window after a dog presses its nose to it.

Telecrastination (tel e kras tin ay' shun) n. The act of always letting the phone ring at least twice before you pick it up, even when you're only six inches away.

Actual Bumper Stickers

I love cats… they taste just like chicken.

Out of my mind. Back in five minutes.

Cover me. I'm changing lanes.

As long as there are tests, there will be prayer in public schools.

Laugh alone and the world thinks you're an idiot.

Sometimes I wake up grumpy; other times I let her sleep.

I want to die in my sleep like my grandfather… not screaming and yelling like the passengers in his car.

I didn't fight my way to the top of the food chain to be a vegetarian.

Your kid may be an honor student, but you're still an idiot!

It's as bad as you think, and they *are* out to get you.

Smile, it's the second-best thing you can do with your lips.

Friends don't let friends drive naked.

Where there's a will, I want to be in it!

If we aren't supposed to eat animals, why are they made of meat?

Time is the best teacher; unfortunately it kills all its students!

It's lonely at the top, but you eat better.

Reality? That's where the pizza delivery guy comes from!

Warning: dates in calendar are closer that they appear.

Be nice to your kids. They'll choose your nursing home.

There are three kinds of people; those who can count and those who can't.

Ever stop to think, and forget to start again?

Diplomacy is the art of saying 'Nice doggie!'... until you can find a rock.

Two plus two equals five for extremely large

values of two.

I like you, but I wouldn't want to see you working with subatomic particles.

I killed a six-pack just to watch it die.

Flight Attendants Can Be Humorous, Too

Occasionally, airline attendants make an effort to make the in-flight safety lecture and other announcements a bit more entertaining. Here are some real examples that have been heard or reported:

'Should the cabin lose pressure, oxygen masks will drop from the overhead area. Please place the bag over your own mouth and nose before assisting children or adults acting like children.'

'To operate your seatbelt, insert the metal tab into the buckle, and pull tight. It works just like every other seatbelt, and if you don't know how to operate one, you probably shouldn't be out in public unsupervised.'

'In the event of a sudden loss of cabin pressure, oxygen masks will descend from the ceiling. Stop screaming, grab the mask, and pull it over your face.'

'If you have a small child traveling with you, secure your mask before assisting with theirs. If you are traveling with two small children, decide now which one you love more.'

'Your seat cushions can be used for flotation, and in the event of an emergency water-landing, please take them with our compliments.'

'Ladies and gentlemen, please remain in your seats with your seatbelts fastened while the Captain taxis what's left of our plane to the gate!'

'We'd like to thank you folks for flying with us today. And, the next time you get the insane urge to go blasting through the skies in a pressurized metal tube, we hope you'll think of us here.'

On a Lighter Note...

The following quotes are from actual medical records dictated by physicians:

By the time he was admitted, his rapid heart had stopped, and he was feeling better.

Patient has chest pain if she lies on her left side for over a year.

On the second day the knee was better and on the third day it had completely disappeared.

She has had no shaking chills, but her husband states she was very hot in bed last night.

The patient has been depressed ever since she began seeing me in 1983.

I will be happy to go into her GI system; she seems ready and anxious.

Patient was released to outpatient department without dressing.

I have suggested he loosen his pants before standing, and then, when he stands with the help of his wife, they should fall to the floor.

The patient is tearful and crying constantly. She also appears to be depressed.

Discharge status: alive without permission.

The patient will need disposition, and therefore we will get Mr Blank to dispose of him.

Healthy-appearing decrepit 69-year-old female, mentally alert but forgetful.

The patient refused an autopsy.

The patient has no past history of suicides.

The patient expired on the floor uneventfully.

Patient has left his white blood cells at another hospital.

Patient was becoming more demented with urinary frequency.

The patient's past medical history has been remarkably insignificant with only a 40-pound weight gain in the past three years.

She slipped on the ice and apparently her legs went in separate directions in early December.

The patient experienced sudden onset of severe shortness of breath with a picture of acute pulmonary oedema at home while having sex which gradually deteriorated in the emergency room.

Actual Answers Given by Contestants on *Family Feud*

Name something a blind person might use...
'A sword.'

Name a song with moon in the title...
'Blue suede moon.'

Name a bird with a long neck...
'Naomi Campbell.'

Name an occupation where you need a torch...
'A burglar.'

Name a famous brother and sister...
'Bonnie & Clyde.'

Name a dangerous race...
'The Arabs'

Name an item of clothing worn by the three musketeers...
'A horse.'

Name something that floats in the bath...
'Water.'

Name something you wear on the beach...
'A deckchair.'

Name something red...
'My cardigan.'

Name a famous cowboy...
'Buck Rogers.'

Name a famous royal...
'Mail.'

Name something you have to memorize...
'7.'

Name something you do before going to bed...
'Sleep.'

Name something you put on walls...
'Rooves.'

Name something in the garden that's green...
'Toolshed.'

Name something that flies that doesn't have an engine...
'A bicycle with wings.'

Name something you might be allergic to...
'Skiing.'

Name a famous bridge...
'The bridge over troubled waters.'

Name something a cat does...
'Goes to the toilet.'

Name something you do in the bathroom...
'Decorate.'

Name an animal you might see at the zoo...
'A dog.'

Name something associated with the police...
'Pigs.'

Name a sign of the zodiac...
'April.'

Name something slippery...
'A conman.'

Name a food that can be brown or white...
'Potato.'

Name a jacket potato topping...
'Jelly.'

Name a famous Scotsman...
'Jock.'

Name something with a hole in it...
'Window.'

Name a non-living object with legs...
'Plant.'

Name a domestic animal...
'Leopard.'

Name a part of the body beginning with 'n'...
'Knee.'

Name something you open other than a door...
'Your bowels.'

Church Bulletins

The Boy Scouts are saving aluminium cans, bottles and other items to be recycled. Proceeds will be used to cripple children.

The Outreach Committee has enlisted 25 visitors to make calls on people who are not afflicted with any church.

The pastor would appreciate it if the ladies of the congregation would lend him their electric girdles for the pancake breakfast next Sunday morning.

Low Self-esteem Group will meet Thursday at 7 p.m. Please use the back door.

Ushers will eat latecomers.

For those of you who have children and don't know it, we have a nursery downstairs.

Reverend Merriweather spoke briefly, much to the delight of the congregation.

The pastor will preach his farewell message, after which the choir will sing 'Break Forth into Joy'.

A songfest was hell at the Methodist Church Wednesday.

Due to the rector's illness, Wednesday's healing service will be discontinued until further notice.

Remember in prayer the many who are sick of our church and community.

The eighth-graders will be presenting Shakespeare's *Hamlet* in the church basement Friday at 7 p.m. The congregation is invited to attend this tragedy.

The concert held in Fellowship hall was a great success. Special thanks are due to the minister's daughter, who labored the whole evening at the piano which as usual fell upon her.

Don't let worry kill you. Let the church help.

Thursday night potluck supper. Prayer and medication to follow.

The rosebud on the altar this morning is to announce the birth of David Alan Belzer, the sin of Reverend and Mrs. Julius Belzer.

This afternoon there will be a meeting in the south and north ends of the church. Children will be baptised at both ends.

Tuesday there will be an ice-cream social at 4 p.m. All ladies giving milk please come early.

Thursday at 5 p.m. there will be a meeting of the Little Mothers Club. All wishing to become Little Mothers, please see the minister in his private study.

This being Easter Sunday, we will ask Mrs Lewis to come forward and lay an egg on the altar.

Next Sunday a special collection will be taken to defray the cost of the new carpet. All those wishing to do something on the new carpet will come forward and get a piece of paper.

The ladies of the church have cast off clothing of every kind and they may be seen in the church basement Friday.

A bean supper will be held on Tuesday evening in the church basement. Music will follow.

At the early evening service tonight, the sermon topic will be 'What is Hell?' Come early and listen to our choir practise.

Weight Watchers will meet at 7 p.m. at the Presbyterian Church. Please use large double door at the side entrance.

Pastor is on vacation. Messages can be given to the church secretary.

Eight new choir robes are needed, due to the addition of several new members and to the deterioration of some older ones.

Mrs Johnson will be entering the hospital this week for testes.

The Senior Choir invites any member of the congregation who enjoys sinning to join the choir.

Please join us as we show our support for Amy and Alan who are preparing for the girth of their first child.

The Lutheran Men's Group will meet at 6 p.m. Steak, mashed potatoes, green beans, bread and dessert will be served for a nominal feel.

★ ★ ★ ★

Dijon vu — the same mustard as before.

★ ★ ★ ★

Puritanism: the haunting fear that someone, somewhere may be happy.

Points to Ponder

Why do we say something is out of whack? What is a whack?

Do infants enjoy infancy as much as adults enjoy adultery?

If a pig loses its voice, is it disgruntled?

If love is blind, why is lingerie so popular?

Why is the man who invests all your money called a broker?

Why do croutons come in airtight packages? It's just stale bread to begin with.

Why are a wise man and a wise guy opposites?

Why do overlook and oversee mean opposite things?

If horrific means to make horrible, does terrific mean to make terrible?

Why is it that if someone tells you that there are one billion stars in the universe you will believe them, but if they tell you a wall has wet paint you have to touch it to be sure?

A bus station is where a bus stops. A train station is where a train stops. On my desk I have a work station...

Can atheists get insurance for acts of God?

I believe five out of four people have trouble with fractions.

How come you never hear about gruntled employees?

How much faith does it take to be an atheist?

If a tin whistle is made out of tin, then what exactly is a fog horn made out of?

If atheists say there is no God, who pops up the next tissue in the box?

If vegetable oil comes from vegetables, where does baby oil come from?

What was the best thing *before* sliced bread?

Reasons Why Alcohol Should Be Served at Work

It's an incentive to show up.

It reduces stress.

It leads to more honest communications.

It reduces complaints about low pay.

It cuts down on time off because you can work with a hangover.

Employees tell management what they think, not what management wants to hear.

It helps save on heating costs in the winter.

It encourages car pooling.

It increases job satisfaction because if you have a bad job, you don't care.

It eliminates vacations because people would rather come to work.

It makes fellow employees look better.

It makes the cafeteria food taste better.

Bosses are more likely to hand out raises when they are wasted.

Salary negotiations are a lot more profitable.

Suddenly, burping during a meeting isn't so embarrassing.

Employees work later since there's no longer a need to relax at the bar.

It makes everyone more open with their ideas.

Everyone agrees the work is of better quality after they've had a couple of drinks.

It eliminates the need for employees to get drunk on their lunch break.

It increases the chance of seeing your boss naked.

The cleaner's closet will finally have a use.

Employees will no longer need coffee to sober up.

Sitting on the photocopier will no longer be seen as gross.

Babbling and mumbling incoherently will be common language.

Actual Label Instructions on Consumer Goods

On a hair dryer: Do not use while sleeping.

On a bag of crisps: You could be a winner! No purchase necessary. Details inside.

On a bar of soap: Directions — use like regular soap.

On frozen dinners: Serving suggestion — defrost.

On a hotel-provided shower cap in a box: Fits one head.

On a tiramisu dessert: Do not turn upside down. (Printed on the bottom of the box.)

On a bread pudding: Product will be hot after heating.

On packaging from an iron: Do not iron clothes on body.

On children's cough medicine: Do not drive car or operate machinery.

On sleeping tablets: Warning — may cause drowsiness.

On a kitchen knife: Warning — keep out of children.

On a string of Christmas lights: For indoor or out-door use only.

On a packet of peanuts: Warning — contains nuts.

On an airline's packet of nuts: Instructions — open packet, eat nuts.

On a chainsaw: Do not attempt to stop chain with your hands.

How to Keep a Healthy Level of Insanity in the Workplace

Page yourself over the intercom. Don't disguise your voice.

Make up nicknames for all your co-workers and refer to them only by these names. That's a good point, Sparky. No, I'm sorry I'm going to have to disagree with you there, Chachi.'

Put up mosquito netting around your cubicle.

Arrive at a meeting late, say you're sorry, but you didn't have time for lunch, and you're going to be nibbling during the meeting. During the meeting eat five entire raw potatoes.

Insist that your e-mail address be
zena_goddess_of_fire@companyname.com

Every time someone asks you to do something, ask them if they want fries with that.

Encourage your colleagues to join you in a little synchronized chair dancing.

Put your waste paper basket on your desk. Label it 'in'.

Determine how many cups of coffee is 'too' many.

Develop an unnatural fear of staplers.

For a relaxing break, get away from it all with a mask and snorkel in the fish tank. If no one notices, take out your snorkel and see how many fish you can catch in your mouth.

Put decaf in the coffeemaker for three weeks. Once everyone has got over their caffeine addictions, switch to espresso.

★ ★ ★ ★

The sex was so good that even the neighbors had a cigarette.

Some Time-honored Truths

Don't sweat the petty things, and don't pet the sweaty things.

One tequila, two tequila, three tequila, floor.

One nice thing about egotists: they don't talk about other people.

To be intoxicated is to feel sophisticated but not be able to say it.

The older you get, the better you realize you were.

I doubt, therefore I might be.

Age is a very high price to pay for maturity.

Procrastination is the art of keeping up with yesterday.

A fool and his money are soon partying.

Before they invented drawing boards, what did they go back to?

If one synchronized swimmer drowns, do the rest have to drown too?

If work is so terrific, how come they have to pay you to do it?

If you're born again, do you have two belly buttons?

If you ate pasta and antipasta, would you still be hungry?

347

Funny Signs

At a restaurant: Tip-ing is not a city in China.

Seen on an electrical appliance store: Go modern! Go Gas! GO BOOM!

Emergency evacuation plan posted in various places around an office building: Run like hell!

At a septic tank service: Call Monday thru Friday, sorry, we haul milk on weekends.

Billboard sign on a highway: Nobody reads billboards... but you just did.

In an airline office in Copenhagen: We take your bags and send them in all directions.

In a hotel in Acapulco: The manager has personally passed all the water served here.

On the door of a Moscow hotel room: If this is your first visit to the USSR, you are welcome to it.

In a Bangkok dry cleaners: Drop your trousers here for best results.

In a hotel in Zurich: Because of the impropriety of entertaining guests of the opposite sex in the bedroom, it is suggested that the lobby be used for this purpose.

On a dock: Safety ladder, climb at own risk.

In a doctor's office in Rome: Specialist in women and other diseases.

In a Bangkok temple: It is forbidden to enter a woman even a foreigner if dressed as a man.

On the menu in a Swiss restaurant: Our wines leave you nothing to hope for.

In a laundry in Rome: Ladies, leave your clothes here and spend the afternoon having a good time.

In the window of a furrier's shop in Sweden: Fur coats made for ladies from their own skin.

At a zoo in Budapest: Please do not feed the animals. If you have any suitable food, give it to the guard on duty.

Woman's Instruction Booklet

Never do housework. No man ever made love to a woman because the house was spotless.

Remember you are known by the idiot you accompany.

Don't imagine you can change a man — unless he's in diapers.

So many men — so many reasons not to sleep with any of them.

If they put a man on the moon, they should be able to put them all there.

Tell him you're not his type — you have a pulse.

Never let your man's mind wander. It's too little to be let out alone.

The only reason men are on this planet is that vibrators can't dance or buy drinks.

Never sleep with a man who's named his penis.

Go for younger men. You might as well. They never mature anyway.

A man who can dress himself without looking like Forrest Gump is unquestionably gay.

Definition of a bachelor: a man who has missed the opportunity to make some woman miserable.

Women don't make fools of men. Most of them are the do-it-yourself types.

The best way to get a man to do something is to suggest they are too old for it.

Love is blind, but marriage is a real eye-opener.

If you want a committed man, look in a mental hospital.

If he asks what sort of books you're interested in, tell him check books.

A man's idea of serious commitment is usually, 'Oh all right, I'll stay the night.'

Women sleep with men, who if they were women, they wouldn't even bother to have lunch with.

Remember a sense of humor does not mean that you tell him jokes, it means you laugh at his.

If he asks you if you're faking it, tell him no — you're just practising.

Sadly, all men are created equal.

When he asks you if he's your first, tell him 'you may be, you look familiar.'

Women don't blink during foreplay because they don't have time.

It takes one million sperm to fertilize one egg because they won't stop to ask for directions.

Men and sperm are similar as they both have a one-in-a-million chance of becoming a human being.

A man shows that he is planning for the future by buying two cases of beer.

Men and government bonds are different as the bonds mature.

Blonde jokes are short so men can remember them.

It is difficult to find men who are sensitive, caring and good looking as they all already have boyfriends.

A woman who knows where her husband is every night is a widow.

After creating man, God said 'I must be able to do better than that.'

Men and parking spots are alike as good ones are always taken and the free ones are mostly handicapped or extremely small.

How to Impress a Woman

Compliment her, cuddle her, kiss her, caress her, love her, stroke her, comfort her, protect her, hold her, spend money on her, wine and dine her, buy things for her, listen to her, care for her, stand by her, support her, go to the ends of the Earth for her.

How to Impress a Man

Show up naked, with beer.

Various Philosophies Explained in Terms of Two Cows

Socialism — You have two cows. You keep one and give one to your neighbor.

Capitalism — You have two cows. You sell one and buy a bull.

Communism — You have two cows. The government takes them both and provides you with milk.

Fascism: You have two cows. The government takes them both and sells you the milk.

Nazism — You have two cows. The government takes them both and shoots you.

Surrealism — You have two giraffes. The government requires you to take harmonica lessons.

Advertising at its Best

2 female Boston terrier puppies. 7 weeks old, perfect markings, 555-1234. Leave mess.

Lost: small apricot poodle. Reward. Neutered. Like one of the family.

A superb and inexpensive restaurant. Fine food expertly served by waitresses in appetizing forms.

Dinner special — turkey $2.35; chicken or beef $2.25; children $2.00.

For sale: an antique desk suitable for lady with thick legs and large drawers.

Four-poster bed, 101 years old. Perfect for antique lover.

Now is your chance to have your ears pierced and get an extra pair to take home, too.

Wanted: 50 girls for stripping machine operators in factory.

Wanted: unmarried girls to pick fresh fruit and produce at night.

We do not tear your clothing with machinery. We do it carefully by hand.

For sale: three canaries of undermined sex.

For sale: eight puppies from a German Shepherd and an Alaskan hussy.

Great dames for sale.

Have several very old dresses from grandmother in beautiful condition.

Tired of cleaning yourself? Let me do it.

Dog for sale: eats anything and is fond of children.

Holiday special: have your home exterminated.

Mt Kilimanjaro, the breathtaking backdrop for the Serena Lodge. Swim in the lovely pool while you drink it all in.

Get rid of aunts: Zap does the job in 24 hours.

Toaster: a gift that every member of the family appreciates. Automatically burns toast.

Sheer stockings. Designed for fancy dress, but so serviceable that lots of women wear nothing else.

Stock up and save. Limit: one

For rent: 6-room hated apartment.

Man, honest. Will take anything.

Wanted: chambermaid in rectory. Love in, $200 a month. References required.

Man wanted to work in dynamite factory. Must be willing to travel.

Used cars: why go elsewhere to be cheated? Come here first.

Christmas sale. Handmade gifts for the hard-to-find person.

Wanted: haircutter. Excellent growth potential.

Wanted: man to take care of cow that does not smoke or drink.

3 year-old teacher needed for pre-school. Experience preferred.

Our experienced Mom will care of your child. Fenced yard, meals and smacks included.

Our bikinis are exciting. They are simply the tops.

Auto repair service. Free pick-up and delivery. Try us once, you'll never go anywhere again.

Illiterate? Write today for free help.

Girl wanted to assist magician in cutting-off-head illusion. Blue Cross and salary.

Wanted: widower with school-age children requires person to assume general housekeeping duties. Must be capable of contributing to growth of family.

And now, the Superstore — unequalled in size, unmatched in variety, unrivalled inconvenience.

We will oil your sewing machine and adjust tension in your home for $1.00

★ ★ ★ ★

He who laughs last thinks the slowest.

★ ★ ★ ★

A torch is a case for holding dead batteries.

Maintenance Complaints

*Here are some actual complaints submitted recently
by pilots to maintenance engineers pertaining to
problems that are to be fixed prior to the aircraft's
next flight. After attending to the complaints, the
maintenance crews are required to log the details of
the action taken to fix these complaints.*

(P) = The problem logged by the pilot
*(S) = The solution and the action taken by
the maintenance engineers.*

(P) Left inside main tire almost needs replacement.
(S) Almost replaced left inside main tire.

(P) Test flight okay, except autoland very rough.
(S) Autoland not installed on this aircraft.

(P) Number 2 propeller seeping prop fluid.
(S) Number 2 propeller seepage normal. Number 1,
3 and 4 propellers lack normal seepage.

(P) Something loose in cockpit.
(S) Something tightened in cockpit.

(P) Evidence of leak on right main landing gear.
(S) Evidence removed.

(P) DME volume unbelievably loud.
(S) Volume set to more believable level.

(P) Dead bugs on windshield.
(S) Live bugs on backorder.

(P) Autopilot in altitude hold mode produces a 200 fpm descent.
(S) Cannot reproduce problem on ground.

(P) IFF inoperative.
(S) IFF always inoperative in off mode.

(P) Friction locks cause throttle levers to stick.
(S) That's what they're there for!

(P) Number three engine missing
(S) Engine found on right wing after brief search.

(P) Aircraft handles funny.
(S) Aircraft warned to straighten up, 'fly right' and be serious!

(P) Target radar hums.
(S) Reprogrammed target radar with the words.

★ ★ ★ ★

I used to have a handle on life. Then it broke.

★ ★ ★ ★

I'd give my right arm to be ambidextrous.

★ ★ ★ ★

I believe in youthenasia.

Men's Guide to Women's English

When Women Say

They Really Mean

When Women Say	They Really Mean
'We need…'	I Want
'It's your decision.'	The correct decision should be obvious by now.
'Do what you want.'	You'll pay for this later.
'We need to talk.'	I need to complain.
'Sure… go ahead'	Don't.
'I'm not upset.'	Of course I'm upset, you moron.
'You're certainly attentive tonight.'	Is sex all you think about?
I'm not emotional! And I'm not overreacting!'	I've got my period.
'Be romantic, turn out the lights.'	I have flabby thighs.
'This kitchen is so inconvenient.'	I want a new house.
'I heard a noise.'	I noticed you were almost asleep.

'Do you love me?'	I'm going to ask for something expensive.
'How much do you love me?'	I did something today you're really not going to like.
'Is my butt huge?'	Tell me I'm beautiful.
'You have to learn to communicate.'	Just agree with me.
'Yes.'	No.
'No.'	No.
'Maybe.'	No.
'I'm sorry.'	You'll be sorry.
'Do you like this recipe?'	It's easy, so you'd better get used to it.
'Was that the baby?'	Why don't you get out of bed and walk him until he goes to sleep?
'Can't we just be friends?'	There is no way in hell I am going to let any part of your body touch any part of mine again.
'I just need some space.'	I just need some space without you in it.

'Do I look fat in this dress?'	We haven't had a fight in a while.
'No, pizza's fine.'	Cheap git.
'I just do not want a boyfriend.'	I just do not want (you as) a boyfriend.
'Oh, no, I will pay for myself.	I'm just pretending it be nice, there is no way I am going Dutch.
'Oh yes! Right there.'	Well, near there. I just want to get this over with.
'I'm just going out with the girls.'	We are gonna get sloppy and make fun of you and your friends.
'There's no one else.'	I am sleeping with your best friend.
'Size doesn't count.'	Size doesn't count unless I want an orgasm.

Women's Guide to Men's English

What Men Say

They Really Mean

What Men Say	They Really Mean
Hello.	Let's cut the talk and go have sex.
'How are you?'	How are you in bed, I mean.
'I'd like a discreet relationship.'	I want sex, but I'm married.
'I'll be out of town for a few days.'	I'll be spending time with the wife.
'I'm a novelist.'	I have 10 unpublished books.
'I'm coming out of a long relationship.'	My wife is divorcing me.
'I'm consulting.'	I'm looking for a job.
'I'm divorced.'	I just slipped off my wedding ring.
'I'm in television.'	I fix them.
'I'm self-employed.'	I just got fired.
'I'm sorry I flirted with caught. your sister.	I'm sorry I got
'I can't leave my wife just yet.'	Be patient forever

'I enjoy reading.'

That's right — *Playboy* and *Penthouse*.

'I like a woman who is intelligent.'

As long as she thinks I'm smarter.

'I love opera.'

I want sex, but I've seen an opera once.

'I work high up in an executive office.'

I'm a window washer.

'I work with computers.'

I'm a cashier at a gas station.

'I'm looking for a satisfying relationship.'

I want sex.

'My job keeps me running.'

I'm a messenger.

'My wife and I are I'm separated.'

She's at home and here at the bar.

'I'm hungry.'

I'm hungry.

'I'm sleepy.'

I'm sleepy.

'I'm tired.'

I'm tired.

'Do you want to go to a movie?'

I'd eventually like to have sex with you.

'Can I take you out to dinner?'

I'd eventually like to have sex with you.

'Can I call you sometime?'

I'd eventually like to have sex with you.

'May I have this dance?' — I'd eventually like to have sex with you.

'Nice dress!' — Nice cleavage!

'You look tense, let me give you a massage.' — I want to fondle you.

'What's wrong?' — I guess sex tonight is out of the question.

'I'm bored.' — Do you want to have sex?

'I love you.' — Let's have sex right now.

'Let's talk.' — I am trying to impress you by showing that I am a very deep person and maybe then you'd agree to have sex with me.

'Will you marry me?' — I want to make it illegal for you to have sex with any other guys.

'I like that one better.' — Pick any damned dress (while shopping) and let's go home!

'I need you.' My hand is tired.

'How do I compare with your other boyfriends?' Is my penis really that small?

'It is just orange juice' Three more shots and she'll have her legs around my head.

'I want you back.' I want you tonight.

'We've been through so much together.' If it weren't for you, I never would have lost my virginity.

'I miss you so much.' I am so horny that my roommate is starting to look good.

'I'm going fishing.' I'm going to drink myself dangerously stupid, and stand by a stream with a stick in my hand, while the fish swim by in complete safety.

'It would take too long to explain.' I have no idea how it works.

'It's a guy thing.'

There is no rational thought pattern connected with it, and you have no chance at all of making it logical.

'What's wrong?'

What meaningless self-inflicted psychological trauma are you going through now?

'Can I help with dinner?'

Why isn't it already on the table?

'Uh huh', 'sure honey' or 'yes, dear'

Absolutely nothing. It's a conditioned response.

'We're going to be late.'

Now I have a legitimate excuse to drive like a maniac.

'I was listening to you. It's just that I have other things on my mind.'

I was wondering if that redhead over there is wearing a bra.

'Take a break, honey, you're working too hard.'

I can't hear the game over the vacuum cleaner.

'That's interesting, dear.'

Are you still talking?

'It's a really good movie.'

It's got guns, knives, fast cars and beautiful naked women.

'That's women's work.'

It's difficult, dirty, and thankless.

'You know how bad my memory is.'

I remember the theme song to 'F Troop', the address of the first girl I ever kissed and the vehicle identification and license plates of every car I've ever owned, but I forgot your birthday.

'I was just thinking about you, and got you these roses.'

The girl selling them on the corner was a babe.

'Oh, don't fuss, I just cut it's no big deal.

I have actually myself, severed a limb, but will bleed to death before I admit I'm hurt.

'Hey, I've got my reasons for what I'm doing.

And I hope I think of some pretty soon.

'I can't find it.'

It didn't fall into my outstretched hands, so I'm completely clueless.

'What did I do this time?'

What did you catch me at?

'I heard you.'

I haven't the foggiest clue what you just said, and am hoping desperately that I can fake it well enough so that you don't spend the next three days yelling at me.

'You know I could never love anyone else.'

I am used to the way you yell at me, and realize it could be worse.

'You look terrific.'

Oh, God, please don't try on one more outfit. I'm starving.

'I'm not lost. I know exactly where we are.'

No one will ever see us alive again.

'We share the housework.'

I make the messes, she cleans them up.

Sex-related Truths

Nothing improves with age.

Sex has no calories.

Sex takes up the least amount of time and causes the most amount of trouble.

Sex is like snow; you never know how many inches you are going to get or how long it is going to last.

Virginity can be cured.

Never sleep with anyone crazier than yourself.

Sex is dirty only if it's done right.

It is always the wrong time of month.

When the lights are out, all women are beautiful.

Sex is hereditary. If your parents never had it, chances are you won't either.

Sow your wild oats on Saturday night — then on Sunday pray for crop failure.

It was not the apple on the tree but the pair on the ground that caused the trouble in the garden.

You shouldn't fake it because men would rather be ineffective than deceived.

Sex discriminates against the shy and the ugly.

Love your neighbor, but don't get caught.

One good turn gets most of the blankets.

You cannot produce a baby in one month by impregnating nine women.

Love is the triumph of imagination over intelligence.

Never lie down with a woman who's got more troubles than you.

Abstain from wine, women and song; mostly song.

Never argue with a women when she's tired — or rested.

It is better to be looked over than overlooked.

A man can be happy with any woman as long as he doesn't love her.

There is no difference between a wise man and a fool when they fall in love.

Never say no.

★ ★ ★ ★

The early bird may get the worm, but it's the second mouse that gets the cheese.

Final University Exam

Instructions: Read each question carefully.
You have two hours to answer all questions.
Begin immediately.

History: Describe the history of the papacy from its origins through to the present day, concentrating especially, but not exclusively, on its social, political, economic, religious and philosophical impact on Europe, Asia, America and Africa. Be brief, concise and specific.

Medicine: You have been provided with a razor blade, a piece of gauze, and a bottle of scotch whisky. Remove your appendix. Do not suture until your work has been inspected.

Public Speaking: 2500 riot-crazed tribal men are storming the classroom. Calm them. You may use any ancient language except Latin or Greek.

Biology: Create life. Estimate the differences in subsequent human culture if this form of life had developed 500 million years earlier, with special attention to its probable effect on the American Ideal. Prove your thesis.

Music: Write a piano concerto. Orchestrate and perform it with flute and drum. You will find a piano under your seat.

Psychology: Based on your knowledge of their works, evaluate the emotional stability, degree of adjustment, and repressed frustration of each of the following: Alexander of Aphrodisis, Rameses II, Hammuarabi. Support your evaluation with quotations from each man's work, making appropriate references. It is not necessary to translate.

Sociology: Estimate the sociological problems which might accompany the end of the world. Construct an experiment to test your theory.

Engineering: The disassembled parts of a high-powered rifle have been placed on your desk. You will also find an instruction manual, printed in Swahili. In 10 minutes, a hungry Bengal tiger will be admitted to the room. Take whatever action you feel necessary. Be prepared to justify your decision.

Physics: Explain the nature of matter. Include in your answer an evaluation of the impact of the development of mathematics on science.

Philosophy: Sketch the development of human thought. Estimate its significance. Compare with the development of any kind of thought.

General Knowledge: Describe in detail. Be objective and specific.

Things Never to Say During Sex

What is *that?*

Is it in?

You're kidding, right?

(Phone rings) Hello? Oh nothing, and you?

Do I have to pay for this?

You look better in the dark.

You have the same bra my mom does (worse if the girl says it).

I hope you don't expect a raise for this...

Did I tell you I have herpes?

Now we must get married.

Are you trying to be funny?

Haven't you ever done this before?

Do you know what some female spiders do after sex?

But you just started!

Don't touch that!

I think my dad is listening at the door.

Smile for the camera, honey!

Get your hand out of there!

I knew you wore a padded bra!

Hold on, let me change the channel...

Stop moaning, you sound so stupid.

I'm sorry, I wasn't listening.

It's okay honey, I can imagine that it's bigger.

God I wish you were a real woman.

By the way, when I drove over here, I ran over your dog...

Oh Susan, Susan... I mean Donna...

Is it okay if after this I never see you again?

Did I forget to tell you I got worms from my cat?

Don't make that face at me!

How come we each have a penis?

Of course you can't be on top, you're too fat. You'll kill me!

No problem, we'll try again later when you can satisfy me too.

The only reason I'm doing this is because I'm drunk.

My mom taught me this...

This is my pet rat, Larry...

I haven't had this much sex since I was a hooker!

Don't squirm, you'll spill my beer.

Did I tell you where my cold sore came from?

Fun Things to do While Driving

At traffic lights, eye the person in the next car suspiciously. With a look of fear, lock your doors.

Stop at green lights.

Pass cars, then drive very slowly.

Honk frequently without motivation.

Wave at people often. If they wave back, offer an angry look and an obscene gesture.

Let pedestrians know who's boss.

Restart your car at every stop light.

Hang numerous car-fresheners on the rear-view mirror. Talk to them, stroking them lovingly.

Have some passengers in the back who are having wild, noisy sex.

Stop and smell the roses along the way.

Politically Correct Terms

Dirty old man = Sexually focused chronologically gifted individual

Perverted = Sexually dysfunctional

Serial killer = Person with difficult-to-meet needs

Lazy = Motivationally deficient

Fat = Horizontally challenged

Fail = Achieve a deficiency

Dishonest = Ethically disoriented

Clumsy = Uniquely co-ordinated

Body odour = Nondiscretionary fragrance

Alive = Temporarily metabolically abled

Worst = Least best

Wrong = Differently logical

Ugly = Cosmetically different

Unemployed = Involuntarily leisured

Dead = Living impaired

Vagrant = Non-specifically destinationed individual

Spendthrift = Negative saver

Stoned = Chemically inconvenienced

Pregnant = Parasitically oppressed

Ignorant = Knowledge-based non-possessor

Dumb and Dumber

The following are questions actually asked of witnesses by attorneys during trials and, in certain cases, the responses given by the insightful witnesses:

Q. What is your date of birth?
A. July fifteenth.
Q. What year?
A. Every year.

Q. What gear were you in at the time of the impact?
A. Gucci sweats and Reeboks.

Q. How old is your son — the one living with you?
A. Thirty-eight or thirty-five, I can't remember which.
Q. How long has he lived with you?
A. Forty-five years.

Q. What was the first thing your husband said to you when he woke that morning?
A. He said, 'Where am I, Cathy?'
Q. Any why did that upset you?
A. My name is Susan.

Q. She had three children, right?
A. Yes.
Q. How many were boys?
A. None.
Q. Were there any girls?

377

Q. You say the stairs went down to the basement?

A. Yes.

Q. And these stairs, did they go up also?

Q. How was your first marriage terminated?

A. By death.

Q. And by whose death was it terminated?

Q. Now doctor, isn't it true that when a person dies in his sleep, he doesn't know about it until the next morning.

Q. Were you present when your picture was taken?

Q. How far apart were the vehicles at the time of the collision?'

Q. You were there until the time you left, is that true?

Q. How many times have you committed suicide?

Q. Doctor, how many autopsies have you performed on dead people?

A. All my autopsies are performed on dead people.

Q. Do you recall the time that you examined the body?

A. The autopsy started around 8.30 p.m.

Q. And Mr Descartes was dead at the time?

A. No, he was sitting on the table wondering why I was doing an autopsy.

Q. Doctor, before you performed the autopsy, did you check for a pulse?

A. No.

Q. Did you check for blood pressure?

A. No.

Q. Did you check for breathing?

A. No.

Q. So, then it is possible that the patient was alive when you began the autopsy.

A. No.

Q. How can you be so sure, Doctor?

A. Because his brain was sitting on my desk in a jar.

Q. But nevertheless, could the patient have still been alive?

A. It is possible that he could have been alive and practising law somewhere.

★ ★ ★ ★

The gene pool could use a little chlorine.

★ ★ ★ ★

Where there's a will, I want to be in it.

Crazy Calls

A transcript of the new call center recently set up for the Acme Mental Health Institute.

Hello and welcome to the Mental Health Hotline.

If you are obsessive-compulsive, press 1 repeatedly.

If you are co-dependent, please ask someone to press 2 for you.

If you have multiple personalities, press 3, 4, 5 and 6.

If you are paranoid, we know who you are and what you want. Stay on the line so we can trace the call.

If you are delusional, press 7 and your call will be transferred to the mothership.

If you are schizophrenic, listen carefully and a small voice will tell you which number to press.

If you are manic-depressive, it doesn't matter which number you press, no one will answer.

If you are dyslexic, press 865325478929136.

If you have a nervous disorder, please fidget with the hash key until a representative comes on the line.

If you have amnesia, press 8 and state your name, address, phone number, date of birth, credit card number and your mother's maiden name.

If you have post-traumatic stress disorder, slowly and

carefully press 911.

If you have bi-polar disorder, please leave a message after the beep, or before the beep. Or after the beep.

If you have short term memory loss, press 9.

If you have short term memory loss, press 9.

If you have short term memory loss, press 9.

If you have low self-esteem, please hang up. All our operators are too busy to talk to you.

Anagrams

An anagram is a word or phrase made by rearranging the letters of another word or phrase. Judging by the following anagrams, someone out there has way too much time on their hands.

Dormitory: Dirty room

Evangelist: Evil's agent

Desperation: A rope ends it

The Morse Code: Here come dots

Slot machines: Cash lost in 'em

Animosity: Is no amity

Mother-in-law: Woman Hitler

Snooze alarms: Alas! No more zs

Semolina: Is no meal

The public art galleries: Large picture halls, I bet

A decimal point: I'm a dot in place

The earthquakes: That queer shake

Eleven plus two: Twelve plus one

Contradiction: Accord not in it

This one's truly amazing: To be or not to be: that is the question, whether tis nobler in the mind to suffer the slings and arrows of outrageous fortune. *The anagram:* In one of the Bard's best-thought-of tragedies, our insistent hero, Hamlet, queries on two fronts about how life turns rotten.

And for the grand finale: That's one small step for man, one giant leap for mankind — Neil Armstrong *The anagram:* This man ran; makes a large stride, left planet, pins flag on moon! On to Mars!

★ ★ ★ ★

Few women admit their age. Few men act theirs.

★ ★ ★ ★

Consciousness: that annoying time between naps.

Answering Machine Messages

'Hi! John's answering machine is broken. This is his refrigerator. Please speak very slowly, and I'll stick your message to myself with one of these magnets.'

'A is for academics, B is for beer. One of those reasons is why we're not here. So leave a message and I'll get back to you.'

'Hi. This is John. If you are the phone company, I already sent the money. If you are my parents, please send money. If you are my financial aid institution, you didn't lend me enough money. If you are my friends, you owe me money. If you are a female, don't worry, I have plenty of money.'

'Hi. Now you say something.'

'Hi, I'm not home right now but my answering machine is, so you can talk to it instead. Wait for the beep.'

'Hello. I am David's answering machine. What are you?'

'Hello, you are talking to a machine. I am capable of receiving messages.'

'This is not an answering machine — this is a tele-pathic thought-recording device. After the tone think about your name, your reason for calling and number where I can reach you, and I'll think about returning your call!'

'My owners do not need their walls painted, windows washed, or their carpets steam-cleaned. They give to charity through their office and do not need their picture taken. If you're still with me, leave your name and number and they will get back to you.'

'Hi. I am probably home, I'm just avoiding someone I don't like. Leave a message, and if I don't call back, it's you.'

'If you are a burglar, then we're probably at home cleaning our weapons right now and can't come to the phone. Otherwise, we probably aren't home and it's safe to leave us a message.'

'Hi, this is George. I'm sorry I can't answer the phone right now. Leave a message, and then wait by your phone until I call you back.'

'Please leave a message. However, you have the right to remain silent. Everything you say will be recorded and will be used by us.'

★ ★ ★ ★

Lottery: a tax on people who are bad at maths.

★ ★ ★ ★

Artificial intelligence usually beats real stupidity.

Guidance Counselor

The following information was gained through much arduous research involving men and women from all backgrounds and walks of life. It consists of the most frequently asked questions of women — relationships, sex, and life in general. All women who read this are encouraged to use the wisdom contained therein to change their behavior in accordance with the truths set out below.

Q. How do I know if I'm ready for sex?

A. Ask your boyfriend. He'll know when the time is right. When it comes to love and sex, men are much more responsible, since they're not as emotionally confused as women. It's a proven fact.

Q. Should I have sex on the first date?

A. Yes. Before if possible.

Q. What exactly happens during the act of sex?

A. Again, this is entirely up to the man. Just remember that you must do whatever he tells you without question. He may ask you to do certain things that may at first seem strange to you. Do them anyway.

Q. How long should the sex act last?

A. This is a natural or normal part of nature, so don't feel ashamed or embarrassed. After you've finished making love, he'll have a natural desire

to leave you suddenly, go out with his buddies
to a pool hall or a really sleazy bar and get drunk.

Q. What is afterplay?
A. After a man has finished making love, he needs
to replenish his manly energy. Afterplay is simply
a list of important activities such as lighting his
cigarette, making him a sandwich or pizza,
bringing him a few beers, or leaving him alone to
sleep while you go out and buy him an expensive
gift.

Q. Does the size of his penis matter?
A. Yes. Although many women believe that quality,
not quantity, is important, studies show this is
simply not true. The average erect male penis
measures about three inches. Anything longer
than that is extremely rare. If by some chance
your lover's sexual organ is four inches or over,
you should go down on your knees and thank
your lucky stars. Do everything possible to please
him, such as doing his laundry, cleaning his
apartment and/or buying him an expensive gift.

Q. What about the female orgasm?
A. What about it? There's no such thing. It's a myth.

It's the Size That Counts...

I've smoked fatter joints than that.

Who circumcised you?

Why don't we just cuddle?

You know they have surgery to fix that.

It's more fun to look at.

Make it dance.

You know, there's a tower in Italy like that.

My last boyfriend was four inches bigger.

It's okay, we'll work around it.

Will it squeak if I squeeze it?

Can I be honest with you?

How sweet, you brought incense.

This explains your car.

You must be a growing boy.

Maybe if we water it, it'll grow.

Have you ever thought of working in a sideshow?

All right, a treasure hunt!

I didn't know they came that small.

Why is God punishing you?

I never saw one like that before.

What do you call this?

But it still works, right?

I hear excessive masturbation shrinks it.

Maybe it looks better in natural light.

Why don't we skip right to the cigarettes?

Oh, I didn't know you were in an accident.

Aww, it's hiding.

Are you cold?

Get me real drunk first.

Is that an optical illusion?

Does it come with an air pump?

So this is why you're supposed to judge people on personality.

★★★★

Does fuzzy logic tickle?

★★★★

'Very funny, Scotty. Now beam me down my clothes.'

The Rules of Bedroom Golf

Each player shall furnish his own equipment for play. Play on a course must be approved by the owner of the hole. Unlike outdoor golf, the object is to get the club in the hole and keep the balls out.

For most effective play, the club should have a firm shaft. Course owners are permitted to check shaft stiffness before play begins. Course owners reserve the right to restrict club length to avoid damage to the hole.

The object of the game is to take as many strokes as necessary until the course owner is satisfied that play is completed. Failure to do so may result in being denied permission to play the course again.

It is considered bad form to begin playing the hole immediately upon arrival at the course. The experienced player will normally take time to admire the entire course with special attention to well-formed bunkers.

Players are cautioned not to mention other courses they have played, or are currently playing, to the owner of the course being played. Upset course owners have been known to damage players equipment for this reason.

Players are encouraged to bring proper rain gear for their own protection.

Players should ensure themselves that their match has been properly scheduled, particularly when a new course is being played for the first time. Previous players have been known to become irate if they discover someone else playing on what they considered to be a private course.

Players should not assume a course is in shape for play at all times. Some players may be embarrassed if they find the course to be temporarily under repair.

Players are advised to be extremely tactful in this situation. More advanced players will find alterna- tive means of play when this is the case.

The course owner is responsible for manicuring and pruning any bush around the hole to allow for improved viewing of alignment with, and approach to the hole.

Slow play is encouraged. However, players should be prepared to proceed at a quicker pace, at least temporarily, at the course owner's request.

It is considered outstanding performance, time permitting, to play the same hole several times in one match.

★ ★ ★ ★

I wouldn't be caught dead with a necrophiliac.

The Best and Worse Country and Western Song Titles

Get Your Biscuits in the Oven and Your Buns in Bed.

Get Your Tongue Outta My Mouth 'Cause I'm Kissing You Goodbye.

Her Teeth Were Stained, But Her Heart Was Pure.

How Can I Miss You If You Won't Go Away?

I Can't Get Over You, So Why Don't You Get Under Me?

I Don't Know Whether to Kill Myself or Go Bowling.

I Just Sold a Car to a Guy that Stole My Girl, The Car Don't Run So I Figure We Got an Even Deal.

I Keep Forgettin' I Forgot About You.

I Liked You Better Before I Knew You So Well.

I Still Miss You Baby, But My Aim's Gettin' Better.

I Wouldn't Take Her to a Dog Fight, Cause I'm Afraid She'd Win.

I'll Marry You Tomorrow, But Let's Honeymoon Tonight.

I'm So Miserable Without You, It's Like Having You Here.

I've Got Tears in My Ears From Lying On My Back While I Cry Over You.

If I Had Shot You When I Wanted To, I'd Be Out By Now.

Mamma Get a Hammer (There's a Fly On Papa's Head).

My Head Hurts, My Feet Stink, and I Don't Love Jesus.

My Wife Ran Off With My Best Friend, and I Sure Do Miss Him.

She Got the Ring and I Got the Finger.

You Done Tore Out My Heart, and Stomped That Sucker Flat.

You're the Reason Our Kids Are So Ugly.

Ways to Annoy People

Leave the photocopier set to reduce 200%, extra dark, A3 paper, 99 copies.

Specify that your drive-through order is 'to go'.

If you have a glass eye, tap on it occasionally with your pen while taking orders.

Insist on keeping your windscreen wipers running in all weather conditions 'to keep them tuned up'.

Reply to everything someone says with 'that's what *you* think'.

Practise making fax and modem noises.

Highlight irrelevant information in scientific papers and 'cc' them to your boss.

Make beeping noises when a large person backs up.

Finish all your sentences with the words 'in accor- dance with the prophesy'.

Signal that a conversation is over by clamping your hands over your ears.

Adjust the tint on your TV so that all the people are green, and insist to others that you 'like it that way'.

Staple papers in the middle of the page.

Publicly investigate just how slowly you can make a 'croaking' noise.

Decline to be seated at a restaurant, and simply eat their complimentary mints by the cash register.

Buy a large quantity of orange traffic cones and re-route whole streets.

Repeat the following conversation a dozen times: 'Do you hear that?' 'What?' 'It's okay, it's gone now.'

Try playing the William Tell Overture by tapping on the bottom of your chin. When nearly done, announce, 'No, wait, I messed it up' and repeat.

Ask people what gender they are.

type only in lower case.

While making presentations, occasionally bob your head like a parakeet.

Sit in your front yard pointing a hairdryer at passing cars to see if they slow down.

Sing along at the opera.

TYPE ONLY IN UPPER CASE.

More Bad Pick-Up Lines

'That dress would look great on the floor next to my bed.'

'Do you want to see something swell?'

'Say, did we go to different schools together?'

'Why don't you come over here, sit on my lap and we'll talk about the first thing that pops up?'

Hand out cards that say: 'Smile if you want to sleep with me.' Watch them try to hold back their laugh.

At the office photocopier: 'Reproducing eh? Can I help? Would you like gin and platonic or do you prefer scotch and sofa?'

'Bond. James Bond.'

'If I told you that you had a great body, would you hold it against me?'

'I'm Irish. Do you have any Irish in you? Would you like some?'

'Do I know you from somewhere, because I don't recognize you with your clothes on?'

'Do you know the essential difference between sex and conversation? (No?) Do you wanna go upstairs and talk?'

More Funny Signs

Sign on an electrician's truck: Let us remove your shorts.

Sign outside a radiator repair shop: Best place in

town to take a leak.

Maternity clothes shop: We are open on Labor Day.

Non-smoking area: If we see you smoking we will assume you are on fire and take appropriate action.

On maternity room door: 'Push, push, push'.

On a front door: Everyone on the premises is a vegetarian except the dog.

Optometrist's office: If you don't see what you're looking for, you've come to the right place.

Scientist's door: Gone fission.

Taxidermist's window: We really know our stuff.

Podiatrist's window: Time wounds all heels.

Butcher's window: Let me meat your needs.

Used-car lot: Second-hand cars in first crash condition.

Sign on fence: Salesmen welcome. Dog food is expensive.

Car dealership: The best way to get back on your feet: miss a car repayment.

Muffler shop: No appointment necessary. We'll hear you coming.

Hotel: Help! We need inn-experienced people.

Butcher's window: Pleased to meat you.

Dry cleaner's: Drop your pants here.

Beauty shop: Dye now!

Veterinarian's waiting room: Be back in 5 minutes. Sit! Stay!

Music teacher's door: Out Chopin

At the electric company: We would be delighted if you send in your bill. However, if you don't, you will be.

Computer store: Out for a quick byte.

Bowling alley: Please be quiet. We need to hear a pin drop.

Music library. Bach in a minuet

Sign in laundromat: Automatic washing machines: please remove all your clothes when the light goes out.

Sign in a New York department store: Bargain basement upstairs.

In an office: Would the person who took the step ladder yesterday please bring it back or further steps will be taken.

Outside a farm: Horse manure 50 cents per pre-packed bag. 20 cents do-it-yourself.

In an office: After tea-break staff should empty the teapot and stand upside down on the draining board.

English sign in a German café: Mothers, please wash your hands before eating.

Outside a second-hand shop: We exchange anything — bicycles, lawn mowers, washing machines etc. Why not bring your wife along and get a wonderful bargain?

Sign outside a new town hall which was to be opened by the Prince of Wales: The town hall is closed until opening. It will remain closed after being opened. Open tomorrow.

Outside a photographer's studio: Out to lunch. If not back by five, out for dinner also.

Sign warning of quicksand: Quicksand. Any person passing this point will be drowned. By order of the district council.

Notice in a dry cleaner's window: Anyone leaving their garments here for more than 30 days will be disposed of.

Sign on gas station: Please do not smoke near our gas pumps. Your life may not be worth much but our gas is.

Notice in health food shop window: Closed due to illness.

Sign on a repair shop door: We can repair anything. (Please knock hard on the door — the bell doesn't work.)

Spotted in a safari park: Elephants please stay in your car.

Spotted in a toilet in a Chicago office block: Toilet out of order. Please use floor below.

Dumb Inventions

Solar-powered flashlight

Inflatable dart board

Sliding doors on a submarine

Reusable condoms

Dehydrated water

Pet rocks

Plastic firewood

Soleless shoes

A book on how to read

A flammable fire extinguisher

A glass baseball bat

Wooden soap

Plasticine wire cutters

A water-proof tea bag

Revolving basement restaurant

Marriage

A successful man is one who makes more money than his wife can spend. A successful woman is one who can find such a man.

Marriage is a three-ring circus: engagement ring, wedding ring, suffering.

My girlfriend told me I should be more affectionate. So I got two girlfriends.

A man meets a genie. The genie tells him he can have whatever he wants provided that his mother-in-law gets double. The man thinks for a moment and then says, 'Okay, give me a million dollars and beat me half to death.'

Men who have pierced ears are better prepared for marriage. They've experienced pain and bought jewelry.

How do most men define marriage? A very expensive way to get your laundry done free.

A little boy asked his father, 'Daddy, how much does it cost to get married?' And the father replied, 'I don't know son, I'm still paying for it.'

A man said his credit card was stolen, but he decided not to report it because the thief was spending less than his wife did.

Love is blind, but marriage is an eye-opener.

The most effective way to remember your wife's birthday is to forget it once.

When a man opens the door of his car for his wife, you can be sure of one thing; either the car is new or the wife is new.

Words to live by: Do not argue with a spouse who is packing your parachute.

Most Common Rejection Lines... and What they Actually Mean

By Women

I think of you as a brother...
You get on my nerves and are always bugging me.

There's a slight difference in our ages.

You are one Jurassic geezer who looked a lot younger in the nightclub.

I'm not attracted to you in 'that' way.
You are the ugliest loser I've ever laid eyes on.

My life is too complicated right now.
I don't want you spending the whole night or else you may hear phone calls from all the other guys I'm seeing.

I've already got a boyfriend.
Who's really my male cat and a cheap cask of wine.

I don't date men where I work.
I wouldn't even date you if you were in the same solar system, let alone building.

It's not you, it's me.
It's not me, it's you.

I'm concentrating on my career.
Even something as boring and unfulfilling as my job is better than a jerk like you.

By men

I think of you as a sister.
You're ugly.

There's a slight difference in our ages.
You're ugly.

I'm not attracted to you in 'that' way.
You're ugly.

My life is too complicated right now.
You're ugly.

I've got a girlfriend.
You're ugly.

I don't date women where I work.
You're ugly.

It's not you, it's me...
You're ugly.

I'm concentrating on my career.
You're ugly.

I'm celibate.
You're ugly.

Special One-liners

Well, this day was a total waste of make-up.

A hard-on doesn't count as personal growth.

I started out with nothing and still have most of it left.

You! Off my planet!

If I want to hear the pitter patter of tiny feet, I'll put shoes on my cat.

The Bible was written by the same people who said the Earth was flat.

Did the aliens forget to remove your anal probe?

Sarcasm is just one more service we offer.

Whatever kind of look you were going for, you missed.

Suburbia: Where they tear out all the trees and then name the streets after them.

I'm not your type. I'm not inflatable.

Can I trade this job for whatever's behind door number 2?

Nice perfume. Must you marinate in it?

Too many freaks, not enough circuses.

I thought I wanted a career. Turns out I just wanted pay checks.

How do I set the laser printer to stun?

It isn't the size, it's the... no, it's the size.

Children's Books You Will Never See

You Are Different and That's Bad

Dad's New Wife Timothy

Pop! Goes The Kitten... and Other Great Microwave Games

Testing Homemade Parachutes Using Only Your Household Pets

The Hardy Boys, the Barbie Twins, and the Vice Squad.

Babar Meets the Taxidermist

Curious George and the High-Voltage Fence

The Boy Who Died from Eating All His Vegetables

Spend up Big With the Change From Your Mom's Purse.

The Pop-up Book of Human Anatomy

Things Rich Kids Have, But You Never Will

Controlling the Playground: Respect through Fear

You Were an Accident

Strangers Have the Best Candy

The Little Sissy Who Snitched

Some Kittens Can Fly!

Kathy Was So Bad Her Mom Stopped Loving Her

All Dogs Go to Hell

The Kid's Guide to Hitch-Hiking

When Mommy and Daddy Don't Know the Answer, They Say God Did It.

Garfield Gets Feline Leukemia

What Is That Dog Doing to That Other Dog?

Why Can't Mr Fork and Ms Electrical Outlet Be Friends?

Boyle's Law in Regards to Hell

This was an actual question given on a university chemistry exam:

'Is Hell exothermic (gives off heat) or endothermic (absorbs heat)? Support your answer with proof.'

Most of the students wrote proofs of their beliefs using Boyle's Law (gas cools off when it expands and heats up when it is compressed) or some variant. One student, however, wrote the following:

'First, we need to know how the mass of Hell is changing in time. So, we need to know the rate that souls are moving into Hell and the rate they are leaving. I think that we can safely assume that once a soul gets to Hell, it will not leave. Therefore no souls are leaving.

As for how many souls are entering Hell, let's look at the different religions that exist in the world today. Some of these religions state that if you are not a member of their religion, you will go to Hell. Since there are more than one of these religions, and since people do not belong to more than one religion, we can project that all people and all souls go to Hell. With birth and death rates as they are we can expect the number of souls in Hell to increase exponentially.

Now, we look at the rate of change of volume in Hell because Boyle's Law states that in order for temperature and the pressure in Hell to stay the same, the volume of Hell has to expand as souls are added.

This gives two possibilities:

1. If Hell is expanding at a slower rate than the rate at which souls enter Hell, then the temperature and pressure in Hell will increase until all Hell breaks loose.

2. Of course, if Hell is expanding at a rate faster than the increase of souls in Hell, then the temperature and pressure will drop until Hell freezes over. So which is it? If we accept the postulate given to me by Ms Tracey Nicholson during my first year at college — 'That it will be a

cold night in Hell before I sleep with you' and take into account the fact that I still have not succeeded in that area, then (2) cannot be true, and so Hell is exothermic.'

This student got the only A.

★ ★ ★ ★

Never try to date a psychic; she'll leave before you meet.

Useful Work Phrases

Thank you. We're all refreshed and challenged by your unique point of view.

The fact that no one understands you doesn't mean you're an artist.

I don't know what your problem is, but I'll bet it's hard to pronounce.

Any connection between your reality and mine is purely coincidental.

I have plenty of talent and vision. I just don't care.

I like you. You remind me of when I was young and stupid.

I'm not being rude. You're just insignificant.

I'm already visualizing the duct tape over your mouth.

I will always cherish the initial misconceptions I had about you.

It's a thankless job, but I've got a lot of karma to burn off.

Yes, I am an agent of Satan, but my duties are largely ceremonial.

No, my powers can only be used for good.

How about never? Is never good enough for you?

I'm really easy to get along with once you people learn to worship me.

You sound reasonable... time to up my medication.

I'll try being nicer if you'll try being smarter.

I'm out of my mind, but feel free to leave me a message.

I don't work here. I'm a consultant.

Who me? I just wander from room to room.

My toys! My toys! I can't do this job without my toys!

It might look like I'm doing nothing, but at a cellular level I'm really quite busy.

At least I have a positive attitude about my destructive habits.

You are validating my inherent mistrust of strangers.

I see you've set aside this special time to humiliate yourself in public.

Someday, we'll look back on this, laugh nervously and change the subject.

★ ★ ★ ★

There are 24 hours in a day and 24 beers in a case...coincidence?

10 Simple Rules for Dating My Daughter

Some thoughtful information for those who ARE daughters, WERE daughters, HAVE daughters, INTEND TO HAVE daughters, or INTEND TO DATE a daughter.

Rule One

If you pull into my driveway and honk, you'd better be delivering a package, because you're sure not picking anything up.

Rule Two

You do not touch my daughter in front of me. You may glance at her, so long as you do not peer at anything below her neck. If you cannot keep your eyes or hands off my daughter's body, I will remove them.

Rule Three

I am aware that it is considered fashionable for boys of your age to wear their trousers so loosely that they appear to be falling off their hips. Please don't take this as an insult, but you and all of your friends are complete idiots. Still, I want to be fair and open minded about this issue, so I propose this compromise: You may come to the door with your underwear showing and your pants 10 sizes too big, and I will not object. However, in order to ensure that your clothes do not, in fact, come off during the course of your date with my daughter, I will take my electric nail gun and fasten your trousers securely in place to your waist.

Rule Four

I'm sure you've been told that in today's world, sex without utilizing a 'barrier method' of some kind can kill you. Let me elaborate: when it comes to sex, I am the barrier, and I will kill you.

Rule Five

In order for us to get to know each other, you may think we should talk about sports, politics, and other issues of the day. Please do not do this. The only information I require from you is an indication of when you expect to have my daughter safely back at my house. The only word I need from you on this subject is 'early'.

Rule Six

I have no doubt you are a popular fellow, with many opportunities to date other girls. This is fine with me as long as it is okay with my daughter. Otherwise, once you have gone out with my little girl, you will continue to date no one else until she is finished with you. If you make her cry, I will make you cry.

Rule Seven

As you stand in my house, waiting for my daughter to appear, and more than an hour goes by, do not sigh and fidget. If you want to be on time for the movie, you should not be dating. My daughter is putting on her makeup, a process that can take longer than painting the Golden Gate Bridge. Instead of just standing there, why don't you do something useful, like change the oil in my car?

Rule Eight

The following places are not appropriate for a date with my daughter:

Places where there are beds, couches, or anything softer than a wooden stool.

Places where there are no parents, police or nuns within eyesight.

Places where there is darkness.

Places where there is dancing, holding hands, or general happiness.

Places where the ambient temperature is warm enough to induce my daughter to wear shorts, midriff t-shirts, or anything other than a boiler suit, leg-warmers, and an Arctic-grade jacket zipped up to her throat.

Football games are okay. Old folks' homes are better.

Any movies with even the slightest of slight references to love, romance or sex must be avoided.

Movies which feature chainsaws are okay.

Rule Nine

Do not lie to me. I may appear to be a pot-bellied, balding, gray-haired, middle-aged, dim-witted has-been. But on issues relating to my daughter, I am the all-knowing, merciless God of your universe. If I ask you where you are going and with whom, you have one chance to tell me the truth, the whole truth and nothing but the truth. I have a shotgun, a shovel, and five acres behind the house. Do not trifle with me.

Rule Ten

Be afraid. Be very afraid. It takes very little for me to mistake the sound of your car in the driveway for a chopper coming in over a rice paddy outside of Hanoi. When my Agent Orange psychosis starts acting up, the voices in my head frequently tell me to clean the guns as I wait for you to bring my daughter home. As soon as you pull into the drive-way you should exit your car with both hands in plain sight. Speak the perimeter password, announce in a clear voice that you have brought my daughter home safely and early, then return to your car — there is no need for you to come inside. The camouflaged face at the window is mine.

Canonical List of Oxymorons

Anarchy rules!

Thank God I'm an atheist

This page intentionally left blank

Act naturally

Airline food

Computer security

Constant change

Construction worker

Definite maybe

Diet icecream

Exact estimate

Found missing

Fresh frozen

Good grief

Graduate student

Great Britain

Half dead

Happily married

Huge market niche

Journalistic integrity

Living dead

Married life

Mature student

Microsoft Works

Plastic glasses

Pretty ugly

Private e-mail

Public school education

Rap music

Religious science

Resident alien

Safe sex

Same difference

Second best

Sensitive male

Silent scream

Smart bomb

Tax return

Uncontested divorce

Coping With Stress

Jam miniature marshmallows up your nose and sneeze them out. See how many you can do at once.

Use your MasterCard to pay your Visa and vice-versa.

Pop some popcorn without putting the lid on.

When someone says 'have a nice day', tell them you have other plans.

Make a list of things to do that you've already done.

Dance naked in front of your pets.

Put all your toddler's best clothes on backwards and send him off to pre-school as if nothing is out of the ordinary.

Fill out your tax forms using roman numerals.

Tape pictures of your boss on watermelons and launch them from high places. Leaf through

National Geographic and draw underwear on the natives.

Tattoo 'out to lunch' on your forehead.

Go shopping. Buy everything. Sweat in it. Return it the next day.

Buy a subscription of *Sleazoid Weekly* and send it to your boss's wife.

Pay your electric bill in five-cent pieces.

Drive to work in reverse.

Tell your boss to 'blow it out of your mule' and let them figure it out.

Polish your car with ear wax.

Read the dictionary upside down and look for secret messages.

Start a nasty rumor and see if you recognize it when it comes back to you.

Braid the hairs in each nostril.

Write a short story using alphabet soup.

Stare at people through the tines of a fork and pretend they're in jail.

Make up a language and ask people for directions.

A Few Good Books

The Lion Attacked, Claude Yarmoff

How to Write Big Books, Warren Peace

The Art of Archery, Beau N. Arrow

Songs for Children, Barbara Blacksheep

Irish Heart Surgery, Angie O'Plasty

Split Personalities, Jacqueline Hyde

Under the Bleachers, Seymour Butts

Desert Crossing, I. Rhoda Camel

School Truancy, Marcus Absent

I was a Cloakroom Attendant, Mahatma Coate

I Lost My Balance, Eileen Dover and Phil Down

Mystery in the Barnyard, Hu Flung Dung

Positive Reinforcement, Wade Ago

Shhh!, Danielle Soloud

The Philippines Post Office, Imelda Letter

Things to Do at a Party, Bob Frapples

Stop Arguing, Xavier Breath

Come on In!, Doris Open

Things You Don't Want to Hear During Surgery

Better save that. We'll need it for the autopsy.

Someone call the cleaner — we're going to need a mop.

Wait a minute... if this is his spleen, then what in the hell is that?

Hand me that... uh... thing.

Yeah, I've developed this strange spasm in my hands. Whoah! There she goes.

Rats, there go the lights again...

You know, there's big money in kidneys. Heck, the guy's got two of 'em.

Everybody stand back! I lost my contact lens!

Could you stop that thing from beating? It's throwing my concentration off!

What's this doing here?

That's cool! Now can you make his leg twitch?

I wish I hadn't forgotten my glasses.

Well, folks, this will be an experiment for all of us.

Sterile, schmerile. The floor's clean, right?

Anyone see where I left that scalpel?

Okay, now take a picture from this angle. This is truly a freak of nature.

Nurse, did this patient sign the organ donation card?

Don't worry. I think it is sharp enough.

She's gonna blow! Everyone take cover!

Rats! Page 47 of the manual is missing!

Fire! Fire! Everyone get out!

Five Questions Most Feared by Men

1. What are you thinking about?
2. Do you love me?
3. Do I look fat?
4. Do you think she is prettier than me?
5. What would you do if I died?

Tech Support

Dear Tech Support,
Last year I upgraded from Girlfriend 7.0 to Wife 1.0 and noticed that the new program began unexpected child processing that took up a lot of new space and valuable resources. No mention of this phenomenon was included in the product brochure.

In addition, Wife 1.0 installs itself into all other programs and launches during system initialization, where it monitors all other system activity. Applications such as Poker Night 10.3, Drunken Boys Night 2.5 and Saturday Football 5.0 no longer run, crashing the system whenever selected.

I cannot seem to keep Wife 1.0 in the background while attempting to run some of my other favorite applications. I am thinking about going back to Girlfield 7.0, but the uninstall does not work on this program.

Can you please help me!!!???

Thanks,

A Troubled User

Excuses for Missing Work

If it is all the same to you, I won't be coming in to work. The voices told me to clean all my guns today.

On Saturday, I set half the clocks in my house ahead an hour, and the other half back an hour and spent 18 hours in some freaky kind of space-time continuum loop, reliving Sunday (right up until the explosion). I was able to exit the loop only by reversing the polarity of the power source in the house, while simultaneously rapping my dog on the snout with a rolled up newspaper. Accordingly, I will be in either late, or early.

I can't come in to work today because I'll be stalking my previous boss. He fired me for not showing up at work.

Yes, I seem to have contracted some attention-deficit disorder. And, hey, how about that game Saturday night, huh? So, I won't be able to, yes, could I help you? No, no, I'll be sticking with my existing telecommunications carrier, but thank you for calling.

Constipation has made me a walking time bomb.

I just found out that I was switched at birth. Legally, I shouldn't come to work knowing my employee records may now contain false information.

The psychiatrist said it was an excellent session. He even gave me this jaw restraint so I won't bite things when I am startled.

The dog ate my car keys. We're going to hitchhike to the vet.

I prefer to remain an enigma.

My stepmother has come back as one of the undead. We must attract her to her coffin to drive a stake through her heart and give her eternal peace. One day should do it.

I am converting my calendar from Julian to Gregorian.

I am extremely sensitive to a rise in the interest rates.

I've used up all my sick days, so I'm calling in dead.

Ways to be Offensive at a Funeral

Tell the widow that the deceased's last wish was that she have sex with you.

Tell the undertaker that he can't close the coffin until you find your contact lens.

Punch the deceased and tell people he hit you first.

Tell the widow that you're the deceased's gay lover.

Ask someone to take a snapshot of you shaking hands with the deceased.

At the cemetery, play taps on a kazoo.

Walk around telling people that you've seen the will and they're not in it.

Drive behind the widow's limousine and keep honking your horn.

Tell the undertaker that your dog just died and ask if he can sneak him into the coffin.

Place a hard-boiled egg into the mouth of the deceased.

Walk around telling people that the deceased didn't like them.

Use the deceased's tongue to lick a stamp.

Ask the widow for money which the deceased owes you.

The Biggest Lies

The check is in the mail.

I'll respect you in the morning.

This won't hurt a bit.

I'm from your government, and I am here to help you.

It's only a cold sore.

You get this one, I'll pay next time.

My wife doesn't understand me.

Trust me, I'll take care of everything.

Of course I love you.

I am getting a divorce. We lead separate lives anyway.

Drinking? Why, no, Officer.

It's not the money, it's the principle of the thing.

But we can still be good friends.

She means nothing to me.

Don't worry, he's never bitten anyone.

I'll call you later.

I've never done anything like this before.

Now, I'm going to tell you the truth.

It's supposed to make that noise.

...then take a left. You can't miss it.

Yes, I did.

Thoughts to Get You Through Almost Any Crisis

Insanity is hereditary — you get it from your kids.

There is absolutely no substitute for a genuine lack of preparation.

Happiness is merely the remission of pain and absence of worry.

Nostalgia isn't what it used to be.

The facts, although interesting, are irrelevant.

Someone who thinks logically provides a nice contrast to the real world.

Things are more like they are today than they have ever been before.

Anything worth fighting for is worth fighting dirty for.

Everything should be made as simple as possible, but no simpler.

Friends may come and go, and indeed they do, but enemies accumulate.

I have seen the truth and it makes no sense.

Suicide is the most sincere form of self-criticism.

If you think that there is good in everybody, you haven't met everybody.

All things being equal, fat people use more soap.

If you can smile when things go wrong, you have someone in mind to blame.

One-seventh of your life is spent on Monday.

By the time you can make ends meet, they move the ends.

Not one shred of evidence supports the notion that life is serious.

There is always one more imbecile than you counted on.

Never wrestle with a pig. You both get dirty and the pig likes it.

★ ★ ★ ★

I am not a perfectionist. But I'm happy to say my parents were.

★ ★ ★ ★

Many people stop looking for work when they find a job.

A Few Ways to be Annoying

Practice the art of limp handshakes.

Tell the ending of movies.

Blow out other people's birthday candles.

When giving directions, leave out a turn or two.

Before exiting the elevator, push all the buttons, including the buttons on the emergency phone.

Draw moustaches on posters.

Bite your dentist's finger.

Dance fast to slow music and vice-versa.

Tell people they have bad breath.

Smell smoke often and announce it.

Eat out at an expensive restaurant with friends and 'forget' your wallet.

Put everyone on speakerphone.

Step on the back of the shoe of the person in front of you.

Make scary faces at babies.

Flirt with a friend's spouse.

Pretend you're listening.

Shake with your left hand.

Love and Sex

The more beautiful the woman is who loves you, the easier it is to leave her with no hard feelings.

Nothing improves with age.

No matter how many times you've had it, if it's offered take it, because it'll never be quite the same again.

Sex has no calories.

Sex takes up the least amount of time and causes the most amount of trouble.

There is no remedy for sex but more sex.

Sex appeal is 50% what you've got and 50% what people think you've got.

Sex is like snow: you never know how many inches you are going to get or how long it is going to last.

If you get them by the balls, their hearts and minds will follow.

Virginity can be cured.

When a man's wife learns to understand him, she usually stops listening to him.

Never sleep with anyone crazier than yourself.

The qualities that most attract a woman to a man are the same ones she can't stand years later.

It is always the wrong time of month.

When the lights are out, everyone is beautiful.

Sex is hereditary. If your parents never had it, chances are you won't either.

Sow your wild oats on Saturday night — then on Sunday pray for crop failure.

The game of love is never called off on account of darkness.

It was not the apple on the tree but the pair on the ground that caused the trouble in the garden.

Sex discriminates against the shy and the ugly.

Before you find your handsome prince, you've got to kiss a lot of frogs.

There may be some things better than sex, and some things worse than sex. But there is nothing exactly like it.

Love your neighbor, but don't get caught.

Love is a matter of chemistry, sex is a matter of physics.

Do it only with the best.

Sex is a three-letter word which needs some old-fashioned four-letter words to convey its full meaning.

One good turn gets most of the blankets.

Love is the triumph of imagination over intelligence.

It is better to have loved and lost than never to have loved at all.

Thou shalt not commit adultery... unless in the mood.

Never lie down with a woman who's got more troubles than you.

Never argue with a women when she's tired — or rested.

A woman never forgets the men she could have had; a man, the women he couldn't get.

What matters is not the length of the wand, but the magic in the stick.

Never say no.

Beauty is skin deep; ugly goes right to the bone.

Sex is one of the nine reasons for reincarnation; the other eight are unimportant.

Smile, it makes people wonder what you are thinking.

There is no difference between a wise man and a fool when they fall in love.

Never go to bed mad. Stay up and fight.

Love is the delusion that one woman differs from another.

★ ★ ★ ★

Love defenceless animals, especially in a good gravy.

★ ★ ★ ★

Beauty is in the eye of the beer holder.

Memo to All Employees

New Company Policies: Sickness and Related Leave

We will no longer accept a doctor's statement as proof of sickness. If you are able to go to a doctor, you are able to come to work.

Surgery: Operations are now banned. As long as you are an employee here, you need all your organs. You should not consider removing anything. We hired you intact. To have something removed constitutes a breach of employment.

Your Own Death: This will be accepted as an excuse. However, we require at least two weeks notice as it is your duty to train your replacement.

Bathroom Use: Entirely too much time is being spent in the rest room. In the future, we will follow the practice of going in alphabetical order. For instance, those whose names begin with 'A' will go from 8.00 to 8.10, employees whose names begin with 'B' will go from 8.10 to 8.20 and so on. If you're unable to go at your time, it will be necessary to wait until the next day when your time comes again. In extreme emergencies employees may swap their time with a co-worker. Both employees' supervisors must approve this exchange in writing. In addition, there is now a strict three-minute time limit in the cubicle. At the end of three minutes, an alarm bell will sound, the toilet paper roll will retract, and the cubicle door will open.

Romance Points System

In the world of romance, one single rule applies: make the woman happy. Do something she likes, and you get points. Do something she dislikes and points are subtracted. You don't get any points for doing something she expects. Sorry, that's the way the game is played. Here is a guide to the points system:

Simple Duties

You leave the toilet seat up   -5

You replace the toilet paper roll when it is empty 0

When the toilet paper roll is barren, you resort to Kleenex   -1

When the Kleenex runs out you use the next bathroom   -2

You go out to buy her extra-light panty liners with wings   +5

In the snow   +8

...but return with beer   -5

...and no panty liners   -25

You check out a suspicious noise at night   0

You check out a suspicious noise and it is nothing   0

You check out a suspicious noise and it is something   +5

You pummel it with a six iron   +10

...it's her cat   -40

Social Engagements

You stay by her side for the entire party   0

You stay by her side for a while, then leave to chat with a college drinking buddy   -2

...named Tiffany   -4

Tiffany is a dancer   -6

...with breast implants   -18

Her Birthday

You take her out to dinner   0

You take her out to dinner and it's not a sports bar   +1

Okay, it is a sports bar   -2

And it's all-you-can-eat night   -3

It's a sports bar, it's all-you-can-eat night, and your face is painted the colors of your favorite team -10

A Night Out with the Boys

Go with a pal	-5
The pal is happily married	-4
Or frighteningly single	-7
And he drives a Mustang	-10
And his name is Kingo	-4

A Night Out

You take her to a movie	+2
You take her to a movie she likes	+4
You take her to a movie you hate	+6
You take her to a movie you like	-2
It's called Death Cop 3	-3
...which features Cyborgs that eat humans	-9
You lied and said it was a foreign film about orphans	-15

Your Physique

You develop a noticeable pot belly	-15
You develop a noticeable pot belly and exercise to get rid of it	+10
You develop a noticeable pot belly and resort to loose jeans and baggy Hawaiian shirts	-30
You say, 'It doesn't matter, you have one too.'	-800

The Big Question

She asks, 'Do I look fat?':

You hesitate in responding	-10
You reply, 'Where?'	-35
Any other response	-20

Communication

When she wants to talk about a problem:

You listen, displaying a concerned expression	0
You listen for over 30 minutes	+5
You listen for more than 30 minutes without looking at the TV	+100
She realizes this is because you have fallen asleep	-200

★ ★ ★ ★

If you choke a smurf, what color does it turn?

★ ★ ★ ★

What happens if you get scared half to death... twice?

★ ★ ★ ★

My inferiority complex is not as good as yours.

Why Bicycles Are Better Than Women

Bicycles don't get pregnant.

You can ride your bicycle any old time.

Bicycles don't have parents.

Bicycles don't whine unless something is really wrong.

You can share your bicycle with your friends.

Bicycles don't care how many other bicycles you've ridden.

When riding, you and your bicycle can arrive at the same time.

Bicycles don't care how many other bicycles you have.

Bicycles don't care if you look at other bicycles.

Bicycles don't care if you buy bicycle magazines.

If your bicycle goes flat you can fix it.

You don't have to be jealous of the guy who works on your bicycle.

If you say bad things to your bicycle, you don't have to apologize before you ride it again.

You can ride your bicycle the first time you meet it, without having to take it to dinner, see a movie, or meet its mother.

The only protection you have to wear when riding your bicycle is a decent helmet.

When in mixed company, you can talk about what a great ride you had the last time you were on your bicycle.

Bicycles don't try to take you shopping to create a 'new you'.

Bicycles don't care about the anniversary of when you first met.

Bicycles never hassle you about the buns of steel you 'used to have'.

Bicycles don't try to make you jealous by flirting with other bicycles.

When a bicycle gets shrill and squeaky, it's easily silenced.

Why Bicycles Are Better Than Men

Bicycles don't work late.

Your bicycle stays as clean as you want it to.

Bicycles don't have parents.

Bicycles don't get sick.

Bicycles don't get overweight, except as per your convenience.

You can check out the guy who works on your bicycle.

Your bicycle always has time for you.

Bicycles don't complain and don't ride away from you when the road gets rough.

Bicycles don't watch TV.

Bicycles don't shave.

Bicycles don't snore.

Bicycles don't leave a mess in the kitchen or bathroom.

Bicycles are better protection in a bad neighborhood.

If you don't like the size of your bicycle you can get a new one.

You can stop riding your bicycle as soon as you want and it won't get frustrated.

Your parents won't remain in touch with your old bicycle after you dump it.

Bicycles don't get headaches.

Bicycles don't insult you if you're a bad rider.

Your bicycle never wants a night out with the other bicycles.

Bicycles don't care if you're late.

If your bicycle doesn't look good you can paint it or get better parts.

You can try out as many bikes as you like before you get your own.

You don't have to feed your bicycle.

Bicycles never argue, you are always right.

Bicycles never wake you up in the middle of the night, for any reason.

Bicycles never try to show you off to their friends.

Bicycles don't sneak around with other bicycles.

Bicycles don't care what you look like or what your age is.

Bicycles don't care and don't comment about what you spend your money on.

When you go riding, your bicycle doesn't care if other bicycles are bigger or better.

Bicycles don't care about their performance.

Bicycles don't get you pregnant.

When you've finished a ride, you can get off.

You don't have to praise a bike after a ride.

Bicycles don't sulk.

Bicycles don't bore you.

Bicycles don't abandon you at gatherings for more interesting riders.

Bicycles don't have to prove anything.

Bicycles don't try to change you once you've bought them.

Bicycles never interrogate you.

Bicycles don't leave smelly inner tubes lying around on the floor.

Second-hand bikes don't brag about previous owners.

Second-hand bikes don't go to see previous owners for a ride when you're out of town.

You don't have to explain to a bike if you don't feel like a ride.

Guide to Safe Fax

Q. Do I have to be married to have safe fax?

A. Although married people fax quite often, there are many single people who fax complete and utter strangers every day.

Q. If I fax by myself will I go blind?

A. Certainly not, as far as we can see.

Q. There is a place on our street where you can go and pay for fax. Is this legal?

A. Yes, many people have no outlet for their fax needs and must pay a 'professional'.

Q. Should a cover always be used for faxing?

A. Unless you are really sure of the one you are faxing, a cover sheet should always be used to ensure safe fax.

Q. What happens when I incorrectly perform the procedure, and I fax prematurely?

A. Don't panic. Many people prematurely fax when they haven't faxed in a long time. Just start all over. Most people won't mind if you try again.

Q. I have a personal and a business fax. Can the transmission become mixed up?

A .Being bi-faxual can be confusing, but as long as you use a cover with each one, you shouldn't transmit anything you're not supposed to.

10 Ways to Terrorize a Telemarketer

When they ask 'How are you today?', tell them! 'I'm so glad you asked because no one these days seems to care, and I have all these problems; my arthritis is acting up, my eyelashes are sore, my dog just died...'

If they say they're John Doe from XYZ Company, ask them to spell their name. Then ask them to spell the company name. Then ask them where it is located. Continue asking them personal questions or questions about their company for as long as necessary.

Cry out in surprise, 'Judy! Is that you? Oh my God! Judy, how have you been?' Hopefully, this will give Judy a few brief moments of pause as she tries to figure out where she could know you from.

Tell the telemarketer you are on 'home incarceration' and ask if they could bring you beer and corn chips.

After the telemarketer gives their spiel, ask him or her to marry you. When they get all flustered, tell them that you could not just give your credit card number to a complete stranger.

Tell the telemarketer you are busy at the moment and ask them if they will give you their *home* phone number so you can call them back. When the telemarketer explains that they cannot give out their home number, you say, 'I guess you don't want anyone bothering you at home, right?' The telemarketer will agree and you say, 'Now you know how I feel!' Say goodbye — and hang up.

Insist that the caller is really your buddy Leon, playing a joke. 'Come on Leon, cut it out! Seriously, Leon, how's your mom?'

Tell them to talk v-e-r-y s-l-o-w-l-y, because you want to write every word down.

For Those Who Take Life Too Seriously

On the other hand, you have different fingers.

I just got lost in thought. It was unfamiliar territory.

42.7 percent of all statistics are made up on the spot.

99 percent of lawyers give the rest a bad name.

I feel like I'm diagonally parked in a parallel universe.

You have the right to remain silent. Anything you say will be misquoted, then used against you.

I wonder how much deeper the ocean would be without sponges.

Remember, half the people you know are below average.

Despite the cost of living, have you noticed how popular it remains?

Nothing is foolproof to a talented fool.

Eagles may soar, but weasels don't get sucked into jet engines.

The early bird may get the worm, but the second mouse gets the cheese.

I drive way too fast to worry about cholesterol.

If Barbie is so popular, why do you have to buy her friends?

The only substitute for good manners is fast reflexes.

Support bacteria — they're the only culture some people have.

When everything's coming your way, you're driving in the wrong lane and going the wrong way.

A conclusion is the place where you got tired of thinking.

Experience is something you don't get until just after you need it.

For every action there is an equal and opposite criticism.

Bills travel through the mail at twice the speed of checks.

No one is listening until you make a mistake.

Success always occurs in private and failure in full view.

The colder the x-ray table the more of your body is required on it.

The hardness of butter is directly proportional to the softness of the bread.

The severity of the itch is inversely proportional to the ability to reach it.

To steal ideas from one person is plagiarism; to steal from many is research.

Two wrongs are only the beginning.

The sooner you fall behind the more time you'll have to catch up.

A clear conscience is usually the sign of a bad memory.

Change is inevitable except from vending machines.

Plan to be spontaneous — tomorrow.

If you think nobody cares, try missing a couple of payments.

Honk if you love peace and quiet.

Beer Troubleshooting

SYMPTOM: Beer unusually pale and tasteless.
FAULT: Glass empty.
ACTION: Get someone to buy you another beer.

SYMPTOM: Opposite wall covered with fluorescent
              lights.
FAULT: You have fallen over backwards.
ACTION: Have yourself leashed to bar.

SYMPTOM: Mouth contains cigarette butts.
FAULT: You have fallen forward.
ACTION: See above.

SYMPTOM: Can't taste beer, front of your shirt is
              wet.
FAULT: Mouth not open, or glass applied to
              wrong part of face.
ACTION: Retire to rest room, practise in mirror.

SYMPTOM: Floor blurred.
FAULT: You are looking through bottom of
              empty glass.
ACTION: Get someone to buy you another beer.

SYMPTOM: Floor moving.
FAULT: You are being carried out.
ACTION: Find out if you are being taken to
              another bar.

SYMPTOM: Room seems unusually dark.
FAULT: Bar has closed.
ACTION: Confirm home address with bartender.

SYMPTOM: Taxi suddenly takes on colorful textures and aspect.
FAULT: Beer consumption has exceeded personal limitations.
ACTION: Cover mouth.

SYMPTOM: Everyone looks up to you and smiles
FAULT: You are dancing on the table.
ACTION: Fall on somebody cushy-looking.

SYMPTOM: Beer is crystal-clear.
FAULT: It's water. Someone is trying to sober you up.
ACTION: Attack.

SYMPTOM: Hands hurt, nose hurts, mind unusually clear.
FAULT: You have been in a fight.
ACTION: Apologize to everyone you see, just in case it was them.

SYMPTOM: Don't recognize anyone, don't recognize the room you're in.
FAULT: You've wandered into the wrong party.
ACTION: See if they have free beer.

SYMPTOM: Your singing sounds distorted.
FAULT: The beer is too weak.
ACTION: Have more beer until your voice improves.

SYMPTOM: Don't remember the words to the song.
FAULT: Beer is just right.
ACTION: Play air guitar.

Words of Wisdom

A man will pay $2.00 for a $1.00 item he needs.

A woman will pay $1.00 for a $2.00 item that she does not need.

A woman worries about the future until she gets a husband.

A man never worries about the future until he gets a wife.

A successful man is one who makes more money than his wife can spend.

A successful woman is one who can find such a man.

To be happy with a man, you must love him a little and understand him a lot.

To be happy with a woman you must love her a lot and not try to understand her at all.

Men wake up as good-looking as they went to bed. Women somehow deteriorate overnight.

A woman marries a man expecting he will change, but he doesn't.

A man marries a woman expecting she won't change, but she does.

Married men live longer than single men, but married men are more willing to die.

A woman has the last word in any argument.

Anything a man says after that is the beginning of a new argument.

★★★★

I plan on living forever. So far, so good.

★★★★

If you can't repair your brakes, make your horn louder.

Questions Not to Ask in a Job Interview

What's your company's policy on severance pay?

How long does it take your company's bureaucracy to get around to firing somebody for poor performance?

Does your company's life insurance cover suicide?

Who's the ugly woman in that picture on your desk?

Does your company's insurance consider genital herpes a pre-existing condition?

How many sick days do you allow each employee before you stop paying them for not being here?

Does your insurance cover sex-change operations?

Does your LAN have a firewall that blocks triple-X websites?

How frequently do your accountants audit petty cash?

★ ★ ★ ★

Shin: a device for finding furniture in the dark.

★ ★ ★ ★

Why do psychics have to ask you for your name?

Things Men Know

Men know that Mother Nature's best aphrodisiac is still a naked woman.

Men know that PMS is Mother Nature's way of telling you to get out of the house.

Men know that cats are evil and cannot be trusted.

Men know how to change the toilet paper, but to do so would ruin the game.

Men know that from time to time, it is absolutely necessary to adjust oneself.

Men know that a woman will wear a low-cut dress and expect the man to stare at her cleavage. Men also know that the woman will get angry when they do, for reasons not totally clear to them.

Men know that it's never a good idea to tell your father-in-law how good his daughter is in bed.

Men know that men are from here, and women are from way the hell over there.

★ ★ ★ ★

A day without sunshine is like night.

★ ★ ★ ★

Conscience is what hurts when everything else feels so good.

Things Only Women Understand

Cats' facial expressions.

The need for the same style of shoes in different colors.

Fat clothes.

Fat mirrors.

Taking a car trip without trying to beat your best time.

The difference between beige, off-white, stone, bone and eggshell.

Eyelash curlers.

The inaccuracy of every bathroom scale ever made.

Other women.

Ways to Stay Stressed

Never exercise. Exercise wastes a lot of time that could be spent worrying.

Eat anything you like. Hey, if cigarette smoke can't cleanse your system, a balanced diet isn't likely to.

Gain weight. Work hard at staying at least 20 pounds over your recommended weight.

Take plenty of stimulants. The old standards of caffeine, nicotine, sugar and cola will continue to do the job just fine.

Avoid 'woo-hoo' practices. Ignore the evidence suggesting that meditation, yoga, deep breathing, and/or mental imaging help to reduce stress. The Protestant work ethic is good for everyone. Protestant or not.

Get rid of your social support system. Let the few friends who are willing to tolerate you know that you concern yourself with friendships only if you have time, and you never have time. If a few people persist in trying to be your friend, avoid them.

Personalize all criticism. Anyone who criticizes any aspect of your work, family, dog, house, or car is mounting a personal attack. Don't take time to listen —be offended, and then return the attack!

Become a workaholic. Put work before everything else, and be sure to take work home evenings and weekends. Keep reminding yourself that vacations are for sissies.

Discard good time management skills. Schedule in more activities every day than you can possibly get done and then worry about it all whenever you get a chance.

Procrastinate. Putting things off to the last second always produces a marvellous amount of stress.

Worry about things you can't control. Worry about the stock market, earthquakes, the approaching Ice Age, you know, all the big issues.

*Become not only a perfectionist but set impossibly high standards...*and either beat yourself up, or feel guilty, depressed, discouraged, and/or inadequate when you don't meet them.

Throw out your sense of humor. Staying stressed is no laughing matter so don't treat it as one.

Signs You Have a Drinking Problem

You lose arguments with inanimate objects.

You have to hold onto the lawn to keep from falling off the Earth.

Work starts interfering with your drinking.

Your doctor finds traces of blood in your alcohol system.

The back of your head keeps getting hit by the toilet seat.

You sincerely believe alcohol to be the elusive fifth food group.

That damned pink elephant followed you home again.

You believe 'Two hands and just one mouth …that's a drinking problem'.

You can focus better with one eye closed.

Every woman you see has an exact twin.

You fall off the floor or up the stairs.

You discover in the morning that your liquid cleaning supplies have mysteriously disappeared.

Five beers has just as many calories as a burger, so you skip dinner.

Beer: it's not just for breakfast any more.

The glass keeps missing your mouth.

You donate blood and they ask what proof it is.

Mosquitoes and vampires fly into walls after biting you.

You believe your only drinking problem is not having a drink right now.

At AA meetings you begin: 'Hi, my name is…uh…'

You have problems staying on the sidewalk because you walk in the pattern of left, right, stumble, fall.

You tell people, 'I'm not under the affluence of incohol.'

You wake up with a traffic cone between your legs.

You tell people, 'I'm not drunk... you're just sober.'

The bar owner carves your name onto your own bar stool.

Women's Guide to Driving Men Crazy

Do not say what you mean. Ever.

Be ambiguous. Always.

Cry. Cry a lot.

Bring things up that were said, done, or thought years, months or decades ago... or with other boyfriends. Make them apologize for everything.

Stash feminine products in their cars, briefcases and in their books as cute reminders that you were thinking of them.

Look them in the eye and start laughing.

Get mad at them for everything.

Discuss your period in front of them. Watch them squirm.

Demand to be called or e-mailed. Often. Whine when they don't comply.

When complimented, make sure to be paranoid.

Take nothing at face value.

Use Daddy as a weapon. Tell them about his gun collection, his quick-trigger finger, and his affection for his Little Princess.

Be late for everything. However, yell if they're late.

Talk about your ex-boyfriend 24 hours a day, seven days a week. Compare and contrast.

Make them guess what you want and then get mad when they're wrong.

Plan little relationship anniversaries, e.g. the monthly anniversary of the time you saw each other in the library. Then get mad at them for forgetting. Cry.

Gather many female friends and dance to 'I Will Survive' while they are present. Sing all the words. Sing to them. Sing loud.

Constantly claim you're fat. Ask them. Then cry, regardless of their answer.

Leave out the good parts in stories.

Make them wonder. Confusion is a good thing.

Criticize the way they dress.

Criticize the music they listen to.

When asked, 'What's wrong?' tell them that if they don't know, you're not going to tell them.

Try to change them.

Try to mould them.

Try to get them to dance.

When they screw up, never let them forget it.

Blame everything on PMS.

Whenever there is silence ask them, 'What are you thinking?'

Read into everything.

Over-analyze everything.

Things to Say When Caught Napping at Your Desk

'They said at the blood bank that this might happen.'

'This is just a 15 minute power-nap like they raved about in the last time management course you sent me on.'

'Whew! Guess I left the top off the liquid paper.'

'I wasn't sleeping! I was meditating on the mission statement and envisioning a new paradigm!'

'This is one of the seven habits of highly effective people!'

'I was testing the keyboard for drool resistance.'

'I'm actually doing a Stress Level Elimination Exercise Plan (S.L.E.E.P.) which I learned at the last mandatory seminar you made me attend.'

'I was doing a highly specific yoga exercise to relieve work-related stress. Are you discriminatory towards people who practise yoga?'

'Damn! Why did you interrupt me? I had almost figured out a solution to our biggest problem.'

'Boy, that cold medicine I took last night just won't wear off!'

'Aaah, the unique and unpredictable circadian rhythms of the workaholic!'

'Wasn't sleeping. Was trying to pick up my contact lens without hands.'

'Amen.'

★ ★ ★ ★

Black holes are where God divided by zero.

Things That Guys Wished Girls Knew

If you think you're fat, you probably are. Don't ask us.

Learn to work the toilet seat: if it's up, put it down.

Birthdays, Valentine's Day and anniversaries are not quests to see if we can find the perfect present, again.

If you ask a question you don't want an answer to, expect an answer you don't want to hear.

Sometimes, we're not thinking about you. Live with it.

Get rid of your cat. No, it's not different. It's just like every other cat.

Dogs are better than cats. Period.

Your brother is an idiot, your ex-boyfriend is an idiot, and your dad probably is an idiot too.

Ask for what you want. Subtle hints don't work.

Yes, standing is more difficult than peeing from point-blank range. We're bound to miss sometimes.

Yes and no are perfectly acceptable answers.

A headache that lasts seven months is a problem. See a doctor.

Your mom doesn't have to be our best friend.

It is neither in your best interest nor ours to take 'the quiz' from *Cosmopolitan* together.

Anything we said six or eight months ago is inadmissible in an argument. All comments become null and void after 24 hours.

If something we say can be interpreted two ways, and one of the ways makes you sad or angry, we meant the other one.

You can either ask us to do something or tell us how you want it done. But asking us to do both is only going to cause trouble.

Women wearing Wonderbras and low-cut blouses lose their right to complain about having their boobs stared at.

Telling us that the models in the men's magazines are airbrushed make you look jealous and petty, and it's not going to deter us from reading the magazines.

The relationship is never going to be like it was the first two months we were going out.

Cat Wisdom

Cats do what they want, when they want.

They rarely listen to you.

They're totally unpredictable.

They whine when they are not happy.

When you want to play, they want to be alone.

When you want to be alone, they want to play.

They expect you to cater to their every whim.

They're moody.

They leave hair everywhere.

They drive you nuts.

Conclusion: they're like little tiny women in cheap fur coats.

The Little Things That Drive a Sane Person Mad

You have to try on a pair of sunglasses with that stupid little plastic thing in the middle of them.

The person behind you in the supermarket runs his trolley into the back of your ankle.

The elevator stops on every floor and nobody gets on.

There's always a car riding your tail when you're slowing down to find an address.

You open a can of soup and the lid falls in.

It's bad enough that you step in dog mess, but you don't realize it till you walk across your living room rug.

The tiny red string on the Band-Aid wrapper never works for you.

There's a dog in the neighborhood that barks at everything.

You can never put anything back in a box the way it came.

You drink from a can into which someone has extinguished a cigarette.

You slice your tongue licking an envelope.

Your tire gauge lets out half the air while you're trying to get a reading.

A station comes in brilliantly when you're standing near the radio but buzzes, drifts and spits every time you move away.

There are always one or two ice cubes that won't pop out of the tray.

You wash a garment with a Kleenex in the pocket and your entire laundry comes out covered with lint.

You set the alarm on your digital clock for 7 p.m. instead of 7 a.m.

The radio station doesn't tell you who sang that song.

You rub on hand cream and can't turn the bathroom doorknob to get out.

People behind you in a supermarket line dash ahead of you to a counter just opening up.

Your glasses slide off your ears when you perspire.

You can't look up the correct spelling of a word in the dictionary because you don't know how to spell it.

You have to inform five different sales people in the same store that you're just browsing.

You had that pen in your hand only a second ago and now you can't find it.

You reach under the table to pick something off the floor and smash your head on the way up.

★ ★ ★ ★

If you try to fail, and succeed, which have you done?

★ ★ ★ ★

Technology is simply a means of manipulating the world so you don't have to experience it.

'Why Aren't You Married?' Snappy Comebacks

You haven't asked yet.

I was hoping to do something meaningful with my life.

What? And spoil my great sex life?

Nobody would believe me in white.

Just lucky, I guess.

It gives my mother something to live for.

My fiance is awaiting parole.

I'm waiting until I get to be your age.

It didn't seem worth a blood test.

I already have enough laundry to do, thank you.

It would take all the spontaneity out of dating.

I'd have to forfeit my billion-dollar trust fund.

They just opened a great singles bar down the street.

I wouldn't want my parents to drop dead from sheer happiness.

We really want to, but my lover's husband just won't go for it.

Why aren't you thin?

Reasons to Study Martial Arts

Broken masonry makes great drainage for potted plants.

You get beaten up by people half your size and twice your age.

You'll never run out of kindling wood again.

There is no need to wonder what belt to wear.

You get to be on first name basis with the emergency room staff.

The uniforms make nice pajamas.

You get to appreciate the finer points of Chuck Norris's acting.

You learn to count to 10 in three different Asian languages.

★★★★

If at first you do succeed try not to look too astonished.

★★★★

A meeting is an event at which the minutes are kept and the hours are lost.

Baby Boomers – Now and Then

Then: Killer Weed
Now: Weed Killer

Then: Being caught with Hustler magazine
Now: Being caught by Hustler magazine

Then: Getting out to a new, hip joint
Now: Getting a new hip joint

Then: Being called into the principal's office
Now: Storming into the principal's office

Then: Peace Sign
Now: Mercedes Logo

Then: Getting 'blind'
Now: Going blind

Then: Long hair
Now: Longing for hair

Then: Worrying about no one coming to your party
Now: Worrying about no one coming to your funeral

Then: The perfect high
Now: The perfect high-yield mutual fund

Then: Swallowing acid
Now: Swallowing antacid

Then: You're growing pot
Now: Your growing pot

Then: Passing the driving test
Now: Passing the vision test

Then: Seeds and stems
Now: Roughage.

Then: Popping pills, smoking joints.
Now: Popping joints.

Then: Ommmmmmmm.
Now: Ummmmmm.

Secrets of Personal Growth

As I let go of my feelings of guilt, I am in touch with my inner sociopath.

I have the power to channel my imagination into ever-soaring levels of suspicion and paranoia.

I assume full responsibility for my actions, except the ones that are someone else's fault.

I no longer need to punish, deceive, or compromise myself, unless I want to stay employed.

In some cultures what I do would be considered normal.

Having control over myself is almost as good as having control over others.

My intuition nearly makes up for my lack of self-judgment.

I honor my personality flaws for without them I would have no personality at all.

Joan of Arc heard voices too.

I am grateful that I am not as judgmental as all those censorious, self-righteous people around me.

I need not suffer in silence while I can still moan, whimper, and complain.

As I learn the innermost secrets of people around me, they reward me in many ways to keep me quiet.

When someone hurts me, I know that forgiveness is cheaper than a lawsuit, but not nearly as gratifying.

The first step is to say nice things about myself. The second, to do nice things for myself. The third, to find someone to buy me nice things.

As I learn to trust the universe, I no longer need to carry a gun.

All of me is beautiful, even the ugly, stupid and disgusting parts.

I am at one with my duality.

Blessed are the flexible, for they can tie themselves into knots.

Only a lack of imagination saves me from immobilizing myself with imaginary fears.

I honor and express all facets of my being, regardless of state and local laws.

Today I will gladly share my experience and advice with all who care to hear it, for there are no sweeter words than 'I told you so!'

False hope is better than no hope at all.

A good scapegoat is almost as good as a solution.

Why should I waste my time reliving the past when I can spend it worrying about the future?

The complete lack of evidence is the surest sign that the conspiracy is working.

I am learning that criticism is not nearly as effective as sabotage.

Becoming aware of my character defects leads me naturally to the next step of blaming my parents.

To have a successful relationship I must learn to make it look like I'm giving about as much as I'm getting.

I am willing to make the mistakes if someone else is willing to learn from them.

All of the evil that I speak, hear, and see are pleasurable to me.

When counting my blessings, I count backwards from one.

They no longer allow me into the confessional.

When I am here I wish I was there... and I am.

Seminars for Females

Crying and Law Enforcement

Advanced Mathematics Seminar: Programming Your VCR

You CAN Go Shopping for Less Than Four Hours

The Seven-Outfit Week

Telephone Translations (formerly titled 'Me Too' Equals 'I Love You')

Putting the Seat Down by Yourself: Potential Energy is on Your Side.

What Goes Around Comes Around: Why His Credit Card is Not a Toy

Commitment Schmmitment (formerly titled Wedlock Schmedlock)

To Honor and Obey: Remembering the Small Print Above 'I Do'

Why Your Mother Is Unwelcome in the House

Seminars for Males

Combating Stupidity

You, Too, Can Do Housework

PMS: Learn When to Keep Your Mouth Shut

How to Fill an Ice Tray

Understanding the Female Response to Your Coming in Drunk at Four in the Morning.

Parenting: No, It Doesn't End With Conception

Get a Life: Learn to Cook

Understanding Your Financial Incompetence

Reasons to Give Flowers

Why It is Unacceptable to Relieve Yourself Anywhere But the Bathroom

You Can Fall Asleep Without 'It' If You Really Try

How to Put the Toilet Lid Down (formerly titled No, It's Not a Bidet)

'The Weekend' and 'Sports' are Not Synonyms

Give Me A Break: Why We Know Your Excuses are Lies

The Remote Control: Overcoming Your Dependency

Helpful Postural Hints for Couch Potatoes

Mothers-in-Law: They Are People Too

Male Bonding: Leaving Your Friends at Home

You, Too, Can Be a Designated Driver

Changing Your Underwear: It Really Works

The Attainable Goal: Omitting 'Tits' From Your Vocabulary

Fluffing the Blankets After Flatulence is Really Not Necessary

Training Courses Now Available to Women

Silence, the Final Frontier: Where No Woman Has Gone Before

The Undiscovered Side of Banking: Making Deposits

Bathroom Etiquette I: Men Need Space in the Bathroom Cabinet Too

Bathroom Etiquette II: Get Your Own Razor

Parties: Going Without New Outfits

Communication Skills I: Tears — The Last Resort, Not The First

Communication Skills II: Thinking Before Speaking

Communication Skills III: Getting What You Want Without Nagging

Introduction to Parking

Advanced Parking 101: Attempting the Parallel Park

Advanced Parking 201: Attempting the Parallel Park Without Guidance From Passers-by

Cooking I: Bringing Back Bacon, Eggs and Butter

Cooking II: Bran and Tofu Are Not for Human Consumption

Cooking III: How Not to Inflict Your Diets on Other People.

Compliments: Accepting Them Gracefully

PMS: Your Problem... Not His

Dancing: Why Men Don't Like to

Classic Clothing: Wearing Outfits You Already Have in Your Wardrobe

Household Dust: A Harmless Natural Occurrence Only Women Notice.

Integrating Your Laundry: Washing It All Together

★ ★ ★ ★

An optimist thinks that this is the best possible world.

The Five Stages of Drunkenness

Stage 1 – Smart

This is when you suddenly become an expert on every subject in the known universe. You know everything and want to pass on your knowledge to anyone who will listen. At this stage you are always *right*. And of course the person you are talking to is very *wrong*. It makes for an interesting argument when both parties are *smart*.

Stage 2 – Good looking

This is when you realize that you are the *best-looking* person in the entire bar and that people fancy you. You can go up to a perfect stranger knowing they will adore the way you look. Bear in mind that you are still *smart,* so you can talk to this person about any subject under the sun.

Stage 3 – Rich

This is when you suddenly become the richest person in the world. You can buy drinks for the entire bar because you have an armored truck full of money parked behind the bar. You can also make bets at this stage, because of course, you are still *smart,* so naturally you will win all your bets. It doesn't matter how much you bet because you are *rich*.

Stage 4 – Bulletproof

You are now ready to pick fights with anyone and everyone especially those with whom you have been betting or arguing. This is because nothing can hurt you. At this point you can also go up to the partners of the people you fancy and challenge them to a battle of wits or money. You have no fear of losing this battle because not only are you *smart,* you are *rich* and hell, you're *better looking* than they are anyway!

Stage 5 – Invisible

This is the Final Stage of Drunkenness. At this point you can do anything because *no one can see you.* You dance on a table to impress the people you fancy because the rest of the people in the room cannot see you. You are also invisible to the person who wants to fight you. You can walk through the street singing at the top of your lungs because no one can see or hear you. Because you're still *smart,* you know all the words.

★ ★ ★ ★

I have kleptomania, but when it gets bad, I take something for it.

★ ★ ★ ★

Even if you are on the right track, you'll get run over if you just sit there.

477

Baby Talk

Amnesia: A condition that enables a woman who has gone through labor to do it again.

Family planning: The art of spacing your children the proper distance apart to keep you on the edge of financial disaster.

Feedback: The inevitable result when the baby doesn't appreciate the strained carrots.

Full name: What you call your child when you're mad at him or her.

Grandparents: People who think your children are wonderful even though they're sure you're not raising them right.

Hearsay: What toddlers do when anyone mutters a dirty word.

Impregnable: A woman whose memory of labor is still vivid.

Independent: What we want our children to be as long as they do everything we say.

Ow: The first word spoken by children with other siblings.

Prenatal: When your life was still somewhat your own.

Puddle: A small body of water that draws other small bodies wearing dry shoes into it.

Show-off: A child who is more talented than yours.

Sterilize: What you do to your first baby's pacifier by boiling it and to your last baby's pacifier by blowing on it.

Top bunk: Where you should never put a child wearing Superman pajamas.

Two-minute warning: When the baby's face turns red and she begins to make those familiar grunting noises.

I've Learned...

I've learned that you cannot make someone love you. All you can do is stalk them and hope they panic and give in.

I've learned that no matter how much I care, some people are just bastards.

I've learned that it takes years to build up trust, and only suspicion, not proof, to destroy it.

I've learned that it's not what you have in your life that counts, but how much you have in your bank accounts.

I've learned that you shouldn't compare yourself to others — they are more messed up than you think.

I've learned that you can keep puking long after you think you're finished.

I've learned that regardless of how hot and steamy a relationship is at first, the passion fades, and there had better be a lot of money to take its place.

I've learned that money is a great substitute for character.

I've learned that sometimes the people you expect to kick you when you're down will be the ones who do.

I've learned that we don't have to ditch bad friends because their dysfunction makes us feel better about ourselves.

I've learned that no matter how you try to protect your children, they will eventually get arrested and end up in the local paper.

I've learned that overzealous customs agents can change your life in a matter of hours.

I've learned that the people you care most about in life are taken from you too soon. And all the less important ones just never go away.

★ ★ ★ ★

I still miss my ex-husband, but my aim is improving.

Daily Exercise for the Non-Athletic

Calories can be burned by the hundreds by engaging in strenuous activities that do not require physical exercise.

Exercise	Calories/hr
Beating around the bush	75
Jumping to conclusions	100
Climbing the walls	150
Swallowing your pride	50
Passing the buck	25
Throwing your weight around (depending on your weight)	50-300
Dragging your heels	100
Laying down the law	75
Pushing your luck	250
Making mountains out of molehills	500
Hitting the nail on the head	50
Wading through paperwork	300
Falling in love	500
Bending over backwards	75
Jumping on the bandwagon	200
Balancing the books	25
Running around in circles	350

Blowing your own trumpet	25
Climbing the ladder of success	750
Adding fuel to the fire	160
Wrapping it up at the day's end	12
Opening a can of worms	50
Putting your foot in your mouth	300
Starting the ball rolling	90
Twiddling your thumbs	10
Going over the edge	25
Pushing the envelope	50
Picking up the pieces	350

Bumperstickers, Witticisms, One-Liners...

The sex was so good that even the neighbors had a cigarette.

If you smoke after sex, you're doing it too fast.

I don't suffer from insanity, I enjoy every minute of it.

If ignorance is bliss, you must be orgasmic.

The more people I meet, the more I like my dog.

Some people are alive only because it's illegal to kill them.

A bartender is just a pharmacist with a limited inventory.

I used to have a handle on life, but it broke.

Don't take life too seriously. You won't get out alive.

WANTED: Meaningful overnight relationship.

If you can read this, I've lost my trailer.

You're just jealous because the voices only talk to me.

I got a gun for my wife. Best trade I've ever made.

So you're a feminist … isn't that cute?

Jesus may love you, but he won't respect you in the morning.

I don't care, I don't have to.

Earth is the insane asylum for the universe.

To all you virgins, thanks for nothing.

Horn broken, watch for finger.

All men are idiots... I married their king.

The more you complain, the longer God lets you live.

Earth first...we'll mine the other planets later.

Please Mr Bank Manager, how can I be overdrawn, I still have checks!

Work is for people who don't know how to fish.

I'm just driving this way to piss you off.

Jesus paid for our sins... now let's get our money's worth.

Reality is a crutch for people who can't handle drugs.

Missing your cat? Try looking under my tires.

Out of my mind. Back in five minutes.

I want to be like Barbie — that bitch has everything.

This would be really funny it if wasn't happening to me.

I get enough exercise pushing my luck.

If you don't like the news, go out and make your own.

Guns don't kill people... but they sure make it easy.

Ask me about microwaving cats for fun and profit.

I said 'no' to drugs, but they just wouldn't listen.

If we aren't supposed to eat animals, why are they made of meat?

Friends help you move. Real friends help you move bodies.

Sex on television can't hurt you... unless you fall off.

Honk if you do what car bumperstickers tell you to do.

Stress Management

Picture yourself near a stream. Birds are softly chirping in the crisp, cool mountain air. Nothing can bother you here. No one knows this secret place. You are in total seclusion from that place called 'the world'. The soothing sound of a gentle waterfall fills the air with a cascade of serenity. The water is so clear... you can easily make out the face of the person whose head you're holding under the water. There now... feeling better?

Paycheck Guide

The following helpful guide has been prepared to help our employees better understand their paychecks:

Item	Amount
Gross pay	$1,222.02
Income tax	$244.40
Outgoing tax	$45.21
State tax	$11.61
Interstate tax	$61.10
Regional tax	$6.11
City tax	$12.22
Rural tax	$4.44
Back tax	$1.11
Front tax	$1.16
Side tax	$1.61
Up tax	$2.22
Thumb tacks	$3.93
Carpet tacks	$0.98
Stadium tax	$0.69
Flat tax	$8.32
Corporate tax	$2.60
Tic-Tacs	$1.98

World's Best Humor

Parking fee	$5.00
Life insurance	$5.85
Health insurance	$16.23
Dental insurance	$4.50
Mental insurance	$4.33
Reassurance	$0.11
Disability	$2.50
Ability	$0.25
Liability	$3.41
Unreliability	$10.99
Coffee	$6.85
Coffee cups	$66.51
Floor rental	$16.85
Chair rental	$0.32
Desk rental	$4.32
Union dues	$5.85
Union don'ts	$3.77
Cash advances	$0.69
Cash retreats	$121.35
Overtime	$1.26
Undertime	$54.83
Eastern time	$9.00
Central time	$8.00
Mountain time	$7.00

Pacific time	$6.00
Time out	$12.21
Water	$16.54
Heat	$51.42
Cool air	$26.83
Hot air	$20.00
Oxygen	$10.02
Miscellaneous	$113.29
Sundry	$12.09
Various	$8.01
Net Take Home Pay	$0.02

Thank you for your loyalty to our company. We are here to provide a positive employment experience. All questions, comments, concerns, complaints, frustration, irritation, aggravation, insinuations, allegations, accusations, contemplations, consternations, or input should be directed elsewhere. Have a nice week.

Intelligence

All babies start out with the same number of raw cells which, over nine months, develop into a complete female baby. The problem occurs when cells are instructed by the little chromosomes to make a male baby instead. Because there are only so many cells to go around, the cell necessary to develop a male's reproductive organs have to come from cells already assigned elsewhere in the female.

Recent tests have shown that these cells are removed from the communications center of the brain, migrate lower in the body and develop into male sexual organs. If you visualize a normal brain to be similar to a full deck of cards, this means that males are born a few cards short, so to speak, and some of their cards are in their shorts.

This difference between the male and female brain manifests itself in various ways. Little girls will tend to play things like house or learn to read. Little boys, however, will tend to do things like placing a bucket over their heads and running into walls. Little girls will think about doing things before taking any action. Little boys will just punch or kick something, and will look surprised if someone asks them why they just punched their little brother who was half asleep and looking the other way. This basic cognitive difference continues to grow until puberty, when the hormones kick into action and the trouble really begins. After puberty, not only the sizes of the male and female brains differ, but their center of thought also differs. Women think with their heads. Male thoughts often originate lower in their bodies where their ex-brain cells reside.

Of course, the size of this problem varies from man to man. In some men only a small number of brain cells migrate and they are left with nearly full mental capacity, but they tend to be rather dull, sexually speaking. Such men are known in medical terms as 'engineers'. Other men suffer larger brain cell relocation. These men are medically referred to as 'lawyers'. A small number of men suffer massive brain cell migration to their groins. These men are usually referred to as 'congressman'.

You Know You're Over the Hill When...

You find yourself beginning to like accordion music.

Lawn care has become a big highlight of your life.

Your underwear creeps up on you... and you enjoy it.

You tune into the easy listening station... on purpose.

You discover that your measurements are now small, medium and large ... in that order.

You keep repeating yourself.

You start videotaping daytime game shows.

At cafeterias, you complain that the jello is too tough.

Your new easychair has more options than your car.

When you do the 'Hokey Pokey' you put your left hip out... and it stays out.

One of the throw pillows on your bed is a hot water bottle.

Conversations with people your own age often turn into 'duelling ailments'.

You keep repeating yourself.

It takes a couple of tries to get over a speed bump.

You're on a TV game show and you decide to risk it all and go for the rocker.

You begin every other sentence with, 'Nowadays...'

You run out of breath walking *down* a flight of stairs.

You look both ways before crossing a room.

You come to the conclusion that your worst enemy is gravity.

It takes you all night to do what you used to do all night.

You go to a garden party and you're mainly interested in the garden.

You find your mouth making promises your body can't keep.

At parties you attend, 'regularity' is considered the topic of choice.

You start beating everyone else at trivia games.

You frequently find yourself telling people what a loaf of bread *used* to cost.

Your back goes out more than you do.

You keep repeating yourself.

Your childhood toys are now in a museum.

The clothes you've put away until they come back in style... come back in style.

All of your favorite movies are now revised in color.

The car that you bought brand new is now a very valuable antique.

You keep repeating yourself.

You find this list tasteless and insensitive.

You Might Be a Bachelor If...

You can clean engine parts in the bathtub without someone yelling at you.

You amuse yourself by lobbing beer cans so that they bounce off the wall before hitting the trash can.

It takes you 10 minutes every six months to buy new clothes (let's see, I'm out of jeans, white T-shirts, black T-shirts, and socks…)

You don't feel compelled to wear underwear unless you have a date that night.

Your car gets waxed more often than the toilet gets cleaned.

You turn your socks and underwear inside out so you can wear them twice as long.

You have the pizza place on the speed dial.

Instead of cleaning for guests, you just keep the lights low.

Paper towels double as dishes.

Beer is the freshest item in the fridge.

Beer is the only item in the fridge.

You never listen to your messages when a female is around.

Your entire house is trashed except for your TV and stereo, which are lovingly polished every day.

If anything needs to be cooked longer that five minutes, it is a waste of time.

The last time you cleaned the house was when you moved in.

A dress shirt is 'fine' if it only has one or two wrinkles in it.

You don't feel guilty about leaving the toilet seat up.

How to Take a Shower
How to Shower Like a Woman

Take off clothing and place it in sectioned laundry hamper according to whites and coloreds.

Walk to bathroom wearing long dressing gown. If you see your boyfriend/husband along the way, you cover up any exposed flesh and rush to the bathroom.

Look at your womanly physique in the mirror and stick out your gut so that you can complain and whine even more about how you're getting fat.

Get in the shower. Look for facecloth, arm-cloth, long loofah, wide loofah and pumice stone.

Wash your hair once with cucumber shampoo with 83 added vitamins.

Wash your hair again with cucumber shampoo with 83 added vitamins.

Condition your hair with cucumber conditioner enhanced with natural crocus oil. Leave on hair for 15 minutes.

Wash your face with crushed apricot facial scrub for 10 minutes until red raw.

Wash entire rest of body with gingernut body wash.

Rinse conditioner from hair. (This takes at least 15 minutes as you must make sure that it has all come off.)

Shave armpits and legs. Consider shaving bikini area but decide to get it waxed instead.

Scream loudly when your boyfriend/husband flushes the toilet and you lose the water pressure.

Turn off shower.

Squeegee off all wet surfaces in shower. Spray mould spots.

Get out of shower. Dry with towel the size of a small African country. Wrap hair in super-absorbent second towel.

Check entire body for the remotest sign of a zit.

Attack with nails if found.

Return to bedroom wearing long dressing gown and towel on head.

If you see your boyfriend/husband along the way, cover up any exposed flesh and then rush to bedroom to spend at least an hour-and-a-half getting dressed.

How to Shower Like a Man

Take off clothes while sitting on the edge of the bed and leave them in a pile.

Walk naked to the bathroom. If you see your girl-friend/wife along the way, flash her, making the 'woo-woo' sound.

Look at your manly physique in the mirror and suck in your gut and scratch yourself.

Get in the shower.

Don't bother to look for a washcloth. (You don't use one.)

Wash your face.

Wash your armpits.

Wash your bits.

Shampoo your hair. (Do not use conditioner.)

Make a shampoo mohawk.

Pull back shower curtain and look at yourself in the mirror.

Pee (in the shower).

Rinse off and get out of the shower. Fail to notice water on the floor because you left the curtain hanging out of the tub when you checked your mohawk.

Partially dry off.

Look at yourself in the mirror, flex muscles. Admire endowment.

Leave shower curtain open and wet bath mat on the floor.

Leave bathroom fan and light on.

Return to the bedroom with towel around your waist. If you pass your girlfriend/wife, pull off the towel, go 'Yeah baby' and thrust your pelvis at her.

Throw wet towel on the bed. Take two minutes to get dressed.

You Know It's Going to Be a Bad Day When ...

Your twin forgets your birthday.

You wake up face down on the pavement.

You see a 60 Minutes news team waiting in your office.

Your birthday cake collapses from the weight of the candles.

You want to put on the clothes you wore home from the party, and there aren't any.

You turn on the TV news and they're displaying emergency routes out of your city.

Your doctor tells you, 'Well, I have bad news and good news...'

You open the paper and find your picture under a caption that reads: 'Wanted: Dead or Alive'.

Your ex-lover calls and tells you he/she has six days to live, and that you'd better get yourself tested.

You have an appointment in 10 minutes and you just woke up.

You wake up at work naked in front of your co-workers.

Statements to Avoid During a Job Interview

'You could do worse.'

'I'll work so hard you won't even know I'm here.'

'I'll need all my paid annual leave up front so I'll be rested when I start.'

'You can't turn me down because I smell bad. You have to have a reason.'

'That big thing growing on my face isn't my fault.'

'I don't do drugs at work anymore, I swear.'

'I can go all day without peeing once.'

'I won't sue you when you fire me.'

'My arrest record is all a bunch of lies.'

'I was a sniper in the army.'

'I can make explosives from Windex, white-out, and photocopier toner.'

'You don't have the BALLS to hire someone like me!'.

'If you hire me I will show up. That's all I can promise for sure, but maybe it will be better than that and I will sure try.'

'Don't go checking into my record. But if you do, she swore she was 18.'

'I don't hear the voices anymore. Do not. Do not. Do not. SHUT UP!'

'If you give me a job you're okay, but if you don't you suck.'

'I don't *do* applications.'

'If I work here I'll wear the stupid uniform as long as I can wear any kind of underwear I want.'

'I won't have to do anything, will I?'

'Can I bring my goat to the company day care center?'

'I collect guns. You probably want to tell me that I got the job now, right?'

'I'm not what? Oh yeah? Well here's what you can do with your damned job...'

The Rules of Indoor Badminton

In order to score, a player must land his cock in his opponent's court.

Players may only handle the cock before serving or after scoring.

If a player does not get the cock into his opponent's court for any reason, then he does not score and cannot try again until he has service again.

Damaged cocks should not be used as this can cause irritation to the court surface.

Rubber covers are advised for safety, as they are about 99% less likely to damage the court.

Courts with worn or damaged patches should not be used for at least two weeks.

If, while playing, the cock lands out of the court, the players should clean up and carry on with the game unless they are too tired.

The type of cock and size of court should not affect the players enjoyment of the game.

Large courts are not advisable for play as generally they have been overused in the past.

If the opponent is not ready to receive a service for any reason, play should be suspended.

To aid play the players should keep an eye on the cock and court at all times.

To increase service length, the server can use a different type of racquet. This is more likely to stimulate interesting play.

If the game does not involve mixed singles, then the area of play should be changed.

Inspirational Posters

Rome did not create a great empire by having meetings; they did it by killing all those who opposed them.

If you can stay calm, while all around you is chaos... then you probably haven't completely understood the seriousness of the situation.

Doing a job right the first time gets the job done.

Doing a job wrong 14 times gives you job security.

Artificial Intelligence is no match for Natural Stupidity.

A person who smiles in the face of adversity probably has a scapegoat.

If at first you don't succeed, try management.

Never put off until tomorrow what you can avoid altogether.

Teamwork… means never having to take all the blame yourself.

The beatings will continue until morale improves.

Never underestimate the power of very stupid people in large groups.

We waste time, so you don't have to.

Hang in there—retirement is only 30 years away!

Go the extra mile. It makes your boss look like an incompetent slacker.

A snooze button is a poor substitute for no alarm clock at all.

When the going gets tough, the tough take a coffee break.

Indecision is the key to flexibility.

Succeed in spite of management.

Aim low, reach your goals, and you will avoid disappointment.

Never replicate a successful experiment.

Make failure your teacher, not your undertaker.

Letters of Recommendation

Have to write a letter of recommendation for that fired employee? Here are a few suggested phrases:

For the chronically absent:
'A man like him is hard to find.'
'It seemed her career was just taking off.'

For the office drunk:
'I feel his real talent is wasted here.'
'We generally found him loaded with work to do.'
'Every hour with him was a happy hour.'

For an employee with no ambition:
'He could not care less about the number of hours he had to put in.'
'You would indeed be fortunate to get this person to work for you.'

For an employee who is so unproductive that the job is better left unfilled:
'I can assure you that no person would be better for the job.'

For an employee who is not worth further consideration as a job candidate:
'I would urge you to waste no time in making this candidate an offer of employment.'
'All in all, I cannot say enough good things about this candidate or recommend him too highly.'

For a stupid employee:
'There is nothing you can teach a man like him.'
'I most enthusiastically recommend this candidate with no qualifications whatsoever.'

For a dishonest employee:
'Her true ability was deceiving.'
'He's an unbelievable worker.'

Have to read a letter of recommendation? Here are a few translations:

'A keen analyst.'
Thoroughly confused.

'Accepts new job assignments willingly.'
Never finished a job.

'Active socially.'
Drinks heavily.

'Alert to company developments.'
An office gossip.

'Approaches difficult problems with logic.'
Finds someone else to do the job.

'Bridge builder.'
Likes to compromise.

'Character above reproach.'
Still one step ahead of the law.

'Charismatic.'
No interest in any opinion but his own.

'Competent.'
Is still able to get work done if supervisor helps.

'Conscientious and careful.'
Scared.

'Consults with co-workers often.'
Indecisive, confused and clueless.

'Consults with supervisor often.'
Pain in the ass.

'Delegates responsibility effectively.'
Passes the buck well.

'Demonstrates qualities of leadership.'
Has a loud voice.

'Deserves promotion.'
Create new title to make him/her feel appreciated.

'Displays excellent intuitive judgment.'
Knows when to disappear.

'Displays great dexterity and agility.'
Dodges and evades superiors well.

'Enjoys job.'
Needs more to do.

'Excels in sustaining concentration but avoids confrontations.'
Ignores everyone.

'Excels in the effective application of skills.'
Makes a good cup of coffee.

'Exceptionally well qualified.'
Has committed no major blunders to date.

'Expresses self well.'
Can string two sentences together.

'Gets along extremely well with superiors and subordinates alike.'
A coward.

'Happy'
Paid too much.

'Hard worker.'
Usually does it the hard way.

'Identifies major management problems.'
Complains a lot.

'Is well informed.'
Knows all office gossip and where all the skeletons are kept.

'Inspires the cooperation of others.'
Gets everyone else to do the work.

'Is unusually loyal.'
Wanted by no one else.

'Judgment is usually sound.'
Lucky.

'Keen sense of humor.'
Knows lots of dirty jokes.

'Keeps informed on business issues.'
Subscribes to Playboy and National Enquirer.

'Listens well.'
Has no ideas of his own.

'Maintains a high degree of participation.'
Comes to work on time.

'Maintains professional attitude.'
A snob.

'Meticulous in attention to detail.'
A nitpicker.

'Mover and shaker.'
Favors steamroller tactics without regard for other people's opinions.

'Uses all available resources.'
Takes office supplies home for personal use.

'Quick thinking'
Offers plausible excuses for errors.

'Should go far.'
Please.

'Spends extra hours on the job.'
Miserable home life.

'Straightforward.'
Blunt and insensitive.

'Strong adherence to principles.'
Stubborn.

'Tactful in dealing with superiors.'
Knows when to keep mouth shut.

'Takes utmost advantage of every opportunity to progress.'
Buys drinks for superiors.

'Takes pride in work.'
Conceited.

'Uses time effectively.'
Clock watcher.

'Very creative.'
Finds 22 reasons to do anything except original work.

'Will go far.'
Relative of management.

'Willing to take calculated risks.'
Doesn't mind spending someone else's money.

★ ★ ★ ★

It's easier to fight for one's principles than to live up to them.

Marriage One-liners

Marriage is not a word. It is a sentence (a life sentence).

Marriage is very much like a violin; after the sweet music is over, the strings are attached.

Marriage is love. Love is blind. Therefore, marriage is an institution for the blind.

Marriage is a thing that puts a ring on a woman's finger and two under the man's eyes.

Marriage certificate is just another word for a work permit.

Married life is full of excitement and frustration. In the first year of marriage, the man speaks and the woman listens. In the second year, the woman speaks and the man listens. In the third year, they both speak and the neighbors listen.

Getting married is very much like going to a restaurant with friends. You order what you want, and when you see what the other fellow has, you wish you had ordered that.

It's true that all men are born free and equal, but some of them get married!

A happy marriage is a matter of giving and taking: the husband gives and the wife takes.

Son: How much does it cost to get married, Dad?
Father: I don't know son, I'm still paying for it.

Son: Dad, I heard that in ancient China, a man doesn't know his wife until he marries. Is it true?
Father: That happens everywhere, son, EVERYWHERE!

There was a man who said, 'I never knew what happiness was until I got married... and then it was too late!'

Love is one long sweet dream, and marriage is the alarm clock.

They say when a man holds a woman's hand before marriage, it is love; after marriage, it is self-defence.

When a newly married man looks happy, we know why. But when a man who has been married for 10 years looks happy, we wonder why.

What the Doctor Really Means

Doctor says: 'This should be taken care of right away.'

Doctor means: I'd planned a trip to Hawaii next month but this is so easy and profitable that I want to fix it before it cures itself.

Doctor says: 'Well, what have we here.'
Doctor means: Since I haven't the foggiest notion of what it is, I'm hoping you will give me a bit of a clue.

Doctor says: 'We'll see.'
Doctor means: First I have to check my malpractice insurance.

Doctor says: 'Let me check your medical history.'
Doctor means: I want to see if you've paid your last bill before spending any more time with you.

Doctor says: 'Why don't we make another appointment later in the week.'
Doctor means: I'm playing golf this afternoon, and this is a waste of time. *Or*, I need the money, so I'm charging you for another office visit.

Doctor says: 'I really can't recommend seeing a chiropractor.'
Doctor means: I hate those guys mooching in on our fees.

Doctor says: 'We have some good news and some bad news.'
Doctor means: The good news is he's going to buy that new BMW, and the bad news is you're going to pay for it.

Doctor says: 'Let's see how it develops.'
Doctor means: Maybe in a few days it will grow into something that can be cured.

Doctor says: 'Let me schedule you for some tests.'
Doctor means: I have a 40% interest in the lab.

Doctor says: 'How are we today?'
Doctor means: I feel great. You, on the other hand, look like hell.

Doctor says: 'I'd like to prescribe a new drug.'
Doctor means: I'm writing a paper and would like to use you as a guinea pig.

Doctor says: 'If it doesn't clear up in a week, give me a call.'
Doctor means: I don't know what the hell it is. Maybe it will go away by itself.

Doctor says: 'That's quite a nasty-looking wound.'
Doctor means: I think I'm going to throw up.

Doctor says: 'This may sting a little.'
Doctor means: Last week two patients bit through their tongues.

Doctor says: 'This should fix you up.'
Doctor means: The drug salesman guaranteed that it kills all symptoms.

Doctor says: 'Everything seems to be normal.'
Doctor means: I guess I can't buy that new beach house after all.

Doctor says: 'I'd like to run some more tests.'
Doctor means: I can't figure out what's wrong. Maybe the kid in the lab can solve this one.

Doctor says: 'Do you suppose all of this stress could be affecting your nerves?'

Doctor means: He thinks you are crazy and is hoping to find a psychiatrist who will split fees.

What is the Definition of...

Amnesia: What did you ask me?

Apathy: I don't care.

Bigotry: I'm not going to tell someone like you.

Damnation: Go to hell!

Dyslexia: Beeing sackwards.

Egotistical: I'm the best person to answer that question.

Flatulent: That question really stinks!

Hostility: If you ask me just one more question, I'll kill you!

Ignorance: I don't know.

Indifference: It doesn't matter.

Influenza: You've got to be sick to ask me that question.

Insomnia: I stayed awake all last night thinking of the answer.

Irreverent: I swear to God, you ask too many questions!

Masturbation: Your father can handle that question.

Narcissism: Before I answer, tell me, don't I look great?

Over-protective: I don't know if you're ready for the answer.

Paranoid: You probably think I don't know the answer, don't you?

Procrastination: I'll tell you tomorrow.

Repetitive: I already told you the answer once before.

Self-centered: Well, I know the answer, that's all that matters.

Suspicious: Why are you asking me all these questions?

★ ★ ★ ★

It hurts to be on the cutting edge.

★ ★ ★ ★

I don't get even, I get odder.

As Effective As...

A one-legged man in an ass-kicking contest.

Milk shoes

A nuclear-powered computer-controlled intercontinental ballistic duck.

A flammable fire extinguisher.

A glass baseball bat.

A blind lifeguard.

Wooden soap.

A knitted light bulb.

An invisible traffic light.

Plasticine wire cutters.

A neon pink secret door.

A lead balloon.

A water hat.

A steel-reinforced concrete sail.

A silent telephone.

A tap-dancing microprocessor-controlled portrait of a bowl of soup.

A waterproof tea bag.

A liquorice suspension bridge.

Soap false teeth

Ice-cream saucepans.

A soluble drain pipe.

A cubic ball-bearing.

An inflatable dartboard.

A glass hammer.

And a packet of rubber nails.

Revolving basement restaurant.

Objective journalism.

Braille speedometers.

A screen door on a submarine.

An ejector seat in a helicopter.

Boobs on a bull.

A condom with a hole in it.

A box of matches in the desert.

★ ★ ★ ★

In just two days, tomorrow will be yesterday.

So Many Lies, So Little Time

Lies about Love

Everyone does this, it's perfectly normal.

It's dangerous to your health to get excited and then stop.

I'll stop as soon as you say.

I'll tell her/him tonight.

Well, the clinic said I was clear!

Nobody can hear us.

I'll never put myself through this again.

Men's Lies

Sex isn't everything.

It's not your fault.

It's too late.

I read an article today.

I'm allergic to rubber.

We'll try again when we wake up.

It has a mind of its own.

This has never happened before.

Party Lies

I'm not going to drink too much tonight.

They'll all be wearing jeans.

There are no bones in this fish.

The neighbors are very tolerant.

Just half a glass, thanks.

He doesn't normally act like this when he's been drinking.

It's no trouble if you stay the night.

Salesman Lies

You won't see this anywhere else.

This sort of thing never goes out of fashion.

Bring it back if you don't like it.

This is a never-to-be-repeated offer!

Unbelievably low prices.

It's the last one in stock.

You'll have no trouble with it.

Drivers Stopped by the Law Lies

I was just going the speed limit.

I only had one.

What stop sign?

The light was green when I started through the intersection.

He came from nowhere when I changed lanes.

Officer, I can walk without any assistance.

Computer Lies

If you have any problems, just call us.

What you see on the screen, you get on paper.

They don't make those chips anymore.

If kids use them, so can adults.

Oh yeah, it's compatible with everything.

You won't need any special training. There's no harm in trying — nothing can go wrong.

The manual explains everything.

The Parachute Paradigm

You are one of two people on a malfunctioning plane with only one parachute.

Pessimist: you refuse the parachute because you might die in the jump anyway.

Optimist: you refuse the parachute because people have survived jumps just like this before.

World's Best Humor

Procrastinator: you play a game of Monopoly for the parachute.

Bureaucrat: you order the other person to conduct a feasibility study on parachute use in multi-engine aircraft under code red conditions.

Lawyer: you charge one parachute for helping the other person sue the airline.

Doctor: you tell the other person you need to run more tests, then take the parachute in order to make your next appointment.

Sales executive: you sell the other person the parachute at top retail rates and get the names of their friends and relatives who might like one too.

Advertiser: you strip-tease while singing that what the other person needs is a neon parachute with computer altimeter for only $39.99.

Engineer: you make the other person another parachute out of aisle curtains and dental floss.

Scientist: you give the other person the parachute and ask them to send you a report on how well it worked.

Mathematician: you refuse to accept the parachute without proof that it will work in all cases.

Philosopher: you ask how the other person knows the parachute actually exists.

English expert: you explicate simile and metaphor in the parachute instructions.

Comparative literature theorist: you read the parachute instructions in all four languages.

Computer scientist: you design a machine capable of operating a parachute as well as a human being could.

Psychoanalyst: you ask the other person what the shape of the parachute reminds them of.

Dramatist: you tie the other person down so they can watch you develop the character of a person stuck on a falling plane without a parachute.

Artist: you hang the parachute on the wall and sign it.

Environmentalist: you refuse to use the parachute unless it is biodegradable.

Economist: you plot a demand curve by asking them, at regular intervals, how much they would pay for a parachute.

Signs of Life

On an executive's desk: Nobody's perfect. I'm the perfect example.

On a politician's desk: Truth is a precious commodity and therefore should be used as sparingly as possible.

On a secretary's desk: Fact-finding beats fault-finding.

At a health insurance office: Get out reliable health insurance. Don't make your doctor perform a walletectomy.

At a mechanic's: An idealist — one who has both feet firmly planted in the air.

In a manager's office: Sometimes silence is the best way to yell.

On an office desk in a large business: They don't dare fire me. I'm always too far behind in my work.

On an office wall: Even moderation ought not to be practised to excess.

On the same office wall: One of the greatest labor-saving devices of today is tomorrow.

Beside a dentist's office: Patient parking only. All others will be painfully extracted.

Over a barn door: Agriculture is something like farming, only farming is doing it.

In a restaurant: Don't tip the waiters — it upsets them.

In a store: Credit extended to those over 80 if accompanied by their grandparents.

In a science lab: Tragedy is the murder of a beautiful theory by a brutal gang of facts.

On a marriage counsellor's door: Back in an hour. Don't fight.

On a ski slope: Going beyond this point may result in death and/or loss of skiing privileges.

At the entrance to a school administration building: Education will broaden a narrow mind, but there is no known cure for a big head.

In a cemetery: No trespassing. Violators will be haunted.

Murphy's Law of Work

A pat on the back is only a few inches from a kick in the pants.

Don't be irreplaceable. If you can't be replaced, you can't be promoted.

The more crap you put up with, the more crap you are going to get.

You can go anywhere you want if you look serious and carry a clipboard.

Eat one live toad the first thing in the morning, and nothing worse will happen to you for the rest of the day.

Never ask two questions in a business letter. The reply will discuss the one you are least interested in, and say nothing about the other.

When the bosses talk about improving productivity, they are never talking about themselves.

If at first you don't succeed, try again. Then quit. No use being a damn fool about it.

There will always be beer cans rolling on the floor of your car when the boss asks for a ride home from the office.

Mother said there would be days like this, but she never said there would be so many.

Keep your boss's boss off your boss's back.

Everything can be filed under 'miscellaneous.'

Never delay the ending of a meeting or the beginning of a cocktail hour.

Anyone can do any amount of work provided it isn't the work he is supposed to be doing.

Important letters that contain no errors will develop errors in the mail.

The last person that quit or was fired will be the one held responsible for everything that goes wrong... until the next person quits or is fired.

There is never enough time to do it right the first time, but there is always enough time to do it over.

The more pretentious a corporate name, the smaller the organization.

If you are good, you will be assigned all the work. If you are really good, you will get out of it.

If it weren't for the last minute, nothing would get done.

At work, the authority of a person is inversely proportional to the number of pens that person is carrying.

When you don't know what to do, walk fast and look worried.

You will always get the greatest recognition for the job you least like.

No one gets sick on Wednesday.

When confronted by a difficult problem, you can solve it more easily by reducing it to the question. 'How would the Lone Ranger handle this?'

The longer the title, the less important the job.

Machines that have broken down will work perfectly when the repairman arrives.

Once a job is fouled up, anything done to improve it makes it worse.

All vacations create problems, except for one's own.

Success is just a matter of luck, just ask any failure.

The first 90% of the project takes 90% of the time; the last 10% takes the other 90% of the time.

It doesn't matter what you do, it only matters what you say you've done and what you're going to do.

After any salary raise, you will have less money at the end of the month that you did before.

People who go to conferences are the ones who shouldn't.

Following the rules will not get the job done.

Getting the job done is no excuse for not following the rules.

Murphy's Law for Frequent Flyers

No flight ever leaves on time unless you are running late and need the delay to make the flight.

If you are running late for a flight, it will depart from the farthest gate within the terminal.

If you arrive very early for a flight, it inevitably will be delayed.

Flights never leave from Gate #1 at any terminal in the world.

If you must work on your flight, you will experience turbulence as soon as you touch pen to paper.

If you are assigned a middle seat, you can determine who has the seats on the aisle and the window while you are still in the boarding area. Just look for the two largest and noisiest passengers.

Only passengers seated in window seats ever have to get up to go to the toilet.

The crying baby on board your flight is always seated next to you.

The best-looking woman/man on your flight is never seated next to you.

The less carry-on luggage space available on an aircraft, the more carry-on luggage passengers will bring aboard.

You Know You're Drinking Too Much Coffee When...

You get a speeding ticket when you're parked.

You have a bumper sticker that says: 'Coffee drinkers are good in the sack.'

You answer the door before people knock.

You just completed another scarf and you don't

know how to knit.

You grind your coffee beans in your mouth.

You have to watch videos in fast-forward.

You can take a picture of yourself from 10 feet away without using the timer.

You lick your coffee pot clean.

You're the employee of the month at the local coffeehouse and you don't even work there.

The nurse needs a scientific calculator to take your pulse.

Your t-shirt says, 'Decaffeinated coffee is the devil's coffee.'

You're so jittery that people use your hands to blend their margaritas.

You can type 60 words per minute with your feet.

Cocaine is a downer.

Instant coffee takes too long.

You want to be cremated just so you can spend the rest of eternity in a coffee jar.

You go to sleep just so you can wake up and smell the coffee.

You're offended when people use the word 'brew' to mean beer.

You have a picture of your coffee mug on your coffee mug.

You can outlast the Energizer bunny.

Your liver used soft lights, romantic music, and a glass of iced coffee to get you in the mood.

You introduce your spouse as your coffee mate.

Your urine stream bores a hole in the toilet.

You have two complete orgasms whilst brushing your teeth.

You talk so fast your tongue has windburn.

You jog to work and arrive yesterday.

Your eyes are brown... even the white parts.

You personally account for more than 1% of the gross national product of Brazil.

Mosquitoes that bite you can fly through glass.

You bungee jump and go up.

Your coffee breath can etch glass.

You think skydiving is just too damned slow.

★ ★ ★ ★

I am an escapee of a political correction facility.

Tight-ass Tom took the family out to a fancy restaurant. He spent quite a bit of money, and said to the waiter, 'Could I have a bag to take the leftovers home, please?'

Embarrassed that there were only a few morsels left to salvage, his teenage daughter added, 'It's for our dog, Fido.'

Shocked, Tom turned to the girl and exclaimed, 'Since when are we getting a dog?'

★

An urban cowboy was sauntering down the street when he saw a beautiful girl coming towards him. She was wearing the tightest pair of jeans he had ever seen on anyone, even himself!

'Excuse me, ma'am,' he smiled, 'I hope you don't mind me asking, but how could anyone get into such a tight pair of jeans?'

She replied, 'Well, you could start by buying me a glass of wine.'

★

An old man goes to the physician for a routine check up. In passing, he mentions to his physician that he is getting married again to a 22-year-old girl.

The doctor looks quite concerned and feels he could give the old man some advice.

'You know, Jake, sex with such a young girl could be fatal.'

The old man smiled and replied confidently, 'You don't get to my age without a few setbacks, so if she dies, she dies.'

★

A couple are celebrating their golden wedding anniversary when the husband notices his wife is quietly crying.
'What's wrong, honey? Are the tears because of this wonderful occasion?'
'No,' she replies, 'I was just thinking that 50 years ago yesterday, I was still a free woman.'

★

As the honeymoon couple arrive at the hotel, the women turns to her new husband and says, 'I don't think I can face all the remarks we're going to get; is there some way we can pretend we've been married for years?'
'Of course, darlin'. You carry the bags,' he replies.

★

A woman comes out of court having just endured a divorce settlement. As she takes a deep breath of fresh air, she mutters to herself, 'It's about time my luck changed.'
All of a sudden, a genie appeared and spoke to her.
'Madam, I am the genie of the air and I grant you three wishes. But please take care with your wishes because whatever you get, your ex-husband will get double.'

'I'd like to look ten years younger,' she said.
'Your wish is granted, but remember your ex-husband is now 20 years younger.'
'Okay, I'd also like to have $10 million.'
'Your wish is granted, and your ex now has $20 million. What is your last wish?'
'I'd like to be run down by a car and half killed.'

★

When man was first made, he only had twenty years of normal sex life. To him, this was horrifying. Meanwhile, the monkey had also been given twenty years normal sex life, but he said he only needed ten years, so he gave the gave the other ten to the man.

Likewise, the lion, also with twenty years, gave ten years to the man as well. He agreed that ten years was plenty.

Finally the donkey, agreeing with the other animals that ten years was enough, gave the man another ten years.

So all this explains today's modern man. He has twenty years of normal sex left, ten years of monkeying around, a further ten years of lion about it and finally ten years of making a complete ass of himself.

★

A young businessman was returning home when his car broke down and he sought shelter in a nearby house. The following day he arrived back at work looking bleary-eyed and constantly yawning. 'What happened to you, then?' asked his pals.

The man explained about his car and the overnight stay at the nearby house.

'A young woman answered the door. She said she lived there alone and I was welcome to stop the night.'

'Little wonder you look tired,' cheered one pal. 'So a little bit of screwing went on, eh?'

'A lot,' replied the man. 'When it was time for bed, she said the lock on her bedroom door was broken, so I spent half the night trying to mend it.'

★

The Procrastinator's Creed

I believe that if anything is worth doing, it would have been done already.

I shall never move quickly, except to avoid more work or find excuses.

I will never rush into a job without a lifetime of consideration.

I shall meet all of my deadlines at work and at home directly in proportion to the amount of bodily injury I could expect to receive from missing them.

I truly believe that all deadlines are unreasonable regardless of the amount of time given.

I firmly believe that tomorrow holds the possibility for new technologies, astounding discoveries, and a reprieve from my obligations.

If at first I don't succeed, there is always next year. And if not next year, the year after that.

I shall always decide not to decide, unless of course I decide to change my mind.

I shall always begin, start, initiate, take the first step, and/or write the first word, when I get around to it.

The Office Prayer

Grant me the serenity

To accept the things I cannot change.

The courage

To change the things I cannot accept.

And the wisdom

To hide the bodies of those people

I had to kill today because they pissed me off.

And help me to be careful

Of the toes I step on today.

As they may be connected to the ass

That I might have to kiss tomorrow.

10 Reasons Women Date Losers Instead of Nice Guys

It is more fun to complain about them.

Guys who actually like you just aren't challenging or exciting.

When you do date nice guys, they turn into losers anyway, so why not save time and go for the loser in the first place?

You won't get as emotionally attached to a loser, so you'll be more in control.

All the other women want them, so they must be worth having.

Affection means more when it comes from a guy who doesn't normally give it.

They are guaranteed to cheat on you, so someone else can endure his lack of lovemaking skills instead.

There is no need to feel guilty for abusing or deceiving them.

Losers will actually tell you when they don't like what you're doing instead of getting mad about it six months later.

You are looking for someone you can't trust, and won't care about too much, who will abuse you mentally and financially, but you don't know any lawyers.

The Dictionary of Dating

Attraction — the act of associating horniness with a particular person.

Birth control—avoiding pregnancy through such tactics as swallowing special pills, inserting a diaphragm, using a condom, dating repulsive men or spending time around children.

Dating — the process of spending huge amounts of money, time, and energy to get better acquainted with a person whom you don't especially like in the present and will learn to like a lot less in the future.

Easy — a term used to describe a woman who has the sexual morals of a man.

Eye contact — a method utilized by a single woman to communicate to a man that she is interested in him. Despite being advised to do so, many women have difficulty looking a man directly in the eyes, not necessarily due to shyness, but usually due to the fact that a woman's eyes are not located in her chest.

Friend — a member of the opposite sex in your acquaintance who has some flaw which makes sleeping with him/her totally unappealing.

Frigid — a man's term for a woman who wants to have sex less often than he does, or who requires more foreplay than ripping her jeans off.

Indifference — a woman's feeling towards a man, which is interpreted by the man as 'playing hard to get'.

Interesting — a word a man uses to describe a woman who lets him do all the talking.

Irritating habit — what the endearing little qualities that initially attract two people to each other turn into after a few months together.

Law of relatively — how attractive a given person appears to be is directly proportional to how unattractive your own date is.

Love at first sight — what occurs when two extremely horny, but not entirely choosy people meet.

Nag — a man's term for a woman who wants more to her life with him than just intercourse.

Nymphomaniac — a man's term for a woman who wants to have sex more often than he does.

Prude — a term used to describe a woman who wants to stay a virgin until married.

Sober — a condition in which it is almost impossible to fall in love.

★ ★ ★ ★

I don't mind going nowhere as long as it's an interesting path.

Similarities Between Men and Dogs

Both take up too much space on the bed.

Both have irrational fears about vacuum cleaning.

Both are threatened by their own kind.

Both like to chew wood.

Both mark their territory.

Both are bad at asking you questions.

Neither tells you what's bothering them.

Both tend to smell riper with age.

The smaller ones tend to be more nervous.

Neither do any dishes.

Neither of them notice when you get your hair cut.

Both like dominance games.

Both are suspicious of the postman.

Neither knows how to talk on the telephone.

Neither understands what you see in cats.

★ ★ ★ ★

If at first you don't succeed, then skydiving isn't for you.

Pick-up Line Rebuttals

Man: I know how to please a woman.
Woman: Then please leave me alone.

Man: I want to give myself to you.
Woman: Sorry, I don't accept cheap gifts.

Man: Your hair color is fabulous.
Woman: Thank you. It's on aisle three at the
       supermarket down the street.

Man: You look like a dream.
Woman: Go back to sleep.

Man: I can tell that you want me.
Woman: Yes, I want you to leave.
Man: I'd go through anything for you.
Woman: Let's start with your bank account.

Man: May I have the last dance?
Woman: You've just had it.

Man: Your place or mine?
Woman: Both. You go to your place, and I'll go to
       mine.

Man: Is this seat empty?
Woman: Yes, and this one will be too if you sit
       down.

Man: Haven't I seen you somewhere before?
Woman: Yeah, that's why I don't go there any
       more.

Why Does He Always Have To...

Be dressed and ready to go before you are?

Get off the phone in a microsecond if he answers when your mother calls?

Pretend he likes stars like Angelina Jolie and Cameron Diaz because of their acting ability?

Drive 20 miles over the speed limit?

Act as if his razor is priceless and should never be touched?

Toss change, keys and credit cards on the dresser, no matter how many charming containers you provide?

Hand you the 'lifestyle section' when you ask for part of the paper?

Make elaborate snacks the minute you've finished cleaning the kitchen?

Be such a charmer with your best friend after you've privately told her what a beast he's been all week?

Drink milk from the carton with great gusto?

Not understand the 'toilet-seat thing'?

Assume you will take care of gifts, cards and flowers for his family?

Want you to make a fuss when he does some little household chore unasked?

Say 'I am listening to you' when he's not?

Get lost rather than ask for directions?

Wait until you are dressed and made-up to suggest a quickie?

Wash all the dishes in the sink, but leave the big, dirty pots and pans for you?

Be convinced, no matter what you tell him, bigger is better?

Stand at the refrigerator, shouting, 'Honey, where's the mustard?', when it's right in front of him?

Spend hours measuring and making minute pencil marks on the wall when you ask him to hang up a few framed photos, then plop on the couch for the rest of the weekend with the weariness of a man who's just single-handedly built the railroad?

Take charge of everybody's automatic window buttons in the car?

Say 'I'm starving' the minute you walk in the door?

Revert to the age of two during minor illnesses.

Hit the shower immediately after sex?

Be sent to the store with a detailed shopping list and return with four six-packs and an economy-size bag of corn chips?

Constantly ask, 'Where'd I put my keys?' as though you watch his every move?

Complain there's nothing on TV, but continue watching (and channel surfing) for the rest of the evening?

Observe that you have a closet full of stuff you never wear just as you're leaving to go clothes shopping?

Leave his shoes in the living room?

Eat the last piece of leftover chicken and stick the empty plate back in the fridge?

Adjust his private parts in front of you, as if you're not looking?

Accuse you of having PMS?

Hold an umbrella over you so that the rain invariably drips down your neck?

Tell you to 'Shhh' until the next commercial — even if what you have to say is important?

Facts About Women

Women love to shop. It is the one area of the world where they feel like they're totally in control.

Women especially love a bargain. The question of 'need' is irrelevant, so don't bother pointing it out. Anything on sale is fair game.

Women never have anything to wear. Don't question the racks of clothes in the wardrobe. You 'just don't understand'.

Women need to cry. And they won't do it alone unless they know you can hear them.

Women will always ask questions that have no right answer, in an effort to trap you into feeling guilty.

Women love to talk. Silence intimidates them and they feel a need to fill it, even if they have nothing to say.

Women need to feel like there are people worse off than they are. That's why soap operas and Oprah Winfrey-type shows are so successful.

Women don't need sex as often as men do. This is because sex is more physical for men and more emotional for women. Just knowing that the man *wants* to have sex fulfils the emotional need.

Women hate bugs. Even female martial arts experts need a man around when there's a spider or a wasp involved.

Women can't keep secrets. They eat away at them from the inside. And they don't view their gabbing as being untrustworthy, providing they only tell two or three people.

Women always go to public toilets in groups. It gives them a chance to gossip.

Women can't refuse to answer a ringing phone, no matter what she's doing.

Women never understand why men love toys. Men understand that they wouldn't need toys if women had an 'on/off' switch.

Women think all beer is the same.

Women keep three different shampoos and two different conditioners in the shower, as well as at least 10 sundry items.

After a woman showers, the bathroom will smell like a tropical rainforest.

Women don't understand the appeal of contact sports. Men seek entertainment that allows them to escape reality. Women seek entertainment that reminds them of how horrible things could be.

If a man goes on a seven-day trip, he'll pack five days worth of clothes and will wear some things twice; if a woman goes on a seven-day trip, she'll pack 21 outfits because she doesn't know what she'll feel like wearing each day.

Women brush their hair *before* bed.

Watch a woman eat an ice-cream cone and you'll have a pretty good idea about how she'll be in bed.

Women have better rest rooms. They get the nice chairs and red carpet.

The average number of items in a typical woman's bathroom is 437. A man would not be able to identify most of these items.

Women love cats. Men say they love cats, but when women aren't looking, men kick cats.

Women love to talk on the phone. A woman can visit her girlfriend for two weeks, and upon returning home, she will call the same friend and they will talk for three hours.

A woman will dress up to go shopping, water the plants, empty the trash, answer the phone, read a book, or get the mail.

Women will drive miles out of their way to avoid the possibility of getting lost using a shortcut.

Women do not want an honest answer to the question, 'How do I look?'

PMS stands for: Permissible Man-Slaughter. (Or at least men think it means that. PMS also stands for Punish My Spouse).

The first naked man women see is 'Ken'.

Women are insecure about their weight, butt and breast-size.

Women will make three left-hand turns to avoid making one right-hand turn.

'Oh, nothing,' has an entirely different meaning in woman-language than it does in man-language.

Women cannot use a map without turning the map to correspond to the direction that they are heading.

All women are overweight by definition, don't argue with them about it.

All women are overweight by definition, don't agree with them about it.

If it is not Valentine's Day, and you see a man in a flower shop, you can probably start up a conversation by asking, 'What did you do?'

Only women understand the reason for 'guest towels' and 'good china'.

Women can get out of speeding tickets by pouting. This will get men arrested.

★ ★ ★ ★

If marriage were outlawed, only outlaws would have in-laws.

Facts About Men

Men like to barbecue. Men will cook if danger is involved.

Men who have pierced ears are better prepared for marriage. They've experienced pain and bought jewelry.

Marrying a divorced man is ecologically responsible. In a world where there are more women than men, it pays to recycle.

Men are very confident people. Usually they are so confident that when they watch sports on television, they think that if they concentrate they can help their team.

Men love to be the first to read the newspaper in the morning. Not being the first is upsetting to their psyches.

The way a man looks at himself in a mirror will tell you if he can ever care about anyone else.

A good place to meet a man is at the dry cleaner. These men usually have jobs and bathe.

Men love watches with multiple functions, preferably ones that have a combination address book, telescope and piano.

Men are sensitive in strange ways. If a man has

built a fire and the last log does not burn, he will take it personally.

Men are brave enough to go to war, but they are not brave enough to get a bikini wax.

Men have an easier time buying bathing suits.

Women have two types of bathing suit available to them: depressing and more depressing. Men have two types: nerdy and not nerdy.

Women take clothing much more seriously than men. Men never walk into a party and say 'Oh, my God, I'm so embarrassed... get me out of here. There's another man wearing a black tuxedo.'

Most men hate to shop. That's why the men's department is usually on the first floor of a department store, two inches from the door.

If a man prepares dinner for you and the salad contains three or more types of lettuce, he is serious.

The cocoon-to-butterfly theory only works on cocoons and butterflies.

When four or more men get together, they talk about sports.

When four or more women get together, they talk about men.

Not one man in a beer commercial has a beer belly.

Men who can eat anything they want and not gain weight should do it out of sight of women.

Getting rid of a man without hurting his masculinity is a problem.

'Get out' and 'I never want to see you again' might sound like a challenge. However, one of the most effective calls is, 'I love you. I want to marry you. I want to have your children.'

Only men who have worn a ski suit understand how complicated it is for a woman to go to the bathroom when she's wearing a jumpsuit.

Men are self-confident because they grow up identifying with superheros.

Women have bad self-images because they grow up identifying with Barbie.

When a woman tries on clothing from her closet that feels tight, she will assume she has gained weight. When a man tries something from his closet that feels tight, he will assume the clothing has shrunk.

Male menopause is a lot more fun than female menopause. With female menopause you gain weight and get hot flushes. With male menopause you get to date young girls and drive motorcycles.

Men forget everything; women remember everything. That's why men need instant replays in sports. They've already forgotten what happened.

Men would like monogamy better if it sounded less like monotony.

Fun Things to Do in a Public Toilet

Compliment people on their shoes.

Introduce yourself to the person in the next cubicle.

Strike up a conversation.

Provide 'strenuous' sound effects.

Ask the person in the next stall if there's anything swimming in *their* bowl.

Discuss the pros and cons of laxatives.

Scream 'Oh my God! What the hell is that?'

Simulate a drug deal.

Pretend to fall in (with appropriate sound effects).

Roll Easter eggs under the doors.

Start a sing-a-long

Knock on the doors of occupied stalls and ask if there is anyone in there. Ask if they are busy.

Masquerade as a door-to-door salesman.

Ask loudly, 'When does the movie start?'

Write 'nerdy' graffiti like 'Please wash your hands. Thank you'.

Kick the cubicle doors, camera in hand.

Pour water over the cubicle door onto occupant.

Say, 'Oops missed' while syringing water out around the bowl and under the walls and door into other stalls.

Fake an orgasm.

At night, switch off the lights.

Run around naked, yelling 'Where's the fish?'

Ask, in a small trembling voice, 'Is there a doctor in the house?'

Impersonate Elvis. Be convincing.

Write essay questions on the toilet paper.

Offer refreshments.

Replace rolls of toilet paper with rolls of sand paper.

Electrify metal urinals.

Leave a ladle in the toilet bowl.

Remove cubicle doors.

Glue seat and cover down to bowl.

Place signs warning of 24-hour video surveillance.

Make cubicle doors lockable only from the outside.

Put itching powder on the toilet seats.

Leave a fried egg floating in the bowl.

Replace soap in dispenser with custard.

Completely soak the towel in the towel dispenser, or the paper towels if available.

Make kitty litter trays that fit into toilet boils. Install.

Replace condoms in vending machine with tampons (or vice versa).

Create a crime scene complete with police tape and chalk silhouette.

★ ★ ★ ★

If it weren't for me, there'd just be a pile of my clothes on the floor.

Travel Agent Translations

Travel Agent Term	Translation
Old world charm	Room with a bath
Tropical	Rainy
Majestic setting	A long way from town, at end of dirt road
Options galore	Nothing is included in the itinerary
Secluded hideaway	Directions to locate unclear
Some budget rooms	Sorry, already occupied
Explore on your own	At your own expense
Knowledgeable trip hosts	They've flown in a plane before
No extra fees	No extras
Nominal fee	Outrageous charge
Standard	Sub-standard
Deluxe	Barely standard
Superior accommodations	One complimentary chocolate and free shower cap
All the amenities	Two chocolates and two shower caps.

Gentle breezes	In hurricane alley
Light and airy	No air conditioning
Picturesque	Theme park nearby
24 hour bar	Ice cubes at additional cost (when available)

Working in the New Millennium

Cleaning up the dining area means getting the fast food bags out of the back seat of your car.

Your reason for not staying in touch with family is that they do not have e-mail addresses.

You have a 'to do list' that includes entries for lunch and bathroom breaks and they are usually the ones that never get crossed off.

Pick-up lines now include a reference to liquid assets and capital gains.

You consider overnight mail to be painfully slow.

Your idea of being organized is multiple colored post-it notes.

Your grocery list has been on your refrigerator so long some of the products don't even exist any more.

You lecture the neighborhood kids selling lemonade on ways to improve their profitability.

You get all excited when it's Saturday so you can go to work in casual clothes.

You refer to the tomatoes grown in your garden as deliverables.

You find you really need Power Point to explain what you do for a living.

You normally eat out of vending machines and at the most expensive restaurant in town within the same week.

You think that 'progressing an action plan' and 'calendarizing a project' are acceptable English phrases.

You know the people at the airport hotels better than your next-door neighbors.

You ask your friends to 'think out of the box' when making Friday night plans.

You think Einstein would have been more effective had he put his ideas into a matrix.

You think a 'half day' means leaving at five o'clock.

Things That May Be Overhead in the Darkroom

Hey, careful with that thing.

You can't expose it to the light.

Is it stiff yet?

Don't open the door.

I can't get it in.

How much time is left?

I just can't enlarge it to that size.

Would you like to see my exposures?

Don't go anywhere, we're not finished yet.

So how does it go in there?

It doesn't work the way you say.

Check the chart.

I always prefer manual enlarging.

★ ★ ★ ★

Ever stop to think, and forget to start again?

The 10 Commandments of the Frisbee

1. The most powerful force in the world is that of a frisbee straining to get under a car.

2. The better the catch the worse the re-throw (a.k.a. 'good catch, bad throw').

3. One must never precede any maneuvre by a comment more predictive than, 'watch this!'

4. The higher the costs of hitting any object the greater the certainty it will be struck.

5. The best catches are never seen.

6. The greatest single aid to distance is for the frisbee to be going in the wrong direction (a.k.a. goes the wrong way, goes a long way').

7. The most powerful hex words in the world of sport are: 'I really have this sussed — watch' (a.k.a. 'know it, blow it').

8. In any crowd of spectators at least one will suggest that razor blades could be attached to the frisbee.

9. The greater your need to make a good catch the greater the probability your partner will deliver his worst throw.

10. The single most difficult move with a frisbee is to put it down (a.k.a. 'just one more throw').

Laws of Documentation

1. If it should exist, it doesn't.

2. If it does exist, it's out of date.

3. Only documentation for useless programs transcends the first two laws.

Laws of Love

People to whom you are attracted invariably think you remind them of someone else.

The love letter you finally got the courage to send will be delayed in the mail long enough for you to make a fool of yourself in person.

The probability of a young man meeting a desirable and receptive young female increases by pyramidal progression when he is already in the company of:

1. a date

2. his wife

3. a better-looking and richer male friend.

Bored in a Lecture at College?

Fake a seizure.

Make loud animal noises then deny doing it.

Think of new pick-up lines. See if they work.

Churn some butter.

Create a brand new language.

Walls made of brick: count them.

Plot revenge against someone.

Think of nicknames for everyone you know.

Punch the person next to you in the mouth.

See how long you can hold your breath.

Take your pants off and give them to the lecturer.

Chew on your arm until someone notices.

Change seats every three minutes.

Run across the room, tag someone and say 'You're it.'

Announce to the class that you are God and that you are angry.

Think of five new ways to use your shoes.

Run to the window, then say, 'Sorry, I thought I saw the bat-signal'.

Ask the person in front of you to marry you.

Start laughing really hard and say, 'Oh, now I get it.'

Make a sundial.

Sell stolen goods.

Bite people.

Summarize the teaching of Socrates in 50 words or less.

Give yourself a new identity.

Write a screenplay about a diabetic Swedish girl who can't swim.

Start a Mexican wave.

Dig an escape tunnel.

Learn voodoo.

Lick yourself clean.

Lick someone else clean.

Learn to tie your shoes with one hand.

See how many push-ups you can do.

Experiment with your sexuality.

Run with scissors.

Write stupid lists.

Space Age Product Warnings

Warning: This product warps space and time in its vicinity.

Warning: This product attracts every other piece of matter in the universe, including the products of other manufacturers, with a force proportional to the product of the masses and inversely proportional to the distance between them.

Caution: The mass of this product contains the energy equivalent of 85 million tonnes of TNT per net ounce of weight.

Handle with extreme care: This product contains minute electrically charged particles moving at velocities in excess of five hundred million miles per hour.

Consumer notice: Because of the 'Uncertainty Principle', it is impossible for the consumer to find out at the same time both precisely where this product is and how fast it is moving.

Advisory: There is an extremely small but non-zero chance that, through a process known as 'tunnelling', this product may spontaneously disappear from its present location and reappear at any random place in the universe, including your neighbor's domicile. The manufacturer will not be responsible for any damages or inconvenience that may result.

Read this before opening package: According to certain suggested versions of the grand unified theory, the primary particles constituting this product may decay to nothingness within the next four hundred million years.

This is a 100% matter product: In the unlikely event that this merchandise should contact anti-matter in any form, a catastrophic explosion will result.

Public notice as required by law: Any use of this product, in any manner whatsoever, will increase the amount of disorder in the universe. Although no liability is implied herein, the consumer is warned that this process will ultimately lead to the heat death of the universe.

Note: The most fundamental particles in this product are held together by a 'gluing' force about which little is currently known, and whose adhesive power can therefore not be permanently guaranteed.

Attention: Despite any other listing of product contents found herein, the consumer is advised that, in actuality, this product consists of 99.9999% empty space.

New grand unified theory disclaimer: The manufacturer may technically be entitled to claim that this product is 10-dimensional. However, the consumer is reminded that this confers no legal rights above and beyond those applicable to three-dimensional objects, since the seven new dimensions are 'rolled up' into such a small 'area' that they cannot be detected.

Please note: Some quantum physics theories suggest that when the consumer is not directly observing this product, it may cease to exist or will exist only in a vague and undetermined state. No responsibility is taken by the manufacturers of the product should this occur.

Component equivalency notice: The subatomic particles (electrons, protons, etc.) comprising this product are exactly the same in every measurable respect as those used in the products of other manufacturers, and no claim to the contrary may legitimately be expressed or implied.

Health warning: Care should be taken when lifting this product, since its mass, and thus its weight, is dependent on its velocity relative to the user.

Important note to purchasers: The entire physical universe, including this product, may one day collapse back into an infinitesimally small space. Should another universe subsequently re-emerge, the existence of this product in that universe cannot be guaranteed.

Laws of Life

It is easier to get forgiveness than permission.

Under the most rigorously controlled conditions of pressure, temperature, volume, humidity, and other variables, the organism will do as it damn well pleases.

Research is what I'm doing when I don't know what I'm doing.

It is not an optical illusion, it just looks like one.

There are two rules for success... 1. Never tell everything you know.

When in doubt, predict that the present trend will continue.

Don't force it; get a larger hammer.

Any tool when dropped will roll into the least accessible corner of the workshop.

An alcoholic is a person who drinks more than his own physician.

If all you have is a hammer, everything looks like a nail.

If you're feeling good, don't worry. You'll get over it.

Project teams detest weekly progress reporting because it so vividly manifests their lack of progress.

Never go to a doctor whose office plants have died.

You always find something in the last place you look.

When in charge, ponder. When in trouble, delegate. When in doubt, mumble.

If computers get too powerful, we can organize them into a committee — that will do them in.

No good deed goes unpunished.

Whenever a system becomes completely refined, some damn fool discovers something which either abolishes the system or expands it beyond recognition.

Nothing is ever accomplished by a reasonable man.

When all else fails, read the instructions.

You can fool all of the people some of the time, and some of the people all of the time, but you can't fool your mom.

The amount of time required to complete a government project is precisely equal to the length of time already spent on it.

When things just can't possibly get any worse, they will.

Man will occasionally stumble over the truth, but most of the time he will pick himself up and continue on.

All probabilities are 50%. Either a thing will happen or it won't. This is especially true when dealing with someone you're attracted to.

In any organization, there will always be one person who knows what's going on. This person must be fired.

Virtue is its own punishment.

If you hit two keys on the typewriter, the one you don't want hits the paper.

The first bug to hit a clean windshield lands directly in front of your eyes.

If you view your problem closely enough you will recognize yourself as part of the problem.

Opportunity always knocks at the least opportune moment.

Our chief want in life is somebody who shall make us do what we can. Having found them, we shall then hate them for it.

If you are given an open-book exam, you will forget your book. If you are given a take-home exam, you will forget where you live.

Procrastination avoids boredom; one never has the feeling that there is nothing important to do.

Science is true. Don't be misled by facts.

If an experiment works, something has gone wrong.

No matter what the anticipated result, there will always be someone eager to misinterpret it, fake it, or believe it happened according to his own pet theory.

In any collection of data, the figure most obviously correct, beyond all need of checking, is the mistake.

Once a job is fouled up, anything done to improve it only makes it worse.

A closed mouth gathers no feet.

No matter which way you ride, it's uphill and against the wind.

Procrastination shortens the job and places the responsibility for its termination on someone else (namely the authority who imposed the deadline).

Celibacy is not hereditary.

History doesn't repeat itself — historians merely repeat each other.

The time when you need to knock on wood is when you realize that the world is composed of vinyl, glass and aluminium.

Push something hard and it will fall over.

If you knew what you were doing you'd probably be bored.

An object in motion will always be headed in the wrong direction.

An object at rest will always be in the wrong place.

The secret to success is sincerity. Once you can fake that, you've got it made.

If the shoe fits, it's ugly.

Always hire a rich attorney. Never buy from a rich salesman.

If a string has one end, it has another.

You never really learn to swear until you learn to drive.

Anything is possible if you don't know what you're talking about.

Eighty per cent of all people consider themselves to be above-average drivers.

The belief that enhanced understanding will necessarily stir a nation to action is one of mankind's oldest illusions.

Never attribute to malice that which is adequately explained by stupidity.

There are never enough hours in a day, but always too many days before Saturday.

Experience is directly proportional to the amount of equipment ruined.

For every action, there is an equal and opposite criticism.

You can lead a horse to water, but if you can get him to float on his back, you've got something.

The first myth of management is that it exists.

If you have a difficult task, give it to a lazy person — they will find an easier way to do it.

Inside every large problem is a small problem struggling to get out.

Among economists, the real world is often a special case.

Everyone has a scheme that will not work.

The chance of forgetting something is directly proportional to...to...uh...

You can never tell which way the train went by looking at the track.

Everybody lies, but nobody listens.

When the going gets tough, everyone leaves.

The one day you'd sell your soul for something, there's a glut of souls on the market.

When we try to pick out anything by itself, we find it hitched to everything else in the universe.

Cleanliness is next to impossible.

No matter where you go, there you are.

It is a mistake to let any mechanical object realize that you are in a hurry.

On the way to the far-flung corner, any dropped tool will first strike your toes.

People who love sausages and respect the law should never watch either one being made.

The correct advice to give is the advice that is desired.

The purpose of the communication is to advance the communicator.

The information conveyed is less important than the impression.

Change is the status quo.

A manager cannot tell if he is leading an innovative mob or being chased by it.

A decision is judged by the conviction with which it is uttered.

To protect your position, fire the fastest rising employees first.

Decisions are justified by the benefits to the organization, but they are made by considering the benefits to the decision-makers.

Anyone else who can be blamed should be blamed.

Anything that can go wrong will go wrong faster with computers.

Whenever a computer can be blamed, it should be blamed.

In any decision situation, the amount of relevant information available is inversely proportional to the importance of the decision.

You cannot successfully determine beforehand which side of the bread to butter.

Bare feet magnetize sharp metal objects so they always point upwards from the floor — especially in the dark.

A memorandum is written not to inform the reader but to protect the writer.

Trouble strikes in series of threes, but the next job after a series of three is not the fourth job — it's the start of a brand new series of three.

Complaints to the Landlord

Below is a series of complaints sent in by various tenants to their landlords.

I wish to complain that my father hurt his ankle very badly when he put his foot in the hole in his back passage.

The lavatory is blocked; this is caused by the boys next door throwing their balls on the roof.

This is to let you know that there is a smell coming from the man next door.

The toilet seat is cracked: where do I stand?

I am writing on behalf of my sink, which is running away from the wall.

I request your permission to remove my drawers in the kitchen.

Our lavatory seat is broken in half and is now in three pieces.

Can you please tell me when our repairs are going to be done, as my wife is about to become an expectant mother?

I want some repairs done to my stove as it has backfired and burnt my knob off.

I am still having trouble with smoke in my built-in drawers.

The toilet is blocked and we cannot bathe the children until it is cleared.

The person next door has a large erection in his back garden, which is unsightly and dangerous.

Will you please send someone to mend our cracked sidewalk? Yesterday my wife tripped on it and is now pregnant.

Our kitchen floor is very damp, we have two children and would like a third, so will you please send someone to do something about it.

Will you please send a man to look at my water, it is a funny color and not fit to drink.

Would you please send a man to repair my down-spout. I am an old age pensioner and need it straight away.

Could you please send someone to fix our bath tap? My wife got her toe stuck in it and it is very uncomfortable for us.

I want to complain about the farmer across the road. Every morning at 5.30 his cock wakes me up, and it is getting too much.

When the workmen were here they put their tools in my wife's new drawers and made a mess. Please send men with clean tools to finish the job and keep my wife happy.

Infamous Last Words

Let it down slowly.

Rat poison only kills rats.

I'll get your toast out.

It's strong enough for both of us.

This doesn't taste right.

I can make this light before it changes.

Nice doggie.

I can do that with my eyes closed.

I've done this before.

Well we've made it this far.

That's odd.

Okay this is the last time.

With those guns, those guys couldn't hit the side of a...

Don't be so superstitious.

Now watch this.

This planet has an atmosphere just like on Earth.

What duck?